Kant and the Role of
Pleasure in Moral Action

·······································

IAIN P. D. MORRISSON

OHIO UNIVERSITY PRESS   ATHENS

Ohio University Press, Athens, Ohio 45701
www.ohioswallow.com
© 2008 by Ohio University Press

To obtain permission to quote, reprint, or otherwise reproduce or distribute
material from Ohio University Press publications, please contact our rights and
permissions department at (740) 593-1154 or (740) 593-4536 (fax).

Portions of this work appeared in a slightly different form in "Moral and
Non-moral Freedom in Kant," *Southern Journal of Philosophy* 45, no. 1
(2007): 129–48; "The Intelligible World and the Practical Standpoint,"
Southwest Philosophy Review 23, no. 1 (2007): 137–46; "Pleasure in Kant: An
Analysis of Desire Formation," *Journal of Philosophical Research* 31 (2006):
219–32; "On Kantian Maxims: A Reconciliation of the Incorporation Thesis
and Weakness of the Will," *History of Philosophy Quarterly* 22, no. 1 (2005):
73–89; and "Respect in Kant: How the Moral Feeling of Respect Acts as an
Incentive to Moral Action," *Southwest Philosophy Review* 20,
no. 2 (2004): 1–26.

Printed in the United States of America
Ohio University Press books are printed on acid-free paper ∞ ™

15 14 13 12 11 10 09 08   5 4 3 2 1

Library of Congress Cataloging-in-Publication Data

Morrisson, Iain P. D.
Kant and the role of pleasure in moral action / Iain P.D. Morrisson.
    p. cm. — (Series in Continental thought ; 35)
Includes bibliographical references (p.   ) and index.
ISBN 978-0-8214-1830-7 (cloth : alk. paper)
1. Kant, Immanuel, 1724–1804. 2. Moral motivation. I. Title.
B2799.E8M67 2008
170.92—dc22

2008025726

To Leona

CONTENTS

ACKNOWLEDGMENTS

Daniel Guevara and Mehmet Erginel helped me immensely through their conversations, comments, and criticisms. They have both suffered a barrage of questions from me over the last number of years, and their answers and arguments were often critical in deciding issues. A debt of gratitude is also owed to Kathleen Higgins and Brian Leiter, who helped me progress as a thinker and gave me some input on this project when it was just part of a chapter of my dissertation. For comments on some of the manuscript and helpful discussion, I thank Rachel Zuckert. I am also grateful to Patrick Frierson for some very constructive criticism during a conference and in communication.

I received useful criticisms on various parts of my argument from anonymous referees at the following journals: *History of Philosophy Quarterly, Journal of Philosophical Research, Southern Journal of Philosophy,* and *Southwest Philosophy Review.* I am also grateful to commentators at a number of APA conferences as well as the Midsouth Philosophy Conference and the Southwestern Philosophical Society Conference.

Finally, I would like to thank my wife Leona Hammill and my family, who, perhaps unbeknownst to them, helped me through periods of writing this manuscript that were frustrating and difficult. Thank you for your encouragement and tolerance.

METHODOLOGY AND TWO KINDS OF ETHICS

Kant's theory of moral motivation is notoriously controversial. Indeed, few areas of Kant scholarship have drawn as much attention or prompted as much disagreement. Kant himself was so confounded by the issue of how the moral law can provide an incentive that moves the will to action that he refers to this problem as the "philosophers' stone" (LE 27:1428). Unfortunately, Kant's perplexity ultimately translates into an unusually elusive theory of moral motivation. As a result, the list of scholars who have presented divergent, often mutually exclusive interpretations of Kant's account of moral motivation is long and distinguished.[1] In this study, I want to contribute to the debate over how Kant thinks we are moved to act morally by approaching the issue in a new and, I argue, wholly enlightening way.

The problem that is perhaps central to this debate is as follows: how can Kant account for moral motivation while divorcing the basis of morality from the pathological, and therefore motivational, side of human agents?[2] To put this pivotal question another way: if Kant thinks that morality is not grounded in our sensuous and affective natures (as the British moral sense theorists suggest), then how does he think we are *moved* by moral considerations at all? Kant (notoriously) introduces the concept of respect (*Achtung*) as an answer to this question. On the face of it, his solution seems to be that respect is a moral *feeling*, and, as such, bridges the gap between the moral law and the capacity of humans—as sensuously affected beings—to be motivated. But, to get to the heart of the matter, it has proven extremely difficult for readers of Kant to grasp the precise nature and function of this bridging feeling of respect.

In what follows I will not rehearse the scholarly debate that has sur-
rounded this particular issue in any great detail; this has been adequately
done elsewhere.[3] In the most general terms, then, the central disagreement
in the secondary literature is over whether respect *as a feeling* is the actual motive to moral action. Most commentators argue that, in fact,
respect is only a moral motive insofar as it has a *nonfeeling* dimension.
There are numerous variations on this position, but the basic view is that
Kantian respect involves a recognition or consciousness of the moral
law, and that it is this recognition that actually motivates moral choice.[4]
Now, there is evidence supporting the identification of respect with a
kind of consciousness in the *Groundwork for the Metaphysics of Morals*,
when Kant writes, "The direct determination of the will by law and the
consciousness of this determination is respect" (G 4:401n). Furthermore,
Kant's well-known insistence that moral actions are performed purely for
the sake of, or from, duty seems to be linked to this cognitive characterization of respect. In insisting that moral actions are done for the sake
of duty, Kant appears to be indicating that the mere thought or recognition of our duty can motivate moral action. Finally, this interpretation is
also supported by passages such as the following: "If the determination
of the will occurs in accordance with the moral law but only by means
of a feeling of any kind whatsoever, which must be presupposed in order
that the law may become a determining ground of the will, and if the action thus occurs not for the sake of the law, it has legality but not morality" (Pr. R 5:72). This passage seems to make it clear that, for Kant, even
if moral motivation *involves* the feeling of respect, this feeling cannot
do the actual motivating in any given moral action. If it does, then this
action is not properly moral.

According to the primary alternative to this interpretation—an alternative that I will ultimately defend—Kant's moral *feeling* of respect can
and does motivate moral action.[5] This understanding of respect is consistent with Kant's claim that a moral action is done for the sake of duty,
and not from feeling, so long as the latter is taken to mean *pathological*
feeling.[6] A pathological feeling is one that is caused by our susceptibility
to sensible objects. A nonpathological feeling is one that is caused independently of our sensible susceptibility to objects.[7] Thus, when Kant says
that we cannot be morally moved by a feeling of any kind, he means a
pathological feeling of any kind, and is primarily referring to the notion

of a moral sense or feeling proposed by Hutcheson, Shaftesbury, and Hume (against whom Kant's Critical ethics is to a large extent formed). One central virtue of this interpretation of Kant's notion of respect (as an effective nonpathological feeling) is that it, too, is supported by quite a bit of textual evidence. For example, in the *Critique of Practical Reason,* Kant says of the moral law that it "has an influence on the sensibility of the subject and effects a feeling which promotes the influence of the law on the will" (Pr. R 5:75). The implication here is that the moral feeling of respect is a mediating force between the moral law and the human will. In the *Metaphysics of Morals,* Kant writes that in a moral person "feelings arising from sensible impressions lose their influence on moral feeling only because respect for the law is more powerful [*mächtiger*] than all such feelings together" (MM 6:408). But if respect does not move us as a moral feeling, then in what sense is it "more powerful" than feelings arising from our sensibility?

This evidence for the idea that respect motivates as a feeling is, on its own, inconclusive, in that Kant offers no real account of *how* such a moral feeling might actually move us. At best, he just says *that* it does, leaving us with an unexplained view that seems to contradict some of his fundamental claims about morality (such as those referred to above). Those critics who argue that Kant thinks that respect motivates as a feeling have failed to supply any account of precisely *how* this feeling motivates.[8] Without such an account there does not seem to be any compelling reason to accept the view that Kant's feeling of respect motivates.[9] In this study I want to present just such an account. Thus, although I will refer to the textual evidence supporting the view *that* Kant's feeling of respect motivates as a feeling, my focus will be on explaining precisely *how* it motivates.

What are some of the concerns that arise in trying to explain *how* Kant's moral feeling of respect motivates? The main issues can be framed in terms of the following kinds of questions:

1. Is respect a nonpathological feeling? If so (and leaving aside the thorny issue of how a nonpathological feeling might arise), then how does it motivate? Presumably, on such an account, respect does not motivate in the same way that ordinary pathological feelings of pleasure and pain motivate. Is there, then, a special kind of motivational mechanism operating in moral actions that differs from the mechanism operating in the

case of nonmoral actions?[10] (Some scholars—thinking along these lines and referring to the *Critique of Judgment*—have pointed to Kant's account of the sublime for help in articulating what such an alternative mechanism might look like.)

2. Or, is respect essentially the same as a pathological feeling but with a different—that is, nonpathological—origin? Kant does seem to indicate that respect is a *practical* feeling, only differing from pathological feelings in its origins. If this is so, and it is *only* in its origin that the feeling of respect differs from nonmoral feelings, then does it follow that moral and nonmoral feelings motivate in essentially the same way? In other words, does moral motivation somehow share a common structure with nonmoral motivation? If so, then what is this common structure?

Ultimately, I will argue that for Kant respect is a nonpathological feeling that motivates moral action in a way that is identical (in crucial respects) to the way in which pathological feelings motivate desire-based actions (and in a way that does not compromise the notion that moral actions are done for the sake of duty). I will contend that respect motivates moral choice in a way that can be illuminated by looking at how nonmoral feelings motivate nonmoral choice. Of course, in order to defend such a contention I must first present an account of how nonmoral feelings motivate. It is this requirement that prompts my methodological approach.

I. METHODOLOGY

The question of motivation in Kant's ethical theory will be addressed explicitly only in the final two chapters of this book, yet this question (or, more specifically, the question of *how* the moral motive actually motivates) is still the central focus of this study. Putting off a direct analysis in this way is part of the methodology that I will adopt in articulating Kant's view of moral motivation.

Broadly speaking, there are two distinct (but not exclusive) methodological ways of approaching philosophical problems such as that of interpreting Kant's theory of moral motivation. On the one hand, texts in which the philosopher discusses the disputed issue can be closely examined, compared, contextualized, and weighed against each other. This approach can produce interpretive conclusions based on a variety of possible criteria, such as the weight of the evidence or whether the relevant text expresses the author's *mature* position. Unfortunately, this method has not yielded much success in interpreting Kant's theory of moral motivation.[11] There are a number of reasons for this, but two are perhaps most important. First, Kant *consistently* maintains what appear to be contrary positions on this issue. For example, as I indicated in the last section, he repeatedly says things to suggest that a moral action is one that is done for the sake of duty and without any influencing feeling. And yet, at the same time he consistently tells us that respect is a feeling that moves us to moral action. Second, Kant is virtually silent when it comes to articulating explicitly *how* respect actually motivates the agent. As a result, there really is no direct evidence to resolve the disagreement over whether it is a cognitive or noncognitive dimension of respect that does the actual motivating.

Kant's most focused discussion of the feeling of respect—in the chapter called "The Incentives of Pure Practical Reason" from the second *Critique*—provides a good illustration of the first difficulty outlined above, insofar as it can be read in support of at least the following three interpretations of respect. First, there is evidence in this chapter for the view that the feeling of respect *represents* the direct determination of the will by the law. Thus, the moral law does not *cause* the feeling of respect so much as it is *represented* in a sensuous way by this feeling. On this reading, the feeling of respect is just the moral law in a sensible form.[12] Second (and this is the position for which I will ultimately argue), it is possible to read Kant as saying that respect is a complex feeling—made up of feelings of pleasure and pain—that is *somehow* produced or caused by (and, therefore, distinct from) the moral law.[13] On this view, respect is not identified with the moral law. Instead, it is a feeling caused by the moral law, and it motivates insofar as it is made up of a combination of feelings of pleasure and pain. Finally, one could also argue that Kant contends in this chapter that while respect is distinct from the moral law, it is the cognitive dimension of respect that does the actual motivational work. The *feeling* aspect of respect only clears the (sensuous) way for this cognitive motivation by attacking our self-love and self-conceit.[14]

And so—to get back to the methodological issue—Kant's theory of moral motivation appears to be one of those thorny philosophical areas in which a balanced and close reading of the immediately relevant texts just does not resolve the issue at hand. Indeed, a balanced and close engagement with these texts appears to complicate the matter further. It seems necessary, then, to approach Kant's understanding of respect by a more circuitous methodological route. This route is as follows: one can project what Kant *should* have said (in order to be consistent) about respect as the moral motive by looking at those areas of his thinking that provide the relevant context for his account of moral motivation. This is the method that I will adopt in interpreting Kant's thinking on how respect functions as the moral motive. Now, of course, this approach might fail if it turns out that the view that Kant *ought* to hold, on such an account, cannot be reconciled with any of the things that he actually says on respect. Fortunately, this is not the case. In chapter 5, I will argue that Kant usually says exactly what one might expect him to say about the feeling of respect in view of the relevant contextual background to his theory of moral motivation. This background throws a clarifying light on Kant's discussions of respect, and allows us to read them as part of a systematic and coherent account of moral action.

Establishing the contextual background relevant to this particular issue involves asking the following questions. First, how exactly does Kant think that nonmoral motivation works for a free but sensuously affected being (such as a human being)? Second, how does Kant understand the distinction between moral and nonmoral motivation for such beings? If the points at which moral and nonmoral motivation differ are made clear, then an account of nonmoral motivation should provide a framework in terms of which we can understand Kant's ambiguous and often conflicting hints on how moral motivation works.

Ultimately, I will contend that for Kant the a priori moral law moves us by causing a feeling that is partly pleasurable and partly painful. This feeling is incorporated into moral maxims and these maxims affect choice insofar as they contain a moral pleasure that tends to maintain itself. The choice to act morally is still "for the sake of duty alone" because it is only as such that moral pleasure maintains itself. I will argue for this position by first laying out the philosophical background relevant to Kant's theory of moral motivation, and then moving to this theory (chapter 5). In articulating this background I will address in some detail Kant's thinking on human psychology (chapter 1), his account of desire formation (chapter 2), his purported hedonism (chapter 2), and, finally, his account of free and rational nonmoral choice, focusing specifically on his understanding of the role of maxims in choice (chapters 3 and 4).[15] I will conclude by defending my reading of respect against a representative of the dominant contemporary interpretation.

Before turning to any of this, though, I want to explain why Kant's theory of nonmoral motivation (including his empirical account of desires and feelings) provides us with the *relevant* background to his understanding of how respect functions as the moral motive.

II. EMPIRICAL ETHICS AND A PRIORI ETHICS

In the preface to his first mature ethical work—the *Groundwork*—Kant divides ethics into an a priori part and an empirical part.[16] According to this division, ethical thinking is concerned either with the moral law and the derivation of this law from some ground (the a priori part), or with the nature of human beings and how this nature bears on their ability to live according to the moral law (the empirical part). Broadly speaking, Kant refers to this empirical part as "anthropology."[17] For Kant, previous philosophers made a mistake insofar as they did not strictly adhere to this clear and programmatic division. This was especially true in the cases of those philosophers—Kant likes to use Epicurus and Hutcheson as examples—who started their ethical thinking with an account of human nature and then tried to derive moral principles from this account.[18] In so doing, Kant argues, these thinkers jumbled the two sides of the division in such a way as to prevent any possibility of grasping the true moral principle. In many respects this division between the a priori and the empirical is the hallmark of Kantian ethics. At the very least, I will argue, it is at the heart of the Kantian problem of moral motivation, and provides a framework for the justification of my methodological approach.

Kant's Focus on A Priori Ethics

Kant scholars concerned with understanding and articulating his ethical theory have typically abided by the a priori/empirical distinction in their expository accounts. But, until recently, interest in the empirical side of Kant's ethics has been very limited and quite critical. Commentators usually

focused on the a priori moral law and often only went as far as the link
between this dimension and the empirical in discussing the problems associated with Kant's real-world applications of the categorical imperative
in the second section of the *Groundwork*. However, in contemporary
scholarship there have been a few attempts to look more closely, and
charitably, at Kant's empirical ethics.[19]

These attempts are to some degree justified by an important histori-
cal consideration. Recent work done by Werner Stark and Reinhard Brandt
indicates that Kant ran his series of lectures on anthropology contempo-
raneously with his lectures on pure ethics.[20] In spite of Kant's emphasis
on a distinction between empirical and a priori ethics, Stark argues that
he actually conceived of a complex relationship between the two kinds
of enquiry. The appearance of a total separation between these two realms
of enquiry—an appearance that is partly a product of Kant's exaggerated
insistence, and partly of scholars' tendency to read the a priori works in
isolation from the empirical works—misrepresents Kant's understanding
of a deeper connection between the two.

Why, then, in view of the closeness that may actually exist between
Kant's empirical and a priori ethics, have scholars not been more interested in his empirical ethics? Many factors have probably contributed to
this lack of interest, and I will just touch on a few here by way of introducing the question of how the two dimensions of moral investigation
relate.[21] First, the neglect of Kant's empirical ethics may be explained in
part by early criticisms, from the likes of Schiller and Schopenhauer,
leveled against Kant's abilities as an empirical thinker. The popular image
of Kant studiously and fastidiously working out a formally beautiful but
practically inapplicable moral theory may have warned off those with
any interest in exploring his empirical thinking. Indeed, as a result of this
common portrayal, many ethicists still regard themselves as *reacting* to
Kant in presenting nonuniversalist, virtue-based theories that are more
sensitive to human psychology and everyday life.[22] Second, it is not at all
obvious *how* Kant's empirical ethics can be systematically connected to
his a priori moral thinking. Kant conceives of the moral agent as transcendentally free, and transcendental freedom involves the freedom of
one's choices from all antecedent causal determination.[23] But, in view of
these considerations, we might ask how the study of empirical factors
(such as human psychology or education) is relevant to morality at all.[24]

It might be argued that it is not relevant to moral deliberation since empirical matters cannot causally influence one's free choices. Nor, it could be said, is it relevant to moral assessment since Kant thinks that the agent's free choices, and not any empirical consequences, should be the focus of this assessment. The fact that scholars have largely ignored Kant's empirical ethics may indicate that these problems, noted by early critics such as Fichte and Hegel, have been taken seriously.

Probably more important than either of these two considerations is the fact that Kant himself seems to privilege the pure dimension of his moral philosophy over the empirical. For example, in the preface to the *Groundwork* he writes, "In ethics . . . the empirical part may be called more specifically practical anthropology; the rational part, morals proper [*eigentlich Moral*]" (G 4:388). Kant not only places the emphasis on the a priori part by referring to it as "proper" or "real" morals, but he also goes on to portray the empirical as somehow getting in the way of this pure enquiry. He continues, "Since my purpose here is directed to moral philosophy, I narrow my proposed question to this: Is it not of the utmost necessity to construct a pure moral philosophy which is completely freed from everything which may be only empirical and thus belong to anthropology? . . . [T]he ground of obligation here must not be sought in the nature of man or in the circumstances in which he is placed but a priori solely in the concepts of pure reason" (G 4:389). Of course, this prioritization is not just a matter of blind favoritism on Kant's part, but rather reflects something crucial about his ethical thinking: the a priori part of morals is morality *proper* because the moral law, given the requirements that it be universal and necessary, cannot be empirically (or contingently) grounded. Kant posits this distinction after some twenty years of pre-Critical grappling with the difficulty of grounding a moral law, so his exaggerated emphasis is perhaps understandable.

But what is fundamental and new, and therefore prioritized, is at the same time (and by Kant's own account) only half of the story. Kant is a systematic philosopher, and, I want to argue, his empirical thinking on human beings connects in direct and systematic ways to his pure ethics. This is a critical claim for my project since the methodological principle guiding this study is that a crucial extension of Kant's a priori ethics— the question of how the purely rational moral law motivates—cannot be properly understood without reference to a contextual background, and

I am going to argue that Kant's empirical thinking on human psychology provides us with the first part of this background. In what follows, I will try to establish the link between certain dimensions of Kant's empirical ethics and his theory of moral motivation by looking at the larger connection that he draws between empirical and a priori ethics. In concluding this discussion I will turn briefly to the more general, and very thorny, issue of Kant's two worlds/standpoints.

The Relation between Empirical and A Priori Ethics

Kant is concerned with the relationship between the empirical and a priori dimensions of ethics in both his early and late Critical period. So, for example, in one of his *Lectures on Ethics* from 1784–85 he says:

> The science of the rules of how man ought to behave is practical philosophy, and the science of the rules of his actual behavior is anthropology; these two sciences are closely connected, and morality cannot exist without anthropology, for one must first know of the agent whether he is also in a position [*im Stande*] to accomplish what it is required from him that he should do. One can, indeed, certainly consider practical philosophy even without anthropology, or without knowledge of the agent, only then it is speculative, or an Idea; so man must at least be studied accordingly. (LE 27:244)[25]

What does Kant mean by the investigation into "whether [man] is also in a position to accomplish what it is required from him that he should do"? Surely, he cannot be suggesting that anthropology explore whether humans are *fundamentally* capable of being moral. Ultimately, this suggestion would mean that anthropology is an investigation into whether humans are free—but it seems highly unlikely that Kant would refer to such an investigation as a science of "the rules of [man's] actual behavior." Moreover, even a cursory glance at Kant's anthropological works indicates that they are most certainly not a study of whether humans are free.

In drawing this connection between anthropology and practical philosophy, then, does Kant simply mean that anthropology is the study of whether man is, in fact, ever moral? Kant's anthropology does *involve* some documenting, or surveying, of moral tendencies, but this only constitutes a very small part of his anthropological project. More importantly, Kant consistently maintains that the morality of an action lies in a deep choice of maxims, and as such we can never know with certainty whether any action is truly moral. With this in mind, we might ask, then, whether Kant is suggesting that anthropology investigate whether people *appear* to be moral. But it is not at all clear how an investigation of whether people appear to be moral would supplement morality proper, such that the latter "cannot exist without" the former.

Perhaps the best way to discover what Kant means by this elusive characterization of the relationship between anthropology and practical philosophy is to check it against the central issues actually discussed in his anthropological work.[26] One of the main focuses of Kant's anthropological thinking is the psychology of the agent. Thus, the faculties of desire and feeling—two of Kant's three powers of the mind—are central to his most comprehensive anthropological account in *Anthropology from a Pragmatic Point of View*. Maybe Kant's point, then, is that anthropology includes the study of whether humans (as free agents) are in a *psychological* position to act morally. More precisely, anthropology may involve an empirical study of whether, and how, our psychological makeup hinders moral action. This reading seems to be confirmed in the *Metaphysics* when Kant says that moral anthropology deals with "the subjective conditions in human nature that hinder people or help them in fulfilling the laws of a metaphysics of morals" (MM 6:217). Typically, Kant puts this question of hindrance in terms of whether, and how, our desires and feelings impede our *morality, reason,* and *freedom.* So, for example, at the heart of Kant's anthropological discussions of the faculty of desire is his concern that passions can lead to *evil.*[27] Thus, passions can provide a psychological threat to our being moral. Meanwhile, in the third *Critique,* Kant addresses the relation between *rational* principles and psychology, saying that the passions "belong to the faculty of desire, and are inclinations that make all determinability of the faculty of desire by means of principles difficult or impossible" (CJ 5:272n). Finally, he also describes the passions as "enchantments" that can "do the greatest harm to *freedom*" (A 7:266; emphasis added). Kant's point is that our psychological makeup can impair our ability to choose freely actions that are based on principles of reason (including the moral principle).

The suggestion here that anthropology studies man understood as a free and rational being capable of choosing morally seems to contravene Kant's radical distinction between the empirical sciences and a priori (or practical) philosophy. Anthropology is an *empirical* kind of study, and, as such, surely it analyzes humans as beings that are entirely governed by mechanistic causal laws? In the *Prolegomena to Any Future Metaphysics,* Kant tells us that the basis for the division of the sciences is determined by "the difference of its object [*Objekt*], or of the sources of knowledge, or of the kind of knowledge, or of some if not all of these together" (Prol 4:265). With this in mind, we might say that anthropology gives us an empirical kind of knowledge, the object of which is man. On this account, anthropology is largely synonymous with what Kant calls empirical psychology. Anthropology would thus yield a theoretical, as opposed to practical, kind of knowledge. In line with this interpretation the *Lectures* passage quoted above says that anthropology is *not* a branch of practical philosophy; it studies humans as they are and not as they would or should be. How can I reconcile these considerations with my reading of this passage?

The first thing to note is that Kant uses the term *Objekt* to mean either the subject matter or aim of a science. So, on the same method of classification that Kant uses in the *Prolegomena, pragmatic* anthropology turns out to be a part of practical philosophy, since its object—in the sense of *aim*—is the betterment of man. Kant writes at the start of the *Anthropology* that pragmatic anthropology "aims at what man makes, can, or should make of himself as a freely acting being" (A 7:119). For Kant, *moral* anthropology is that branch of pragmatic anthropology that deals with moral betterment. So, the object—in the sense of subject matter—of anthropology is man. Meanwhile, the object—in the sense of aim—of moral anthropology is moral betterment. But when the object as aim is practical (as in the case of moral anthropology), then the object as subject matter of this same science is the human as a free and moral being. Clearly, it is only as such that humans can improve morally. Thus, the subject matter of moral anthropology is the human as a free agent and not as a determined being. It is surely in view of this that Kant tells us in the *Metaphysics* that practical philosophy "has not nature but freedom of choice for its object," and a few lines later adds, "The counterpart of a metaphysics of morals, the other member of the division of practical philosophy as a whole, would be moral anthropology" (MM 6:216–17). Practical philosophy deals with freedom of choice, and moral anthropology is a branch of practical philosophy.[28] With all of this in mind, we can now draw a fairly concrete distinction: the subject matter of Kant's *anthropology* is nature, and the subject matter of his *moral anthropology* is freedom.[29]

Unfortunately, Kant does not always employ this distinction between anthropology and moral anthropology in a systematic or consistent way. For example, in the *Lectures* passage quoted at the start of this section he refers only to anthropology, but, insofar as this notion of anthropology includes a study of "whether man is in a position to" act morally, it seems to overlap with moral anthropology (and thus, in spite of what Kant says, it is a part of practical philosophy). The rules of action to which Kant refers in this passage are not at all relevant to the issue of acting morally if these rules concern man as a determined being. In the *Anthropology* itself Kant also seems to mix anthropology and moral anthropology.[30] His investigation in this text clearly assumes that man is free to change. But it is also an empirical study in that Kant makes numerous empirical observations, and often draws what appear to be mechanically causal connections within psychological, social, and pedagogical contexts. Moral anthropology, insofar as it has practical ends, assumes that the object of its study (i.e., the human being) is free, and thus that whatever causal relations are (theoretically) described *do not* undermine freedom. When Kant blurs the division between anthropology and moral anthropology he allows freedom into the former. And so, while we might *expect* Kant's anthropology to present an empirical story that traces cause after cause of human behavior, the reality is otherwise. As Allen Wood puts the point, "The truth about Kantian anthropology, however, is very different from this picture. . . . [His] empirical anthropology always proceeds on the fundamental presupposition that human beings are free" (Wood 1999, 181).[31]

On this account, then, both Kant's anthropology and moral anthropology turn out to be concerned with the psychology of moral, and thus free, agents. Now, Kant refers to the kind of freedom that is relevant to actual moral action as *practical freedom*. In one of his lectures, Kant (referring to some earlier comments he made) explains that "Practical or psychological freedom was the independence of the power of choice from the necessitation of stimuli. This is treated in empirical psychology, and this concept of freedom was also sufficient enough for morality" (LM 28:267).[32] Practical freedom is the freedom of the moral agent from being *determined*, though not *affected*, by sensuous impulses. Rather than causally determining our behavior, our desires and feelings only have an *effect* upon the actions—including the moral actions—that we freely choose. In Kant's own terminology, we are free and rational, but *sensuously affected*. It is this sensuous dimension of man that is studied in Kant's anthropological work.[33] It is studied in order to see if man is "in a position" to act morally even while this sensuous nature affects him. Consequently—and this is the basic point of the passage from the *Lectures on Ethics* quoted above—anthropology is relevant to a priori morals insofar as it tells us something about our sensibility, and how this sensibility *affects* moral choices.

This interpretation is borne out by Kant's published comments on the relation between anthropology and morals proper. For example, Kant tells us in the *Groundwork* that "all morals . . . need anthropology for their application [*Anwendung*] to men" (G 4:412). He elaborates on this notion of the "application" of morals in the *Metaphysics* when he says that "a metaphysics of morals cannot dispense with principles of application, and we shall often have to take as our object the particular *nature* of human beings, which is cognized only by experience. . . . The counterpart of a metaphysics of morals, the other member of the division of practical philosophy as a whole, would be moral anthropology, which, however, would deal only with the subjective conditions in human nature that hinder people or help them in fulfilling the laws of a metaphysics of morals" (MM 6:217). Kant characterizes *moral* anthropology here as the study of our psychology ("subjective conditions") and how it impacts our acting morally. Since it is only in view of our free choices that we are moral creatures, Kant's point must be that this anthropology studies the hindering or helping impact of our desires and feelings on our free choices.

My central contention is that this question of the impact of our psychology on our free choices is *also* relevant to the more specific issue of *how* we are morally *motivated*, since the moral motive must combat these psychological hindrances to morality. But why, one might ask, does this make psychology pertinent to the issue of *how* moral motivation works? In other words, why does it follow from the fact that the moral motive must combat desires and feelings that the latter are relevant to *how* respect works? Kant himself comes closest to linking anthropology and moral motivation along these very lines when he says, in the mid-1780s, "Anthropology is pragmatic, but contributes to moral knowledge of the human being because from it one must derive [*schöpfen*] the grounds of movement [*bewegungsGründe*] for morality, and without it morality would be scholastic and not applicable to the world."[34] According to this passage, the basis of moral motivation ("movement") must somehow be drawn (*schöpfen*), or taken, from anthropology. In saying this, Kant cannot mean that the basis for the *existence* of moral motivation must be drawn from anthropology, since this basis is the moral law itself and this law is most certainly not drawn from any empirical investigation. But Kant's point makes sense if we take him to be referring to the basis for the *functioning* of moral "movement" or motivation. In this case, the claim would be that in order to know how the feeling of respect works as the moral motive we must understand how the desires and feelings that threaten it work.

As I will argue in chapter 5, the key reason that the motivational workings of desires and feelings are relevant to the workings of moral motivation is that for Kant the moral incentive functions in essentially the same way as these motive forces with which it competes. There are some essential *structural parallels* between the ways in which pathological forces and respect move the will. Kant seems to say just this in the second *Critique*, when he comments that "respect . . . is hardly an analogue of the feeling of pleasure, *although in relation to the faculty of desire it does the same thing* but from different sources" (Pr. R 5:117; emphasis added). Anthropology, then, shows us what the moral motive must be like in order to impact the agent's motivational mechanism and influence choice. Ultimately, it is in this way that studying anthropology and the psychological hindrances to morality *points* us to the question of how the moral law moves us to action. The empirical part of ethics provides a *background*, then, to the a priori part, in providing a background to the issue of how the law moves us as free but sensibly affected beings.[35]

Subjective and Objective Determination of the Will

Kant's distinction between the objective and subjective determination of the will helps to clarify and support the point just made. For Kant, the objective determining ground of the will is the standard of morality, while the subjective ground is the principle of motivation. Kant tells us, in a lecture from the mid-1780s:

> We have first to take up two points here: (1) The principle of appraisal of obligation, and (2) the principle of its performance or execution. Guideline and motive have here to be distinguished. The guideline is the principle of appraisal, and the motive that of carrying-out the obligation; in that they have been confused, everything in morality has been erroneous. If the question is: What is morally good or not?, that is the principle of appraisal, whereby I judge the goodness or depravity of actions. But if the question is: What moves me to live according to this law?, that is the principle of motive. Appraisal of the action is the objective ground, but not yet the subjective ground. That which impels me to do the thing, of which understanding tells me that I ought to do it, is the *motiva subjective moventia*. . . . This motive is the moral feeling. Such a principle of motive cannot be confused with the principle of judgment. (LE 27:274)

To objectively determine the will is to tell it what it ought to do, morally or prudentially. To subjectively determine the will is to move it to perform an action. This is the most important (and prevalent) use of the subjective/objective distinction that Kant makes in the ethical context. For Kant, the moral feeling of respect is the subjective determining ground of the will. Since we are not fully rational, but, rather, partly sensuous, we require a distinct subjective, or motivating, ground that can affect us sensuously. Kant never strays from this view. He tells us in the *Groundwork* that "A maxim is the subjective principle of volition. The objective principle (i.e., that which would serve all rational beings also subjectively as a practical principle if reason had full power over the faculty of desire) is the practical law" (G 4:400n). Thus, insofar as reason does not have full power over the faculty of desire, being moved by the practical law is not an essential and intrinsic feature of our nature. Instead, the practical law *obligates* us, it places a demand upon us, and this demand must somehow matter to us as free but sensuously affected beings. Now, what matters to us as sensuously affected beings are the maxims that we freely adopt by incorporating incentives into "subjective principle[s] of volition." For Kant, then, the moral law can only matter to us if we somehow have an incentive to act morally that we incorporate into our "subjective principles" or maxims. Respect is this incentive, and Kant tells us in the *Religion* that "This capacity for simple respect for the moral law within us would thus be moral feeling, which in and through itself does not constitute an end of the natural predisposition except so far as it is the motivating force of the will. Since this is possible only when *the free will incorporates such moral feeling into its maxim,* the property of such a will is good character" (Rel 6:29; emphasis added). I will argue in chapter 5 that the feeling of respect is incorporated into moral maxims in essentially the same way as nonmoral incentives are incorporated into nonmoral maxims.

Bringing these strands together, we can conclude that insofar as reason qua reason does not have full control over the faculty of desire, the moral law strikes us as an obligation, and that in order for us to meet this obligation the law must in some way sensuously impact our faculty of desire (i.e., through the incorporation of respect into maxims). Thus, we must be moved sensuously by the moral law for precisely the same reason that we are *obligated* by it in the first place—that is, as a result of our partly sensuous nature. It is in view of this that, when Kant reflects on his earlier chapter on the moral feeling of respect as an incentive (in the second *Critique*), he tells us that it is an attempt to understand the "necessary influence" of "pure practical reason on our sensibility" (Pr. R 5:90).[36] Without this necessary influence we would not be able to act morally. Studying the sensuous (i.e., psychological) dimension of our nature is important, then, for an understanding of how reason impacts us psychologically and thus allows us to meet the moral demand or obligation.

At the heart of my methodological approach is the view that Kant's comments on the moral feeling of respect can only be properly understood against the background of his account of our sensibility. It is only with this account in mind that we can grasp how Kant thinks the moral law influences our sensibility such that we are motivated to be moral. Understanding how the moral law functions in our human world is essentially equivalent to comprehending the conditions for the possibility of our acting on the moral law in view of (perhaps in spite of) our sensuous constitutions. But these conditions are part of our motivational mechanism and the psychological forces that operate upon it, so we must understand this motivational mechanism and the forces that act upon it before we can reconstruct Kant's understanding of how respect works as an incentive to moral action. The relevant background to the issue of how Kant thinks respect functions encompasses both the psychological dimension of his anthropology and his theory of action, including his theory of motivation. More specifically, that background is provided in Kant's theory of action (and motivation), understood in the light of his account of psychology.

Two Standpoints

Before saying a little more about both of these areas—Kant's theory of action and his account of human psychology—I want to address briefly an issue that has been lurking (or looming) behind my discussion of the relation between a priori and empirical ethics: Kant's two standpoints on the will. According to what is now quite a common reading, Kant thinks that humans are free agents when seen from the "intelligible standpoint," and causally determined beings when viewed from the "empirical standpoint." I have already argued that Kant's study of anthropology is, in spite of some of the things he says, the empirical study of the human as a moral and free being. On this account, Kant focuses on the empirically discoverable characteristics and conditions of a being that he assumes is not causally necessitated by these characteristics and conditions. But, again, if anthropology really is an empirical study, then the object of this study should be a causally determined being, not a free and merely intelligible one. On my reading, then, Kant is somehow combining both standpoints—empirical and intelligible—in a way that does not *seem* to be legitimate in view of the strictness with which he is supposed to divide these standpoints.[37]

A full defense of my interpretation of the two standpoints is not within the scope of this introduction, but I do want to sketch an explanation of (and present some evidence for) this interpretation. On my account, there are two distinct ways of looking at agents: practically (as free but sensuously affected beings) and theoretically (as determined beings). Notice here that this practical/theoretical distinction does *not* map precisely onto Kant's intelligible/empirical (or noumena/phenomena) distinction.[38] What is the difference between these two distinctions? According to the latter, the intelligible self is beyond all sensible intuition, and thus is not susceptible to tempting desires or urges.[39] Kant writes of the intelligible/empirical distinction as follows:

> Thus in respect to mere perception and receptivity to sensations he must count himself as belonging to the world of sense; but in respect to that which may be pure activity in himself . . . he must reckon himself as belonging to the intellectual world. . . . For this reason a rational being must regard itself qua intelligence (and not from the side of his lower faculties) as belonging to the world of understanding and not to that of the senses. Thus it has two standpoints from which it can consider itself and recognize the laws [governing] the employment of its powers and all its actions: first, as belonging to the world of sense, under the laws of nature (heteronomy), and, second, as belonging to the intelligible world under laws which, independent of nature, are not empirical but founded on reason alone. (G 4:451–52)

Kant's division here between intelligible and sensible selves is not the same as the division between the practical and theoretical (i.e., the morally obligated and the determined) agents referred to above. Instead, the intelligible self provides the condition for the possibility of our being moral creatures, but actual human morality involves a conjunction of the intelligible and sensible. It is surely with this in mind that Kant writes, "But we now see that, if we think of ourselves as free, we transport ourselves into the intelligible world as members of it and know the autonomy of the will together with its consequence, morality; *whereas if we think of ourselves as obligated, we consider ourselves as belonging both to the world of sense and at the same time to the intelligible world*" (G 4:453; emphasis added). Kant is clear here: somehow, both the intelligible world and the world of sense include the obligated self. (I am referring to the standpoint of this obligated self as the *practical* standpoint.[40]) Unlike the intelligible self, the agent that is obligated *does* experience tempting desires; otherwise she would not go through any of the moral conflicts typical of human beings. Of course, this practical agent does not experience these desires as causally determining—but she experiences them nonetheless. They affect her actions insofar as they produce motives between which she must freely choose. The intelligible self, on the other hand, is purely rational and not susceptible (i.e., passive) to sensible experience. It is this intelligible dimension of our total being that legislatively (or, in Kant's terms, "objectively") determines the will.

Kant's distinction between transcendental and practical freedom is relevant here. For Kant, transcendental freedom is defined negatively as "independence from everything empirical and hence from nature generally" (Pr. R 5:97), and positively as "the power of beginning a state spontaneously" (A 533/B 561). Practical freedom is (negatively) the "will's independence of coercion through sensuous impulses" (A 534/B 562), and (positively) the capacity to act on "motives which are represented only by reason" (A 802/B 830). Transcendental freedom is the freedom of the purely intelligible self. Meanwhile, practical freedom is the freedom of the sensuously affected/morally obligated agent.[41] It is through this kind of sensuously affected freedom that the feeling of respect must operate and move us to moral action. It has been argued, however, that Kant abandons his notion of practical freedom after he discovers the principle of autonomy in the *Groundwork,* maligning it (in the second *Critique*) as the compatibilist freedom of a "turnspit." I will contend in chapter 3, however, that Kant maintains essentially the same incompatibilist notion of practical freedom throughout his works, insofar as he never wavers from the idea that it is a sensuously affected free will (i.e., *Willkür*) that makes moral choices.

Of course, none of this should be read as undermining the importance of transcendental freedom in Kant's moral system. Again, transcendental freedom is the freedom of the agent considered as purely intelligible—it is the freedom of a spontaneous first cause, and insofar as we possess it we are the ultimate ground of our moral actions.[42] Transcendental freedom is a purely intelligible concept insofar as it requires us to posit an uncaused cause and thus to suspend our theoretical commitments to a causal chain. Now, Kant tells us that transcendental freedom is an important component of practical freedom but that it "does not by any means constitute the whole content" (A 448/B 476) of this idea. It is this transcendental component of practical freedom that is "the real stumbling-block" (A 448/B 476) for philosophy in that it is a merely intelligible idea. Our discussions of the practically free agent are therefore going to involve explanatory gaps as we approach the intelligible (i.e., transcendental) dimension of this freedom.[43] At the same time, however, this intelligible aspect of practical freedom is required in order to ensure the spontaneity and thus the imputability of the agent.

As I will argue, when Kant speaks of the intelligible world in the *Groundwork,* the relevant notion of freedom is transcendental freedom. But when he speaks of us "belonging both to the world of sense and . . . to the intelligible world" (G 4:453), the relevant notion is practical freedom, for it is this "mainly empirical" (A 448/B 476) notion that has both sensible and intelligible dimensions (captured in the idea of being sensuously *affected*). Ordinarily, when Kant discusses moral *actions* he has the practically free agent in mind. Kant's anthropology, in studying the sensible side of this practically free agent, does not explore psychological factors as causal determinants of behavior; instead, these factors are understood as merely affecting behavior. Ultimately, the effect of our feelings and desires is that they provide motives to nonmoral and, of course, immoral actions, and I will argue in chapter 5 that these motives operate in a way that is (in part) *structurally parallel* to the way in which respect operates in the case of moral action. Kant's anthropology is relevant to my argument, then, insofar as it provides some of the details of his account of the structure of motivation for nonmoral actions.

Kantian Psychology and Theory of Action

In his *Encyclopädisches Wörterbuch der kritischen Philosophie,* Georg Samuel Albert Mellin (a contemporary of Kant) connects Kant's a priori and empirical ethics by saying that practical anthropology "is the application of morality to the characteristic condition and situation of the human faculty of desire [*Begehrungsvermögens*]—to the drives, inclinations, appetites, and passions of the human being, and the hindrances to the carrying-out of the moral law" (Mellin 1970, 277). Mellin correctly sees that the faculty of desire is at the heart of human psychology for Kant.[44] Feeling and desire—Kant's two basic psychological categories— can both be understood in terms of the faculty of desire, since feelings determine, and desires are determinations of, this faculty. Ultimately, then, Kant's account of the faculty of desire and its receptivity to the moral law is critical in understanding how respect works as a motive.

With very few exceptions, analyses of the faculty of desire are new in Kant scholarship.[45] This is not to say that scholars have never talked about Kant's understanding of human psychology. They have, but their focus has all too frequently been on Kant's dismissal of the psychological forces that move us as candidates for grounding moral actions. As a result, scholars have often passed over Kant's finer psychological distinctions. For example, numerous Kantians have treated feeling, emotion, desire, and inclination as though they were interchangeable notions. In one such case, Lawrence Hinman writes, "Once Kant has taken this rather crucial step of placing the emotions quite squarely in the world of causally determined phenomena, he is faced with a very serious problem: showing how pure reason can move the will to action. . . . Not only does he hold that the realm of our feelings and emotions—in this context, Kant calls them 'inclinations' (Neigungen)—is a causally determined one, but he also maintains that it is generally ordered in such a way that it runs counter to the demands of the moral law" (Hinman 1983, 254). But, in actual fact, there is never a context in which Kant refers to our feelings and emotions as our inclinations.[46] Indeed, for Kant, feelings and emotions on the one hand, and desires and inclinations on the other, form the two primary psychological categories. Similarly, Nancy Sherman says that for Kant "the reasons for an agent to act based on emotions such as compassion or friendship are permissible so long as they are constrained by a motive of duty. That is, inclinations can support acting from duty but only within boundaries set by duty" (Sherman 1990, 161). But again, Kant consistently draws a concrete distinction between emotion and inclination, so Sherman's interchangeable use of these terms is unjustified. In what follows, I hope to redress these oversights by clearly drawing the psychological distinctions that Kant has in mind and articulating the role that these distinct psychological elements play in nonmoral, and then moral, action.

Of course, Kant's fully developed theory of nonmoral action is not simply a matter of his account of the faculty of desire and the various psychological forces that determine and are determinations of this faculty. Kant posits a second crucial dimension to action, the essence of which is captured in what Henry Allison dubs the Incorporation Thesis.[47] According to this thesis, the faculty of desire throws up incentives, upon which the agent may or may not act. The process of acting upon incentives, for a free and rational agent, involves the incorporation of these incentives into maxims that govern action. Unfortunately, scholars have only used the Incorporation Thesis to explain how Kant thinks we can be sensuously affected yet free beings. Without further discussion, incorporation has been understood simply as a way of securing freedom for the agent, by inserting a wedge—the somewhat mysterious act of incorporating—between the agent and her desires and feelings. But I think that there is more to consider in, and conclude from, this thesis. Along these lines, I will investigate how we as sensuous beings act out of respect for the law (i.e., the moral incentive) by considering how we act out of any incentive at all. This will involve looking more closely at what incentives really are (i.e., psychology), and at precisely what it means to *incorporate* an incentive into a maxim (i.e., theory of choice/action).

As I mentioned above, many Kant scholars have thought of moral motivation as a kind of motivation that is entirely distinct from nonmoral motivation. But, in fact, Kant's notion of incorporation goes some way toward removing the radical distinction between moral and nonmoral action. According to this thesis, *all* actions are freely chosen insofar as they are grounded in an incentive (moral or nonmoral) that has been incorporated into a maxim. Thus, it is not just nonmoral incentives that are incorporated into maxims. As we saw above, Kant writes, "This capacity for simple respect for the moral law within us would thus be moral feeling, which in and through itself does not constitute an end of the natural predisposition except so far as it is the motivating force of the will. Since this is possible only when *the free will incorporates such moral feeling into its maxim,* the property of such a will is good character" (Rel 6:29; emphasis added). A little later in the same text Kant refers to the "subjective ground for the adoption into our maxims of this respect as a motivating force" (Rel 6:29). So *all* actions, moral and nonmoral, involve the presence of an incentive and the incorporation of this incentive into a maxim. I will attempt to articulate and explain this process in the chapters that follow.

III. THE STRUCTURE OF THE ARGUMENT

The general direction and aim of my study can be outlined as follows. I begin with Kant's analysis of human psychology, and then work toward formulating a theory of *nonmoral* action by connecting this psychology with Kant's views on rational agency. I then discuss the differences between moral agency and nonmoral agency before moving, finally, to a theory of moral action. That is, I intend to illuminate Kant's thinking on respect by placing it in the context of his account of nonmoral agency. In a sense, this reverses the order of inquiry typical in Kant studies, where discussions of Kant's ethics often precede, and spawn, interpretations of his theory of action.[48]

In chapter 1, I describe Kant's treatment of the faculties of desire and feeling in texts such as the *Religion*, the *Metaphysics*, and the *Anthropology*. Rather than merely presenting an inventory of Kant's psychological concepts, I introduce each notion through a discussion of an associated issue. The overall concern of the chapter, however, is to present a broad outline of Kant's understanding of the relationship between the faculty of desire and the faculty of feeling.

In chapter 2, I bring the notion of pleasure into greater focus by pointing to an ambiguity in Kant's understanding of desire formation. Kant presents three distinct accounts of the role of pleasure in the formation of desires. I propose a resolution to this ambiguity by arguing that these accounts are not incompatible, but can actually be reconciled in a single theory. Furthermore, I claim that in spite of Andrews Reath's arguments to the contrary this account of desire formation commits Kant to a form of hedonism. This hedonism allows for a greater understanding of some of the terrain covered in chapter 1, so I refer back to this chapter in order to clarify further the nature of the relationship between feelings and desires.

In chapter 3, I turn my attention to Kant's understanding of rational agency by discussing his account of the freedom of nonmoral actions. According to some scholars, Kant's treatment of freedom commits him to the idea that only moral and immoral actions are free. On this view, choices between nonmoral ends are not free but are determined by the agent's conception of happiness. In response, I argue that Kant actually grounds a nonmoral conception of freedom in the moral concept of autonomy.

In chapter 4, I develop Kant's account of nonmoral rational action by raising the issue of how the Incorporation Thesis can be reconciled with the phenomenon of weakness of the will. According to Kant's Incorporation Thesis, all actions are chosen on the basis of maxims. It follows from this that all actions are principled, and, thus, justified for the agent. But how, then, can weak actions be possible if they are understood as actions that the agent does not think are justified? In tackling this issue I introduce all of the notions relevant to Kant's theory of rational action: maxims, interests, and happiness. I go on (in the second part of this chapter) to bring my accounts of the rationality and freedom of non-moral action together with some of my conclusions from chapters 1 and 2. In doing so, I present an interpretation of Kantian rational action that takes into consideration the psychology of the agent. Thus, I take seriously Kant's persistent claim that we are rational but sensuously affected agents. The focus of the second part of this chapter is on working out exactly what happens when incentives are incorporated into maxims that then determine action.

In chapter 5, I draw on my treatment of nonmoral agency in presenting an account of respect as the moral motive. I argue that Kant's account of nonmoral agency can be used to understand his treatment of respect as a moral motive since this feeling of respect operates in a way that fundamentally parallels the way in which nonmoral motives operate. The only differences between moral and nonmoral motivation lie in the distinct grounds of each, in the intentional objects of the feelings involved, and in the differing intentions the agent has in mind. My account pieces together all of the structural parallels between moral and nonmoral action and concludes by responding to the most serious objection that might be leveled against this interpretation.

In my conclusion, I supplement my argument by challenging Andrews Reath's influential reading of Kant on respect. I argue that Reath's interpretation—which claims that respect does not motivate as a feeling—is not faithful to Kant's texts. I contend that the ultimate source of the misreading is Reath's failure to consider all of the possible ways in which feeling might play a role in action.

· ·

CHAPTER ONE

KANT'S PSYCHOLOGY IN THE NONMORAL CONTEXT

Scholars have become increasingly interested in Kant's theory of nonmoral action. According to one commentator, this is largely a product of Henry Allison's attempt in 1990 to argue that Kant does not conceive of nonmoral action as mechanically deterministic.[1] On Allison's account, the view that an incentive only determines the will if it is incorporated into a maxim (or subjective principle of action) removes the misconception that Kant thought of nonmoral, or desire-based, action in terms of causal forces that simply push us deterministically into heteronomous actions. According to the Incorporation Thesis, a desire, in order to be effective, must be incorporated into a maxim based on some kind of rational assessment of its value. A desire becomes a reason for action when it is so incorporated. Maxims, then, provide us with chosen and principled *reasons* that draw us into action, as opposed to desiderative *causes* that deterministically push us into action. This basic understanding of Kant's position on rational action dominates the contemporary literature.

But the suggestion that reasons and maxims are the key notions in an account of how rational desire-based actions are motivated does not amount to a license to minimize the role played in these same actions by pathological forces such as desires, emotions, and inclinations. Unfortunately, this is precisely what has happened in Allison's account as well as in those interpretations that are close to or influenced by Allison.[2] In a sense, the traditional tendency to overlook Kant's empirical thinking has been further facilitated by Allison's emphasis on the Incorporation Thesis, since this thesis has been taken to suggest that the complex psychological side of human nature can be incorporated *into* clean rational maxims and *out of* Kant's theory of rational action. But, in fact, this is not suggested by a correct understanding of the Incorporation Thesis at all. Instead, as I have indicated, there is a significant closeness between Kant's anthropology and his theory of rational action—his empirical psychology and his account of free, maxim-based agency. The incorporation of incentives into maxims is not equivalent to the annihilation, or even neutralization, of an agent's psychology. I will argue, instead, that our maxims include a pathological dimension that is essential to their functioning.

Approaching the same point from a slightly different angle, we might say that Kant's distinction between anthropology as an empirical investigation of humans, and theory of rational action as a metaphysical inquiry into the merely intelligible realm of freedom, does not mean (as the recent emphasis on the *two standpoints* interpretation of Kant's metaphysics seems to suggest) that the *empirical psychology* of the *free* agent cannot be meaningfully discussed. In actual fact, Kant persistently talks about the psychology of the practically free agent in texts such as the *Religion* and the *Metaphysics*. Moreover, Kant never even tries to present us with two incommensurable accounts of human action—an empirical and an intelligible one. Instead, he consistently offers us a mixed, but "*mainly* empirical" (A 448/B 476), account of a practically free agent. In Kant's actual discussions of rational action, his division between the empirical and the intelligible just translates into the requirement that his empirical observations on human agency and motivation be supplemented by concepts that are merely intelligible. The notion of transcendental freedom is, of course, the most important of these intelligible concepts.

In this chapter, I will approach the conjunction of the psychological and rational from the psychological side. This is the first step in an argument that is designed to show that the empirically accessible psychological forces that seek expression in our actions do *not* simply *undergo* incorporation, and then (effectively) *disappear* into the principled rationality of maxims. To dismiss our psychology in this way, and then to focus only on maxims and their functioning, is to overlook the finer details of Kant's psychology and the difference that these details make in understanding his theory of rational agency. In particular, viewing Kant's thinking on action in this way creates an artificial divide between our pathology and our reason—a divide that is mistakenly institutionalized by the view that in Kant's treatment of action the empirical and the intelligible represent two completely incommensurable ways of seeing things, and thus are never brought together in a meaningful way.[3] So, even though I utilize the division between the psychological and rational dimensions of agency throughout this study, one of my goals in this chapter will be to show how this (initially useful) division starts to break down in Kant's actual analyses. More precisely, I will show how Kant infuses his discussion of psychology—a discussion one might expect to be strictly empirical— with assumptions about freedom and rationality. The truth about Kant's conception of nonmoral rational agency lies somewhere between the excessively rational reading suggested by Allison's interpretation of the Incorporation Thesis, and the excessively empirical reading according to which we are mechanically pushed into determined actions.

Let me begin, then, with the psychology of the agent. My intention in this chapter is to sketch out Kant's primary psychological faculties and their interrelations via a series of separate issues. Section I introduces Kant's notion of the faculty of desire by addressing a central ambiguity surrounding his definition of this faculty. I will present in section II the psychological determinations of the faculty of desire: desire, inclination, instinct, and passion. For Kant, these determinations provide us with the basic drives or incentives (*Triebfedern*) to action. I will argue that free-dom plays a role in the formation of some of these desires. Finally, in section III, I will turn to the faculty of feeling, which is the capacity for feelings and affects. I will explore the nature of an affect in some depth and conclude this chapter by presenting an initial framework for under-standing the relationships between the various forms of desire and feel-ing. We will see that a full understanding of these relationships does not simply involve laying out mechanically causal accounts, but draws us into a picture that includes the concepts of freedom and rationality.

I. THE FACULTY OF DESIRE

Desire

Broadly speaking, Kant thinks that nonmoral actions are grounded in choices made on the basis of desires. Desires are made possible by the faculty of desire (*Begehrungsvermögens*). Thus, Kant tells us in the *Meta-physics* (6:212) that the "determination of the faculty of desire" is a desire (*Begierde*). Kant thinks of the faculty of desire as the ability or power by which we bring things into existence. He writes, "The faculty of desire is the power to cause the objects of one's mental representations by means of these same representations" (MM 6:211).[4] Let desire$_1$ refer to desire in the broad and neutral sense of any determination of the faculty of desire. Since the determination of the faculty of desire is a desire$_1$ for something, it follows that a desire$_1$ is that by which something is brought into existence via the idea that we have of this thing. Kant defines the faculty of desire as a *capacity* to have desires$_1$, simply meaning that regardless of whether we actually have a desire$_1$ at any given moment we have a faculty by which we are capable of having one. For Kant, there are many different kinds of desire$_1$—that is to say, many different determinations of the faculty of desire. These different kinds of desire$_1$ include desires (proper), wishes, instincts, inclinations, and passions.[5] These desires$_1$ are distinguished on the basis of their origins, the frequency with which they are experienced, and the kinds of consciousness that accompanies them, but they are also identical in that they are all ways of bringing things into existence.

Unfortunately, Kant presents a *slightly* different account of desire$_1$ in the *Anthropology* when he writes, "Desire (*appetitio*) is the self-determination of the power of a subject to imagine something in the future as an effect of such imagination" (A 7:251; translation modified). On this account, a desire$_1$ is a determination of the power to imagine something in existence as a result of our imagining it. The faculty of desire, on this definition, is the power or capacity to imagine something in the future as a result of our imagining it. So, to have a desire$_1$ is just to imagine something in existence as a result of imagining it.

Now, how can a desire$_1$ be both that by which things are brought into existence *and* imagining something in existence as a result of our imagining it? How are these seemingly distinct characterizations of desire$_1$ linked? Answering this question, and better understanding Kant's treatment of the faculty of desire, is made more difficult by the fact that neither of these accounts of desire$_1$ are familiar. Ordinarily, we do not think of a desire$_1$ as that by which something is brought into existence via the ideas that we have of this thing, nor do we think of it as imagining something existing as a result of imagining this thing. Common sense tells us (quite phenomenologically) that a desire$_1$ is a kind of feeling.[6] For example, passive or reserved people might describe a desire$_1$ as a feeling of *being drawn* to something. More active or dynamic people might say that a desire$_1$ is a feeling of *striving* or *moving* toward something. But Kant does not think that a desire$_1$ is *fundamentally* either of these things, and, indeed, he says very little about the phenomenology of desires$_1$. In defining a desire$_1$ as imagining something in existence as a result of our imagining it (i.e., the second account), Kant is breaking a desire$_1$ into its component parts in order to get at something essential about its *function:* a desire$_1$ is composed of *something imagined in the future* and *the possibility of this thing coming into being because it is imagined.* Now, this second part—the possibility—is itself a product of the power to bring things into existence, and it is this power, which Kant identifies with a desire$_1$ in the *Metaphysics* passage (i.e., the first account), that is really at the heart of what a desire$_1$ *does.* It is in terms of this function (i.e., what a desire$_1$ does) that Kant defines the faculty of desire and the desires$_1$ that are determinations of it. Thus, imagining something existing as a result of imagining it is contingent upon having a power to bring things about out of our ideas, and this latter power is, for Kant, the functional essence of desiring. The fact that Kant understands the faculty of desire in terms of the function of desires$_1$ will turn out to be very significant in coming to grips with his theory of action.

Now, a functional account of something brackets all of those questions concerning the material or phenomenological nature of this particular thing, and focuses on that which this thing produces or effects. For example, to define a hammer as an object by which one drives or forces hard objects into other hard objects is to offer a functional account of a hammer. This account tells us nothing about what hammers are made of, or what they look or feel like, but it still captures an essential dimension of hammers. Similarly, to define a desire$_1$ as that by which things are brought (or the power to bring things) about through our ideas is to bracket any discussion of the composition of a desire$_1$, or of the agent's experience of desiring.

A short example here might serve to show that, despite its unfamiliarity, Kant's account of desire$_1$ as that by which things are brought into existence as a result of imagining them can be related to some of our commonsense (and phenomenological) intuitions about desires$_1$. Suppose one desires$_1$ a drink of iced water on a hot day. What does it mean to have such a desire$_1$? Phenomenologically speaking, one might have a mental representation of the iced water and experience being drawn toward the object of this representation such that one considers measures toward acquiring it.[7] Now, for Kant, the crucial element of desire$_1$ is that this second part of the experience of desiring a glass of water is predicated upon an assumed power to bring it into existence. Any experience of being drawn toward the iced water or reasoning about how to get it is conditioned by a power.[8] By articulating the notion of desire$_1$ in terms of function Kant is pointing to something deep about desires$_1$: the fact that the possession of the power to produce objects *fundamentally orients us toward* production. Having a faculty of desire, then, amounts to having a kind of deep orientation toward, or focus aimed at, production. This orientation gets imaginative expression in our imagining things existing as a result of our imagination. It is on the basis of this deep orientation that we can experience striving for or being drawn toward objects.

Kant is quite aware of the controversial nature of his function-based approach to the faculty of desire (though, strictly speaking, he does not refer to it as a *function-based* approach). Noting in the *Metaphysics* that an astute critic has taken him to task over this conception, he writes, "What is meant by the faculty of desire? It is, the text says, the capacity to be by means of one's representation the cause of the objects of these representations.—To this exposition he objects 'that it comes to nothing as soon as one abstracts from the external conditions of the result of desire.—But the faculty of desire is something even for an idealist, even though the external world is nothing for him'" (MM 6:356). So the criticism (of the astute critic) is that Kant's account of the faculty of desire makes no sense, since people who do not believe in the existence of external effects in the world (i.e., idealists) still believe in the faculty of desire. Kant responds to this criticism as follows:

> *I reply:* but are there not also intense but still consciously futile longings (e.g., Would to God that man were still alive!), which are *devoid of any deed* but not *devoid of any result,* since they still work powerfully within the subject himself (make him ill), though not on external things? A desire, as a *striving (nisus)* to be a *cause* by means of one's representations, is still always causality, at least within the subject, even when he sees the inadequacy

of his representations for the effect he envisages.—The misunderstanding here amounts to this: that since consciousness of one's capacity *in general* is (in the case mentioned) also consciousness of one's *incapacity* with respect to the external world, the definition is not applicable to the idealist. Since, however, all that is in question here is the relation of a cause (a representation) to an effect (a feeling) in general, the causality of representation (whether the causality is external or internal) with regard to its object must unavoidably be thought in the concept of the faculty of desire. (MM 6:356–57)

Kant introduces the phenomenological component of a $desire_1$ as a striving or endeavoring to be a cause, and argues that it is present even when the agent knows that he cannot cause the object in question.[9] In such a case, feelings of illness may be caused. Is Kant, then, identifying a $desire_1$ with the striving and not with the deeper causality? Has Kant, upon meeting resistance, simply reverted to a more familiar phenomenological view of $desire_1$?

I do not think that he has. Instead, Kant's point appears to be that the striving to which he refers is contingent upon the capacity to be a cause, which again is at the heart of the nature of a $desire_1$ as he defines it. Even though Kant defines a $desire_1$ as that by which an agent brings x into existence by means of the representation of x, it does not follow that a $desire_1$ only becomes a $desire_1$ at the point at which x is produced. To say that the definition of a $desire_1$ is function-based is not to say that we must wait for actual production (or completion of the function) before deciding whether or not a $desire_1$ is present. Kant's account of the faculty of desire is not *production-based*. Instead, we might think of Kant's definition of $desire_1$ as *production-oriented*—to have a $desire_1$ is to orient oneself toward production based on one's capacity to produce things (i.e., based on the functional essence of a $desire_1$).

So, something is a $desire_1$ insofar as it orients us toward production. Striving is simply the phenomenological result of this orientation in a specific instance. Now, Kant's point in his reply seems to be that we are often oriented toward production even when we know that we cannot actually produce something. In other words, we do not actually have to think that we can bring something about in order to have a $desire_1$ for it. All that is relevant is that any striving (however futile) assumes that our representations have causal power. This is what Kant means by saying that "the causality of representation with regard to its object must unavoidably be thought in the concept of the faculty of desire." His point is that the faculty of desire cannot but be thought of as the faculty for causing the object of a representation, because there would be no causality of the feeling of disappointment (or illness) without the presence of a power to bring things about (and orient us toward production on the basis of this presence). Again, the effect of this orientation toward production can be disappointment. Kant concludes, then, that the fact that there are desires$_1$ without external effects does not serve to show that the power to cause is not the essence of desire$_1$. Rather, it serves to show that we are often at odds with ourselves. We are at odds with ourselves when we orient ourselves toward production based on the presence of a causal power, even while we are at the same time aware of our inability to cause the object in question.

Kant addresses this paradox explicitly when he discusses the distinction between a desire (proper) and a wish. Both are kinds of desire$_1$, but, for Kant, to *wish* for something is to orient oneself toward production, even though one does not actually exercise one's power in producing. He writes in the *Anthropology,* "Desiring without emphasis on the production of the object is called wish. Wish may be directed toward objects for whose production the subject feels himself *incapable* [*unvermögend*]; in such a case it is an empty (idle) wish" (A 7:251; emphasis added). So, in the case of an idle wish we do not exercise our productive power because we positively know we are incapable of producing the object in question. An idle wish is just one type of wish, and what distinguishes a wish (in general) as a desire is that it is an orientation toward production without any actual measures taken toward production.[10]

Kant's notion of a wish raises the same problem that the astute critic pointed out: how can a wish, which is by definition ineffectual, be a desire$_1$, if a desire$_1$ is that by which things are brought into existence? Kant addresses this question in the third *Critique*.

[T]he definition of the faculty of desire as *the faculty for being through one's representations the cause of the reality of the objects of these representations* has been criticized because mere wishes are also desires, but yet everyone would concede that he could not produce their object by their means alone.—This, however, proves nothing more than that there are also desires in a human being as a result of which he stands in contradiction with himself, in that he works toward [*hinwirkt*] the production of the object by means of his representation *alone*, from which he can however expect no success because he is aware that his mechanical powers . . . are either inadequate or even aimed at something impossible. (CJ 5:177n)

In the case of a desire (proper), the agent is aware of the adequacy of the faculty of desire to produce the object in question. In the case of a wish, there is no such awareness and no effort at production. The agent who wishes does nothing, and yet, at the same time, "works toward" (or, to use the term that I have employed, is *oriented* toward) production. So, to have a wish is to orient oneself toward the production of something based on the presence of the power to cause, even when one does not exercise this power. A wish is still a desire₁, then, because it would not be possible to wish for something without the presence of a power to bring things into existence—this power allows one to orient oneself toward production. In Kantian language, the faculty of desire is the condition for the possibility of a wish. The agent who wishes is "in contradiction with himself" because he does not exercise his power, and yet he orients himself toward doing so anyway.

Choice

Before looking at the other determinations of the faculty of desire I want to turn briefly to the deep connection that Kant draws between the faculty of desire and the power of choice, or *Willkür*. *Willkür* appears to be the seat of human freedom for Kant. It is that in virtue of which we choose maxims and is thus at the very heart of rational agency. Much has been written on Kant's notion of *Willkür*, particularly in its relation to the concept of *Wille*.[11] Rather than repeating or rehearsing these discussions I will limit my focus here to the somewhat mysterious connection that Kant draws between the faculty of desire and *Willkür*.

Kant writes on this connection in the *Metaphysics*, saying, "The faculty of desire . . . insofar as it is joined with one's consciousness of the ability to bring about its object by one's action is called choice [*Willkür*]; if it is not joined with this consciousness its act is called a wish" (MM 6:213). In other words, the faculty of desire is the same as ("is called") the power to choose when we are conscious that we can produce the object in question. Now, this identification should surprise the reader. On this account, a choice is the determination of the faculty of desire that is accompanied by a consciousness of the capacity to produce an object. But, given that Kant distinguishes wishes from all other desires₁ based on the lack of such a consciousness, the implication seems to be that *all* desires₁, with the exception of wishes, include a consciousness of the ability to bring an object about through action. Clearly, this would mean that a choice is the same as a desire (proper), an inclination, an instinct, and a passion. Is it possible, then, that Kant uses the words "desire" (proper), "inclination," etc., as terms of art such that they refer to the same thing as the term "choice"? In ordinary speech, it seems obvious that desiring something (or being inclined to do something, etc.) and choosing something are simply not the same thing. We live our lives desiring many things that we do not choose. How can we explain Kant's confusing classifications?

In another passage in the *Metaphysics*, Kant seems to present the view that there is not a *strict identity* between the faculty of desire and the power of choice. He says that the power of choice is the faculty of desire "considered . . . in relation to action" (MM 6:213). Kant appears to be indicating here that when you limit the faculty of desire by looking at it in conjunction with an actual action, you are looking at the power of choice. On this account, the consciousness of the ability to bring about an object through a *specific* action is the differentiating feature of a choice. A choice is a desire₁ accompanied by the consciousness of a specific action. We could interpret Kant as saying, then, that the faculty of desire is the larger capacity to bring things into existence, and the *final stage* in the process of doing so is the stage of choosing. On this reading, the faculty of desire contains choice as one determination of it. A prior determination of the same faculty would be a desire (proper). Thus, the faculty of desire *is* a power of choice, in the sense that one of the possible determinations of this faculty is a choice.

There is some reason to think that Kant conceives of the relation between the faculty of desire and the power of choice in this way. But Kant also uses the term "faculty of desire" in a second and distinct (albeit related) way that throws a different light on this issue. According to the account just laid out, Kant sees the faculty of desire as a single, specific psychological capacity that allows each agent to have desires$_1$ and to make choices. The essence of this capacity is the ability to bring things into existence, and each kind of determination (apart from wishes) represents a different way of, or stage in, the process of bringing something into existence. On the other hand (and this is the second account), Kant sometimes conceives of the "faculty of desire" as *any* human capacity to bring things into existence. On this account, choice is *a* faculty of desire distinct from that faculty of desire that allows for inclinations, passions, etc. We will see in chapter 4 that Kant also speaks of reason as *a* faculty of desire. On this picture of things, there are a number of distinct faculties of desire, and it is the nature of the consciousness accompanying each kind of production that differentiates these faculties. The power of choice is a faculty of desire just insofar as it is a power to bring things into existence, and its differentiating dimension is a consciousness of the specific productive action. (In the case of reason, on the other hand, the differentiating consciousness turns out to be a consciousness of the moral law.) Kant can define choice, then, in the same way he defines a desire (proper), since both are desires$_1$—that is to say, both are determinations of distinct faculties of desire (which are just distinct powers to bring things into existence).

Now, it seems that Kant's function-based treatment of the faculty of desire allows him to move (unannounced) from one of these conceptions of the faculty of desire to the other, since on both accounts the essence of the/a faculty of desire as a power to bring things into existence is never challenged. Thus, from the functional perspective upon which Kant's entire conception of the faculty of desire is built, it makes no difference whether the faculty of desire is a single capacity with different ways (and stages in the process) of bringing things into existence, or a number of distinct capacities with distinct ways of bringing things into existence.

II. DETERMINATIONS OF THE FACULTY OF DESIRE

For the most part I am going to speak of Kant's notion of the faculty of desire in the first way just set forth—that is, as a single capacity that is determined in a number of distinct ways. This is a more efficient way of speaking of the faculty of desire, but it should not serve to distract us from the fact that the faculty of desire is primarily a function-based notion—and thus that it is appropriate to speak of different faculties of desire, given that there are different ways in which things are brought into existence. With this in mind, let me turn now to the *pathological* determinations of the faculty of desire. As I mentioned above, there is (in view of the Incorporation Thesis) a temptation to think that for Kant the faculty of desire throws up mere raw materials (so to speak), such as passions and inclinations, for the rational, choosing agent. Along these lines, one might think of the determinations of the faculty of desire as a clamoring mass of motivations *from which* one can choose prudentially, and *against which* one must choose morally. But this way of thinking has only limited usefulness. Kant does emphasize the distinction between the rational and nonrational sides of our nature in order to make a point about the sovereignty of the moral law within us. But, as we will see, he also blurs this distinction insofar as his discussions of the nonrational side of our nature repeatedly call upon notions of freedom and rationality.

Inclinations

Kant discusses inclinations (*Neigungen*) more frequently than any other determination of the faculty of desire. Some commentators understand Kant's notion of *Neigung* in a very broad way, such that it includes positive and negative desires$_1$ of varying degrees and duration. For example, Allison writes, "Inclination encompasses momentary desires, instincts, passions, fear and disinclinations" (Allison 1990, 108). Aside from the fact that Kant often uses the term "inclination" in a very general way, his *definition* of inclination in the *Groundwork* provides good evidence for Allison's broad understanding.[12] Kant writes, "The dependence [*Abhängigkeit*] of the faculty of desire on sensations is called inclination" (G 4:413n). On this definition, inclinations arise from the relation of dependence between the faculty of desire and sensations. For Kant, the relation between sensations and the faculty of desire is a determining relation, and so we can conclude that inclination is the determination of this faculty by sensation. In other words, sensations cause inclinations by determining the faculty of desire.[13] This account of inclination is friendly to Allison's all-encompassing characterization insofar as it suggests that different sensations can determine the faculty of desire and cause distinct kinds of desires$_1$.

But, at the same time, Kant consistently characterizes inclination more specifically as habitual desire$_1$.[14] Thus, in the *Metaphysics,* he writes, "As for practical pleasure, that determination of the faculty of desire which is caused and therefore necessarily preceded by such pleasure is called desire in the narrow sense, habitual desire is called inclination" [*Was aber die praktische Lust betrifft, so wird die Bestimmung des Begehrungsvermögens, vor welcher diese Lust als Ursache notwendig vorhergehen muß, im engen Verstande Begierde, die habituelle Begierde aber Neigung heißen*] (MM 6:212). Very much echoing this account, Kant writes in the *Anthropology,* "Desire (*appetitio*) is the self-determination of the power of a subject to imagine something in the future as an effect of such imagination. *Habitual sensuous desire is called inclination*" (A 7:251; emphasis added). As we saw in section I, a desire$_1$ is just any determination of the faculty of desire. Inclination is identified here with *habitual* desire$_1$. The suggestion, then, is that when one desires$_1$ something very frequently, or habitually, one can be said to have an inclination toward this thing. A desire (proper) is, in contrast, a more momentary desire$_1$.

We might think of the difference between a desire and an inclination in terms of the distinction between wanting to go to a particular film and regularly wanting to go to the movies. (I am dropping the "proper" qualification for the sake of convenience.) On Kant's account, the former is a desire, and the latter is an inclination. Thus, one might *desire* to see a new film without being *inclined* to go to films in general. On the other hand, one might be inclined to watch movies regularly without desiring to watch one particular movie. And, finally, one might be inclined to see films regularly and desire to see one particular film. Desire and inclination are different kinds of desire$_1$ with the distinction hinging on the frequency with which the desire$_1$ is experienced. Of course, this principle of discrimination provides us with a somewhat vague division between desires and inclinations. We can see this if we consider the following kind of case. Suppose one really enjoys a particular kind of ice cream (that one had desired to eat) and wants to eat it again and again. At some point, perhaps difficult to specify, an inclination may come to be out of a desire.

In spite of the looseness of the distinction between desires and inclinations, however, Kant's narrow conception of inclinations clearly indicates that they *are not identical to* momentary desires. Indeed, Kant's more specific notion of inclination can only be fully understood when it is distinguished from momentary desires, passions, and fear—that is to say, three out of the five items on Allison's list. In the *Religion,* Kant defines inclination by drawing the following distinctions: "Between inclination, which presupposes acquaintance with the object of desire, and propensity there still is instinct. Which is a felt want to do or to enjoy something of which one has as yet no conception (such as the constructive impulse in animals, or the sexual impulse). Beyond inclination there is finally a further stage in the faculty of desire, passion [*die Leidenschaft*] (not affect [*der Affekt*], for this has to do with the feeling of pleasure and pain), which is an inclination that excludes the mastery over oneself" (Rel 6:29n).[15] Kant distinguishes here between inclinations, instincts, and affects.[16] Inclinations and instincts belong to the faculty of desire and so are kinds of desire$_1$, while affects are feelings of pleasure or pain. Within the category of inclination itself, Kant parcels off passion as a kind of inclination.

Before addressing the distinction between inclinations and instincts I want to suggest a possible explanation for the presence of two notions of inclination in Kant's psychology (i.e., a broad conception and a narrow conception). It may be the case that Kant distinguishes between inclination in the broader sense and inclination in the narrower sense in much the same way as he distinguishes between desire$_1$ and desire. We have seen that desire$_1$ includes all of the possible determinations of the faculty of desire. It seems that inclination in the broader sense (or, perhaps, inclination$_1$) is not quite *any* determination of the faculty of desire, but any determination that is caused by a sensation. On this account, the concept of an inclination$_1$ would include desires, passions, and inclinations, but not (as we will see now) instincts. Meanwhile, inclinations, more narrowly construed, are distinct from desires and instincts, but include passions.

Instinct and Inclination Formation

Kant draws a distinction between inclinations and instincts on the basis of whether or not an experience of pleasure is required in order to produce the desire$_1$ in question. An inclination requires an experience of pleasure in order to come into existence, while an instinct does not. This is what Kant means when he says that instinct is a "felt want to do or to enjoy something of which one has as yet no conception" (Rel 6:29n). For Kant, the sexual impulse and the animal impulse to build shelter are instincts because they are both spontaneous. That is to say, a person or animal does not need to experience the pleasure associated with the ends of these impulses in order to be moved to the relevant action. A bird does not need to sit in a warm and secure nest in order to build a nest. On the other hand, an inclination requires an experience of pleasure in order to come into being. Thus, earlier in the same footnote from the *Religion*, Kant writes, "A propensity is really only the predisposition to crave a delight which, when once experienced, arouses in the subject an *inclination* to it. Thus all savage peoples have a propensity for intoxicants; for though many of them are wholly ignorant of intoxication [*Rausch*], let them but once sample it and there is aroused in them an almost inextinguishable craving for it" (Rel 6:29n). A propensity is an innate potential for an inclination. It may or may not be actualized by an experience of pleasure and become an inclination.

Kant places instinct *between* inclination and propensity when he says, "Between inclination, which presupposes acquaintance with the object of desire, and propensity there still is instinct" (Rel 6:29n). His point seems to be that instincts share something with both inclinations and propensities, but are not the same as either. An instinct is like a propensity in that it is innate, but it is like an inclination in that it is an actualized or extant desire$_1$.[17]

Kant's account of inclination formation in the *Religion* (quoted above) is not the only one that he lays out in his mature writings. In the *Metaphysics,* he outlines a slightly different process when he writes, "To form a habit is to establish a lasting [*beharrlichen*] inclination apart from any maxim, through frequently repeated gratifications [*Befriedigung*] of that inclination; it is a mechanism of sense rather than a principle of thought" (MM 6:479).[18] This passage suggests that an inclination requires repeated experience of a pleasure or gratification in order to come into existence. We might think of the inclination to drink coffee as an example. Coffee often tastes bad to the first-time drinker, but through repeated (and increasingly gratifying) experiences an inclination to drink it can be formed. Yet, in the *Religion,* Kant tells us that only *one* experience of pleasure is required in order to form an inclination: "let them but once [*einmal*] sample [intoxication] and there is aroused in them an almost inextinguishable craving for it" (Rel 6:29n). So, Kant seems to offer us two distinct accounts of inclination formation. On one account, repeated experiences of pleasure are required and inclinations come about slowly, while on the other account, inclinations are formed immediately through a single experience of pleasure. Now, the account in the *Metaphysics* may be more plausible since it seems that we could not know that an inclination, as an *habitual* desire₁, has been formed from only one experience. To decide that something is habitual seems to require the occurrence of more than one case of this thing. Surely, then, at least the knowledge of the presence of anything habitual takes some time to establish. Perhaps Kant thinks that an inclination can be formed through one experience of pleasure, but that we could only *know* that it has been formed over time. This might explain the presence of the two distinct accounts.[19]

However, according to one commentator, the *Religion* passage does not represent Kant's considered view on inclination formation at all. In a recent article, Stephen Engstrom seems to pick up on the passage from the *Metaphysics* in arguing that inclinations, "unlike instincts, are within our power to regulate in so far as their presence and strength depend on the extent to which, through our attention, our choices, and our actions, we allow them to develop" (Engstrom 2002, 309). Engstrom's suggestion, then, is that insofar as inclinations take time to develop we can actually have a say in the kinds of inclinations that we allow to form in us. Now, as I indicated above, the dominant trend even in recent Kant scholarship is to see sensibility/inclinations/incentives on one side of a radical divide, and rationality/interests/maxims on the other. In the context of Kant's theory of action, this divide is between those pathological forces with which we simply find ourselves, and those motivational principles that we rationally choose. Engstrom's view clearly challenges this division insofar as it suggests that we have rational control over inclination formation.

It could be argued, however, that the passage from the *Metaphysics* (6:479, quoted above) does not help Engstrom's reading as much as it might initially appear. Remember, Kant says that habit establishes an inclination "apart from any maxim," and that it is "a mechanism of sense rather than a principle of thought." The suggestion here is that at least *some* inclinations are formed without any free rational choice from the agent, but just as a matter of blindly imitating a certain kind of behavior. Obviously, the account of instantaneous inclination formation in the

Religion also undermines Engstrom's reading since an inclination formed out of one experience is not an inclination over which we have any *developmental* control. We will see now, however, that Kant does seem to commit to the idea that there are *certain* inclinations—namely, passions—for the development of which the agent is indeed responsible. So, Engstrom may be partly right in that Kant conceives of at least some inclinations that are tied to maxims and choices in their very formation.

Passions

Passions (*Leidenschaften*) are a species of the genus inclination, and are, as such, a particular kind of determination of the faculty of desire. Kant refers to passion as "a frame of mind [*Gemütsstimmung*] belonging to the faculty of desire" (A 7:252). So, passions are habitual desires$_1$ that are accompanied by a particular frame of mind or mood. Kant clarifies the nature of this differentiating mood to some extent when he says that passions are inclinations over which the agent has no mastery or control. In the *Anthropology*, Kant writes, "The inclination which can hardly, or not at all, be controlled by reason is passion" (A 7:251). In the third *Critique*, he appears to be expanding on this thought when he tells us that passions "belong to the faculty of desire, and are inclinations that make all determinability of the faculty of choice by means of principles difficult or impossible" (CJ 5:272n). We will see now that Kant thinks that there are a couple of distinct senses in which passions make life according to rational principles (or reason) difficult or impossible.

One sense in which passions defy our reason is that they tend to produce immoral actions. In fact, Kant writes of the passions themselves that they are "deceitful [*hinterlistig*] and hidden" (A 7:252). Elsewhere, he says that they are "morally reprehensible" and "without exception bad" (A 7:267). Notice here that in saying that passions are immoral Kant is implying that when it comes to the very possession of her passions the agent is imputable. The suggestion is that agents can choose their passions. Presumably, this choice must take place at some point during the formation of a passion. This suggests, however, that passions cannot be formed simply through the single experience of a pleasure (such as the experience of intoxication), since if this were true the possession of a passion would not then be something for which the agent was responsible. Kant says at one point that passions develop out of other preexisting desires$_1$. He writes, "Even the most well-intended desire if it aims at what belongs to virtue, that is to charity, is nevertheless, as soon as it changes to passion, not merely pragmatically pernicious, but also morally reprehensible" (A 7:267).[20] Kant also frequently repeats the point that passions work "like a river digging itself deeper and deeper into its bed" (A 7:252). Again, it appears from this that Kant thinks that we have control over (and thus responsibility for) the slow, river-like development and formation of our passions.

Kant's account of the passions problematizes any radical division drawn between our pathology and rationality. He appears (in line with Engstrom's interpretation) to blur the distinction between a psychological force to which we are passively subjected, and a rational maxim that we actively choose. This blurring is facilitated by the amount of time that it takes to form a passionate inclination. Kant is quite clear on this issue in the *Metaphysics,* saying, "A passion is a sensible desire that has become a lasting [*bleibenden*] inclination (e.g., hatred as opposed to anger). The calm with which one gives oneself up to it permits reflection and allows the mind to form principles upon it and so, if inclination lights upon something contrary to the law, to brood upon it, to get it rooted deeply, and so to take up what is evil (as something premeditated) into its maxim" (MM 6:408). The calm that comes with a passion allows it to fester and grow, even as we brood upon it and choose maxims based on it. Kant tells us in the *Anthropology* that passions "must take roots gradually and even be able to coexist [*zusammen bestehen*] with reason" (A 7:265). He also writes, "Passion always presupposes a maxim of the subject, namely, to act according to a purpose prescribed for him by his inclination. Passion, therefore, is always associated with the purposes of reason" (A 7:266). So, a passion takes time to develop, and in spite of the senses in which passion is resistant to our rationality, reason and reflection are involved in this developmental process.

For Kant, then, we do not simply choose maxims based on preexisting passionate inclinations. If this were true, Kant would not say that passions themselves are evil, but only that the maxims that are based on them are. Instead, Kant's point is that we are essentially responsible for choosing our passions insofar as their development is a rational and (im)moral process over which we have control. There is a kind of dynamic relationship between rational principles and the passions that ground them such that the growth of passions is contingent upon the presence of related maxims. This dynamic relationship undermines the notion of a radical divide between our pathology and rationality; this will become important in chapter 4 when we look more closely at the nature of maxims. We can conclude, then, that passions are contrary to reason as it is expressed in the moral law, but linked to the "purposes of reason" insofar as they develop in conjunction with rationally chosen maxims.

Kant also thinks that passions can be contrary to reason in a nonmoral sense. He argues that they upset the kind of balance and harmony between our inclinations that reason tries to guarantee. Thus, the principle of happiness is one of the rational principles against which the passions operate.[21] Though he does not refer to it by name, Kant speaks of this principle when he says, "In the area of what is sensuously practical, reason proceeds from the general to the particular, according to the axiom not to please only a single inclination by placing all the rest in the shade . . . but rather to see to it that it shares properly with the totality of all inclinations" (A 7:266). But passions block this axiom of our reason; they block the rational principle that aims at ensuring that we take into consideration all our inclinations. This is why Kant refers to passions as "pragmatically pernicious" (A 7:267). He uses the passion of ambition as an example: "The ambition of a person may always be an inclination whose direction is sanctioned by reason; but the ambitious person desires, nevertheless, to be loved by others also; he needs pleasant relations with others, maintenance of his assets, and so forth. But if he is, however, passionately ambitious, then he is blind to those other purposes which his inclinations also offer to him. Consequently he ignores completely that he is hated by others or that he runs the risk of impoverishing himself through his extravagant expenses" (A 7:266). Insofar as reason tries to coordinate and organize the satisfaction of our inclinations, it is defied by blinding passions. Passions tend to have the kind of exclusive focus that interferes with a balanced satisfaction of desires$_1$. Notice, passions are *linked* with reason insofar as they develop in conjunction with maxims, but this time are *contrary* to reason in threatening our happiness.

Natural and Social Passions

Kant gives more substance to his account of the passions when he writes in the *Anthropology*:

Passions are divided into those of natural inclination (innate) and those arising from the culture of mankind (acquired). Passions of the first kind are the inclinations of freedom and sex; both are linked with emotion [*beide mit Affekt verbunden*]. Those of the second kind are ambition, lust of power, and avarice, qualities which are not linked with vehement affect but with the persistence of a maxim meant for a certain purpose. The first kind can be called burning passions (*passiones ardentes*); while the second kind, like avarice, can be called cold passions (*frigidae*). (A 7:267–68)[22]

This passage makes it clear that Kantian passions should not be considered fringe players in our psychological economies. The passions include powerful, long-term desires$_1$ for freedom, sex, money, power, and honor (or the esteem of others). It is not too much of a stretch to say that, for the majority of us, one (or perhaps a combination of two or more) of these passions is actually a *central* source of motivation in our lives.[23]

Kant's main point in the passage just quoted is that some passions are innate while others are socially acquired. Now, we saw above that inclinations differ from instincts insofar as they require a grounding experience (or experiences) of pleasure. Prior to this experience an inclination is just a predisposition. But, since it does not make sense to speak of an innate experience of pleasure, it seems to follow that all inclinations are socially acquired. How, then, can Kant distinguish between innate and socially acquired passions when all passions, as kinds of inclination, require an experience of pleasure in order to come into existence? The key here is the idea that inclinations develop out of predispositions. What Kant must have in mind is that there are some passions that come from innate predispositions, and some that come from socially acquired predispositions. But what does it mean to speak of a socially acquired predisposition?

For Kant, socially acquired passions are grounded in predispositions that arose as a result of man moving from the state of nature into society.[24] Consequently, Kant's point in dividing the passions in this way is not that each *individual* socially acquires the predisposition for the passion of ambition (for example) as she moves into society. Rather, his point is that human beings *in general* acquire predispositions toward ambition, lust for authority, and avarice as they move out of a state of nature and into society. More specifically, Kant's thinking seems to be that the innate predisposition toward freedom, while itself remaining intact, develops under the threat of social constraint into a predisposition to rule over others. Kant writes, "Man's own will is always ready to turn hostile toward his neighbour. He never fails to press his claim to an unconditional freedom; he does not merely want to be independent, but he even wants mastery over others who are equal to him by nature" (A 7:327). Kant holds, along Rousseauian lines, that once we enter into society the innate and passionate predisposition for freedom gives rise to a predisposition to rule over others, since every other will is seen as a potential threat to one's own freedom. Kant then divides this general predisposition to rule over others into three subsidiary predispositions: the predisposition to be ambitious, to lust for authority, and to be avaricious.

Socially acquired passions are, at bottom, aimed at removing the threat that is posed to one's freedom by other social beings. Unfortunately, our unsociability leads us to believe that we can only remove this threat by gaining power over these others.[25] Ambition, for example, is an attempt to gain power over others by having them admire us. It is a desire for the esteem of others.[26] Now, we can see quite clearly from this why Kant thinks that the socially acquired passions are immoral. Each of them implicitly threatens to undermine our respect for others. In the process of developing certain passions (i.e., of allowing passions to dig deeper into our minds) we form desires$_1$ that challenge the respect that we should show to others. Again, in order for this lack of respect for others to be something for which we are held accountable, it has to be something chosen, and Kant indicates that it is in the *Anthropology* 7:266 passage when he associates the socially acquired passions with the "persistence of a maxim." This connection between the socially acquired passions and maxims reinforces the link, discussed above, between passions in general and maxims.

But notice that Kant *contrasts* the naturally acquired passions with socially acquired passions by saying that the former are linked with *affects*, while the latter are linked with the persistence of *maxims*. What does he have in mind here? Have we not already seen Kant link the development of *all* passions with maxims? Why is he only linking some passions with maxims here and others with affects? Now, for Kant, affects are feelings of a particular kind. In order to explore further this connection between natural passions and affects we must first turn to that broad psychological category into which affects fall—feeling (*Gefühl*).

III. FEELING: THE GROUND OF DESIRE₁

Feeling, Feelings, and Inclinations

Kant distinguishes between feeling (*Gefühl*) and feelings (*Gefühlen*). According to this distinction, feeling refers to our sensible susceptibility (*Empfänglichkeit*) to representations, while feelings are specific, concrete states of mind.[27] This distinction mirrors Kant's division between the faculty of desire and actual desires₁, and he represents this parallel by sometimes referring to feeling as the "Faculty of Pleasure and Displeasure."[28] Feeling, then, is simply a power or capacity to experience feelings of pleasure or pain at a representation. Kant writes, "The capacity [*Fähigkeit*] for having pleasure or displeasure in a representation is called 'feeling'" (MM 6:211).

Two preliminary things should be noted about Kant's account of feeling. First, for Kant, there are only two basic feelings—pleasure and pain—and all of the other things that we typically consider distinct feelings (e.g., anger or worry) are simply these two basic feelings in different contexts, or with different causes, or felt in differing degrees. So, for example, love is often considered a distinct (even unique) kind of feeling. But, in the *Metaphysics*, Kant tells us that pathological, or sensuous, love is delight, and he defines this delight as "pleasure joined immediately to the representation of an object's existence" (MM 6:402).[29]

Second, Kant's theory of pleasure and pain develops significantly during his Critical period.[30] Initially, he does not distinguish between sensation and feeling; he views pleasure as a homogenous and simple sensation. The final expression of this view can be found in the second *Critique* when Kant writes that

> the feeling of pleasure always affects one and the same life-force which is manifested in the faculty of desire, and in this respect one determining ground can differ from any other only in degree. . . . A man can return unread an instructive book which

he cannot again obtain, in order not to miss the hunt; he can go away in the middle of a fine speech, in order not to be late for a meal. . . . If the determination of the will rests on the feelings of agreeableness or disagreeableness which he expects from any cause, it is all the same to him through what kind of notion he is affected. The only thing he considers in making a choice is how great, how long lasting, how easily obtained, and how often repeated this agreeableness is. (Pr. R 5:23)

Sometime around 1787–88, Kant posits a more complex notion of pleasure than the one he holds from the 1760s all the way through to this passage. In the third *Critique,* Kant distinguishes between sensation and feeling, classifying pleasure as a feeling. He defines the feeling of pleasure as the "consciousness of the causality of a representation with respect to the state of the subject, for maintaining it in that state" (CJ 5:220). (I will focus on and clarify Kant's new approach to pleasure in the next chapter when I turn my attention to his purported hedonism.) Now, even though Kant's later account of pleasure is more relevant to this study, the shift in his thinking on pleasure does not affect the argument in the rest of this chapter. For the moment it is sufficient just to note that there is such a shift.

For Kant all inclinations are grounded in feeling. He writes in the second *Critique* that "sensuous feeling [*sinnliche Gefühl*] . . . is the basis [*Grunde*] of all our inclinations" (Pr. R 5:75). Earlier, he says, "All inclination and every sensible impulse is grounded [*gegründet*] on feeling" (Pr. R 5:73). Finally, in the same chapter of the second *Critique,* Kant also says, "Now everything in self-love belongs to inclination, and all inclination rests on *feelings* [*alle Neigung aber auf Gefühlen beruht*]; therefore, whatever checks all inclinations in self-love necessarily has, by that fact, an influence on *feeling* [*Gefühl*]" (Pr. R 5:74). According to this passage, *feelings,* and not *feeling,* ground inclination. Of course, we can conclude that feeling is also the basis for inclination insofar as the faculty of feeling allows for feelings. Feeling is the capacity for feelings, and, properly speaking, feelings ground inclinations. This also seems to be what Kant is getting at in the *Metaphysics* when he says, "First, *pleasure* or *displeasure,* susceptibility [*Empfänglichkeit*] to which is called *feeling,* is always connected with desire or aversion"

(MM 6:211). But what is the nature of this grounding relation between feelings and inclinations?

Most obviously, the grounding relation between feelings and inclinations suggests that all inclinations require a foundation of pleasure or pain in order to come into existence. In other words, Kant's point appears to be that inclinations are caused (efficiently) by pleasure or pain.[31] As we have already seen, there is evidence for this account of the role of pleasure in the origins of inclinations in the *Religion* footnote quoted above, in which Kant tells us that an experience of pleasure is required in order to transform a predisposition into an inclination. This interpretation of the grounding relation between feelings and inclinations also explains what Kant means in the *Groundwork* footnote quoted above, when he tells us that sensations (meaning—as per Kant's earlier view of pleasure—sensations of pleasure and pain) determine the faculty of desire causing inclinations.[32]

Affects and Reason

The ambiguous passage in the *Anthropology* with which we finished the previous section mentions a relation between passions and affects. For Kant, an affect (*Affekt*) is a particular kind of feeling of pleasure or pain. Recall that in the footnote from the *Religion* quoted above, Kant writes, "Beyond inclination there is finally a further stage in the faculty of desire, passion [*die Leidenschaft*] (not affect [*der Affekt*], for this has to do with the feeling of pleasure and pain), which is an inclination that excludes the mastery over oneself" (Rel 6:29n). Affects and passions are distinct insofar as they belong to different faculties—the faculty of pleasure and displeasure, and the faculty of desire, respectively. Kant also characterizes affects by contrasting them with passions in the third *Critique:* "Affects [*Affekten*] are specifically different from passions. The former are related merely to feeling; the latter belong to the faculty of desire" (CJ 5:272n; translation modified slightly).[33] But, at the same time, Kant *compares* affects and passions by indicating that "both affect and passion, exclude the sovereignty of reason" (A 7:251). In the *Anthropology*, he says that affect "is the feeling of a pleasure or displeasure at a particular moment, which does not give rise to reflection (namely the process of reason whether one should submit to it or reject it)" (A 7:251). Kant echoes this point in the *Metaphysics*, saying, "Affects belong to feeling insofar as, preceding reflection, it makes this impossible or more difficult" (MM 6:407; translation modified). Kant thinks of affects as unpremeditated bursts of pleasure or pain that block, or make difficult, any rational reflection.

Before turning to the relation between affects and passions let us look more closely at affects. Kant elaborates on this central point about the disruptive nature of affects in the third *Critique*: "Every affect is blind, either in the choice of its end, or, even if this is given by reason, in its implementation [*Ausführung*]; for it is that movement of the mind that makes it incapable of engaging in free consideration of principles, in order to determine itself in accordance with them" (CJ 5:272; translation modified). Kant argues here that affects make it difficult to engage in any reflection in choosing an end, or in choosing how to act upon an end that is already given. So, for example, if one is faced by a grave danger, the affect of fear can make it very difficult to decide on one's end, or, if one's end is to avoid danger at all costs and never meet it head on, fear can impair one's ability to reflect on how best to do this.

Kant's account of how affects arise gives us some insight into how and why they inhibit calm reasoning.

> On the whole, it is not the intensity of a certain feeling which creates the emotional state, but the want of reflection in the comparison of this feeling with the sum of all feelings (of pleasure or displeasure) in one's own condition. The rich person, whose servant clumsily smashes a beautiful and rare crystal goblet while waiting on table, would consider this incident of no importance if he compared at that moment this loss of a single gratification with the multitude of all gratifications which his fortunate position as a rich person affords him. But if he completely leaves himself to this one feeling of grief [*Nun überläßt er sich aber ganz allein diesem einen Gefühl des Schmerzes*] (without making such a quick survey in his thoughts), then it is no wonder that he feels as if his whole state of happiness [*Glückseligkeit*] were lost. (A 7:254; translation modified)

Kant's point here is that affects *result from* a lack of reflection. They not only lead to a lack of rational reflection, but they also *arise* from a lack of reflection. When the rich person experiences pain at the loss of the expensive object, this ordinary feeling of pain *becomes* an affect if there is not an intervening thought about the relative value of the pleasure associated with this object. Kant thinks that we are capable of rational reflection immediately after we experience a feeling of pleasure or displeasure. If there is no such reflection, then the agent is just leaving himself to the feeling without any modification that might come from reflecting upon his other pleasures. This lack of reflection can turn a feeling of pain at the loss of an expensive object, for example, into an affect of grief.

The reason that affects block reflection is that affects are those very things that arise from a lack of reflection. It is perhaps more accurate to say, then, that affects themselves do not cause the inhibition of reflection so much as they arise through this inhibition, and then prevent reflection through their continued presence. The implication here, of course, is that any of our pleasures or pains, if they are not reflected upon and given their relative weight in the larger scheme of our lives, can turn into affects. Kant's picture of our inner lives, then, includes a portrayal of pleasure and pain as feelings that can develop into affective outbursts unless they are controlled by a kind of reflection that brings the bigger picture of the agent's pleasures and pains (i.e., the agent's happiness) to mind. The rational and the nonrational are clearly interwoven in this account.

Now, for Kant, reflective control of our affects—controlling the outburst of affects (through reflection) and the reaction to affects (also, presumably, through reflection)—are only possible after *long-term* efforts to master our feelings. Kant discusses this issue in the following passage from the *Anthropology:*

> Hot temper can be controlled *gradually* by inner discipline of the mind; but the weakness of an oversensitive feeling of honor at moments of shyness does not lend itself so easily to control. Hume says (who himself was afflicted with such an infirmity, namely shyness of making public statements), that if the first attempt at boldness fails, the result is more bashfulness. As remedy, nothing else remains but to begin to be with persons whose judgment concerning behavior one does not care much

about, *so that one can gradually overcome the supposed important judgment of others.* (A 7:260; emphasis added)

In this example, Kant thinks that one can train oneself not to give way to
the affect of excessive bashfulness. Employing Kant's own model from the
"rich man" example, it seems that this affect is caused when the thought
of the negative judgments of one's audience produces a pain that is allowed to develop into an affect. Perhaps one allows this development by
failing to consider the years of positive feedback that one has received
from others. Kant's solution is to block the outburst of the affect over
time through a particular way of practicing not caring so much about
these perceived judgments. There seem to be two parts to this solution.
First (and Kant leaves this part implicit), one must develop some kind of
reflective response to the initial experience of pain. We might imagine
that this response could include thoughts such as "other people's judgments do not matter" or "most people actually respond positively to my
speaking." The basic point of these reflections is that they allow one to
see one's pain relative to some larger picture of pleasures and pains. Second, one must integrate these thoughts by rehearsing them in situations
where the judgments of others *really* do not matter to one. Kant implies, then, that one can integrate these kinds of considerations into
one's life (and block emotion) by putting oneself in a situation where it
is easier to see that certain thoughts are true.

We see that these sustained efforts to inhibit the outburst of affects, or
to prevent ill-conceived action in response to these affects, involve the integration of rational reflection into our daily lives. More specifically, they
involve training ourselves to incorporate particular thoughts into the
economy of our feelings, rather than simply giving way or "leaving ourselves" to feelings. Clearly, Kant's psychology of feeling involves a kind of
fluidity. Pleasures and pain intermingle with our thoughts; they can shape,
alter, and inhibit these thoughts and can, in turn, be shaped, etc., by them.
We must keep this fluid nature of the mind in the background as we think
about Kant's accounts of maxims, interests, and choices in later chapters.

Affects and Passions

With all of this in mind let us return to that passage in the *Anthropology*
in which Kant links some passions with affects and others with the per-

sistence of a maxim. Again, he writes, "Passions are divided into those of natural inclination (innate) and those arising from the culture of mankind (acquired). Passions of the first kind are the inclinations of freedom and sex; both are linked with affect. Those of the second kind are ambition, lust of power, and avarice, qualities which are not linked with vehement affect but with the persistence [*Beharrlichkeit*] of a maxim meant for a certain purpose" (A 7:267–68). In what sense are the passions for freedom and sex "linked" (*verbunden*) with affect, and the other passions with persistent maxims? As a working hypothesis let us consider two possibilities: either passions are *caused by* affects or the persistence of maxims, or they *cause* affects or the persistence of maxims.

There is evidence to suggest that Kant thinks that affects can ground, or cause, passions in the same way that other feelings of pleasure and pain ground inclinations. For example, Kant classifies fear as an affect—it is the feeling of pain in the face of a danger. Kant writes of the lust for authority, "This passion is unjust per se, and its manifestation aligns everything against it. It arises from the fear of being ruled by others, and it then concerns itself with gaining a vantage point over this danger before it is too late" (A 7:273). Kant claims here that our passionate lust for authority or power arises from, or is grounded in, a painful feeling of fear of being ruled over by others. It seems from this example, then, that affects are experiences of pleasure or pain that can cause passions in the same way that the experience of the pleasure of intoxication can cause an inclination to drink (in Kant's own example from the *Religion*).

Further reflection reveals, however, that this is not what Kant has in mind in the *Anthropology* passage in question. In his causal account of the lust for authority, Kant writes that this passion "arises from the fear of being ruled by others" (A 7:273). But lust for authority is a *socially acquired* passion. Consequently, the point of this passage cannot be that innate passions, as opposed to socially acquired ones, are grounded in affects, since lust for authority is a socially acquired passion and is grounded in an affect. Kant does *not* think that innate passions differ from socially acquired ones insofar as affects cause the former, and the persistence of maxims causes the latter.

Perhaps, then, Kant's point is that the distinct kinds of passion are the cause or ground of affects or the persistence of maxims. Ostensibly, this is a plausible suggestion. Kant believes that when a passion is frustrated it can result in a sudden experience of pain. He appeals to this idea when he tells us that the passion for freedom grounds a newborn's affect of frustration: "In fact, the child who has just come from its mother's womb, unlike all other animals, seems to enter the world with a loud shriek just because it considers the inability to make use of its limbs a restraint; consequently it announces this claim to freedom" (A 7:268). According to this passage, the basis for the baby's loud shriek is the passion for freedom. Kant follows up on these comments by adding in a footnote, "However, the fact that the baby's feeling of discomfort does not originate from bodily pain, but from a vague idea (or an analogous representation) of freedom and its suppression, perceived as an injustice, is disclosed a few months after the birth by tears which accompany the shrieking. This indicates a sort of exasperation when he strives to get near certain objects or only tries to change his position and finds himself hindered" (A 7:268n). Kant is reiterating the point that a baby's strong affect (i.e., exasperation) can be traced to an inhibited or frustrated passion for freedom. Thus, a passion can cause an affect. Recall, Kant thinks that affects come about through a lack of reflection on the relative value of certain pleasures and pains. Kant's point must be that when the natural passions for freedom and sex are frustrated, this pain tends to disallow any reflection and can lead to an affect.

The kind of pain that is linked with (or caused by) the frustration of a passion is just the kind of explosive pain that Kant identifies with affect. On the other hand, the frustration of some passions does not ground affects so much as it results in the persistence of their associated maxims. The overall picture is clearer now: the passions for freedom and sex, when frustrated, give rise to feelings of pain that can prevent reflection and produce affects. When the social passions are frustrated, however, there is no outburst of affect but just the seething persistence of the relevant maxims. The ambitious agent, upon being rebuked, does not fly into a rage, but is instead further consumed by the principled pursuit of her ends. Social passions are thereby more strongly associated with reason and maxims.[34] But, of course, it is not necessarily the case that Kant thinks it *impossible* for the frustration of natural passions to result in the persistence of their maxims. Instead, we can understand his point to be that the frustration of some passions is *more likely* to result in an affective outburst, and the frustration of others is *more likely* to result in the tightened grip of certain maxims.

In the remainder of this study, I will draw on several of the conclusions reached in this chapter. Let me conclude, then, by highlighting two.

First, the dynamic links between passions and maxims, as well as between affects and reflection, undermine the idea of a radical or unbridgeable divide between the pathological and the rational. Kant does not think that our pathology exists in its own self-contained space, to be morally resisted or prudentially controlled in the act of incorporation. Instead, our maxims, desires$_1$, and feelings are closely linked and, at least in the case of passions and affects, constantly feed off each other. Of course, it should be noted that this is a separate matter from the question of how morality is grounded. Kant *does* think that our inclinations and affects are radically distinct from the *grounds* of moral maxims.

Second, it is worth highlighting the general point that the categories of feeling and desire$_1$ provide us with the basic elements in Kant's account of human psychology. Our psychology is a play of desires$_1$ and feelings, with feelings causing desires$_1$, and the frustration or satisfaction of desires$_1$ leading, in turn, to feelings of various kinds. Now, insofar as this psychology is at the root of motivation, these categories will turn out to be central to Kant's theory of nonmoral motivation as well. With this in mind, let me turn now in more detail to the causal link between feelings of pleasure or pain and our desires$_1$.

· ·

CHAPTER TWO

DESIRE FORMATION AND HEDONISM

It is time now to begin to piece together Kant's theory of nonmoral motivation. For Kant, desires, inclinations, passions, and instincts are all determinations of the faculty of desire, and thus they provide us with a good place to start an account of how we are moved nonmorally. Of course, Kant does not think that the pathological desires$_1$ fully determine a rational agent's faculty of desire, so any analysis of these desires$_1$ *only* gives us a place to start. We might begin our account of nonmoral action, then, with the following question: what is it about each of the pathological desires$_1$ that allows it to play a role in moving the human agent? The short answer, for Kant, is that our pathological desires$_1$ play a role in moving us because they are structurally connected to feelings of pleasure. It follows from this that Kant's treatment of pleasure is central for an understanding of how he thinks nonmoral motivation actually works.

In fact, I will argue in this chapter that when it comes to nonmoral action Kant is a hedonist, and that pleasure is *the* central notion in his account of nonmoral motivation. My approach to establishing this claim will be to look at Kant's account of the formation of pathological desires$_1$ for evidence regarding that toward which he thinks these desires$_1$ are really aimed. More specifically, I will look at Kant's treatment of the formation of desires and inclinations. For convenience, in this chapter I will simply refer to both these two as "desires," since Kant does not maintain any *essential* distinction between desire formation and inclination formation. Passions and instincts, however, are a separate matter when it comes to their grounds, since passions seem to come into being out of already existing inclinations, while instincts are innate and therefore not caused at all. But it should be noted that this exclusion of passions and instincts only applies to the issue of how these desires$_1$ are formed; at bottom, passions and instincts share the same hedonistic structure as the other desires$_1$.

Before introducing my argument in greater detail let me briefly turn to the notion of hedonism. *The Cambridge Dictionary of Philosophy* includes the following concise and useful account of hedonism: "Psychological Hedonism itself admits of a variety of possible forms. One may hold, e.g., that all motivation is based on the prospect of present or future pleasure. More plausibly, some philosophers have held that all choices of future actions are based on one's presently taking greater pleasure in the thought of doing one act rather than another" (Audi 1999, 364). The author indicates here that the latter version of hedonism, according to which our choices are based on the pleasure that we take in the *thought* of doing something, is the "more plausible" version. However, it is, broadly speaking, true that the version resting on the "prospect of present or future pleasure" was the more popular and well-known version for Enlightenment thinkers such as Kant. We will see Kant employ *both* versions in what follows.

Scholars such as Andrews Reath, Henry Allison, and Christine Korsgaard, who argue that Kant is not a hedonist at all, have dominated recent discussions on the role of pleasure in Kant's theory of action. According to their view, the removal of the misconception that nonmoral actions are mechanically caused by inclinations calls for a reconsideration of Kant's references to pleasure.[1] What must be reconsidered, they argue, is the traditionally-held view that, for Kant, nonmoral actions are caused by what promises most pleasure.[2] The traditional view (maintained at one point or another by scholars such as Lewis White Beck, Terence Irwin, and Allen Wood) insists that for Kant the anticipation of pleasure associated with a particular end motivates all nonmoral action.[3] It is the attribution of this form of hedonism to Kant that has come under attack recently. For scholars such as Reath and Allison, the Kantian passages upon which this traditional hedonistic reading is based must be reinterpreted. Perhaps the key article addressing such a reinterpretation is Reath's "Hedonism, Heteronomy and Kant's Principle of Happiness."[4] One of Reath's central arguments in this paper is that when Kant refers to pleasure he is sometimes referring to the role of pleasure in the *origin* of desire, and not (as scholars had believed) the role of pleasure as an *object* of desire (i.e., hedonism). Reath points to the *Metaphysics* 6:212 as his primary piece of textual evidence for this view and argues that this account of the role of pleasure in the origin of desire commits Kant to nothing whatsoever regarding the object of these desires. As an independent claim this is absolutely true: arguing that pleasure plays a role in the origin of desires does not *necessarily* commit Kant to hedonism. However, I will contend—in view of my treatment of Kant's thinking on pleasure and its role in desire formation—that a commitment to a particular form of hedonism is *in fact* entailed in his account.

The main focus of this chapter, then, will be on Kant's theory of desire formation. I will argue for a new way of understanding this theory, and then use this understanding as a basis for the claim that Kant is committed to hedonism. However, I will not be defending the traditional understanding of Kant's hedonism, according to which an anticipation of pleasure moves us to nonmoral action. Instead, my intention is to reconstruct an alternative Kantian hedonism based on a revised understanding of his treatment of desire formation. I will begin in section I by pointing to a substantial ambiguity in Kant's account of desire formation. Kant appears to understand the role of pleasure in the formation of desires in three different ways. I will lay out these three distinct ways and present textual evidence for each. I will piece these three accounts together in section II, arguing that the resulting theory both provides us with a defensible understanding of desire formation (one that is left implicit in Kant's writing) and commits Kant to hedonism.[5] Finally, in section III, I will present support for my interpretation by introducing Kant's mature understanding of pleasure (briefly referred to in chapter 1) and elaborating on his view of the place of pleasure in our psychological makeup.

I. THE AMBIGUOUS ROLE OF PLEASURE IN DESIRE FORMATION

When Kant talks about the causal relationship between pleasure and desire he often seems to be talking about three distinct kinds of things. That is to say, Kant appears to conceive of three distinct causal roles for pleasure in the formation of desires. Sometimes he talks as though a feeling of pleasure at an actual experience of some object or action were a necessary prerequisite for the determination of the faculty of desire and the production of a desire (i.e., the account Reath highlights). On other occasions, he appears to suggest that a feeling of pleasure at the mere *thought* of some object or action in the future can cause a desire. Finally, and perhaps most frequently, Kant also indicates that it is an *anticipation* of some present or future pleasure that causes desire. Thus, Kant seems to have three different accounts of how pleasure (or the thought of pleasure) causes desire, without ever discussing how or even if these accounts are related. What is going on here? Was Kant just being careless, or is there a way of connecting these accounts such that they form a coherent whole?

The Feeling of Pleasure at the Experience of an Object or Action

The primary piece of evidence that Reath uses to support his claim that an experience of pleasure plays a role in causing desires (but is not necessarily the object of desires) is in the *Metaphysics*. Kant writes:

> That pleasure which is necessarily connected with desire (for an object whose representation affects feeling in this way) can be called practical pleasure, whether it is the cause or the effect of the desire. On the other hand, that pleasure which is not necessarily connected with desire for an object, and so is not at bottom a pleasure in the existence of the object of a representation but is attached only to the representation by itself, can be called merely contemplative pleasure or *inactive delight*. . . . As for practical pleasure, that determination of the faculty of desire which is caused [*Ursache*] and therefore necessarily preceded by such pleasure is called desire in the narrow sense, habitual desire is called inclination. (MM 6:212)

Reath argues that for Kant "inclinations presuppose some previously experienced satisfactions; in this sense they are 'preceded by this pleasure as cause'" (Reath 1989a, 47). He goes on to give an example of enjoying watching baseball and forming a desire to watch more of it. Crucially, for Reath, none of this commits one to the idea that the object of one's baseball-related desire is pleasure. Reath seems to be right here, both in his interpretation of the passage from the *Metaphysics* and in his assertion that there is no commitment to hedonism entailed in this interpretation.

In fact, there appears to be even better evidence for Reath's account of the formation of desires through an experience of pleasure in that revealing footnote from the *Religion* that we looked at several times in the last chapter. "A propensity is really only the predisposition to crave a delight which, when once experienced, arouses in the subject an *inclination* to it. Thus all savage peoples have a propensity for intoxicants; for though many of them are wholly ignorant of intoxication, let them but once sample it and there is aroused in them an almost inextinguishable craving for it" (Rel 6:29n). Kant argues here that an inclination is aroused from what is initially only a predisposition. His point is that a *potential* to be inclined to something (i.e., intoxicants) is transformed into an actual inclination if one experiences a pleasure associated with this thing (i.e., intoxication).

Finally, in the *Metaphysics* passage on inclination formation, also discussed in the previous chapter, Kant emphasizes the role of *repeated* gratifications in establishing lasting desires. He tells us that "[t]o form a habit is to establish a lasting inclination apart from any maxim, through frequently repeated gratifications of that inclination; it is a mechanism of sense rather than a principle of thought" (MM 6:479). Kant cannot literally mean, as he appears to indicate, that an inclination is formed through repeated gratifications of that inclination, since obviously the inclination would already have been formed if we were engaged in repeated gratifications of it. Instead, he must mean that an inclination is formed through repeated experiences of the kind of gratification that is *associated* with this inclination, and that these gratifications are experienced by repeatedly engaging in the *activities* linked with this inclination. Kant seems to be talking about acquiring a taste for some object, or developing one's sensibility such that one finds something increasingly pleasant. The result of this development is the formation of an inclination toward the object in question.

As I noted in the previous chapter, these latter two accounts of inclination formation do not match up fully, since the *Religion* passage allows for the formation of an inclination after only a single experience of pleasure. Given that an inclination is a *habitual* desire$_1$ it does seem that it would take more than one occasion of desiring something in response to an experience of pleasure in order to establish the actual presence of an inclination. I suggested that perhaps one experience of pleasure might be all that is needed to *cause* an inclination, but that for the agent a number of such experiences might be needed before she can be *certain* that she possesses an inclination toward something. In either case, the central point remains the same: a feeling of pleasure at an actual experience of an object is required in order to cause a desire for this object.

The Feeling of Pleasure at the Thought of an Object or Action

Elsewhere in his Critical works (and, indeed, often in the same text), Kant presents a different account of how an experience of pleasure plays a role in the origins of a desire. For example, in the *Metaphysics* he writes, "Every determination of choice [*Willkür*] proceeds *from* the representation of a possible action *to* the deed through [*durch*] the feeling of pleasure or displeasure, taking an interest in the action or its effect" (MM 6:399). Now, for Kant, interests are based on desires in the sense that they are our desires reflected upon and judged to be worth pursuing in some way. I will turn to interests at some length in chapter 4, but if we think of interests as rational desires (for now), then Kant appears to be pointing to a causal link between a feeling of pleasure at the thought (or "representation") of a possible action or object, and an interest in, or rational desire for, this action or object.[6] More clearly, Kant writes in the second *Critique*, "Pleasure from the conception of the existence of a thing . . . is a determining ground of the desire for this thing" (Pr. R 5:22). Kant is saying here that a desire is caused when a pleasure at the thought of something in the future determines the faculty of desire. So, for example, my desire to attend tomorrow's sports event comes about when my thoughts about or conception of being at this event and cheering for my team are accompanied by pleasure. In the *Anthropology*, Kant seems to have this kind of pleasure in mind when he writes of the situation in which "the prospect of entering a future state awakens in us the sensation of gratification" (A 7:231). In what follows, I will refer to this pleasure at the mere thought of some future object or action as an *anticipatory* pleasure (or pain). Remember, in the passages quoted in the previous subsection from the *Metaphysics* and the *Religion*, it is the actual experience of an object or action that produces the causal feeling of pleasure, and not simply the thought of a possible object or action in the future.

The Anticipation of Pleasure

In spite of Reath's argument to the contrary (which I will return to in section II below), Kant frequently says things to suggest that when we desire an object it is in virtue of the pleasure associated with this object that we desire it. For example, he writes that "if . . . we desire [begehren] or avoid an object, we do so only in so far as it is related to our sensibility and to the feeling of pleasure or displeasure [das Gefühl der Lust und Unlust] which it produces" (Pr. R 5:60). In the third Critique, he writes that our faculties' "assessment of things and their value . . . [pertains] to the gratification [Vergnügen] that they promise [versprechen]" (CJ 5:206). Along the same hedonistic lines, Kant writes in the Groundwork that the "object of the action (so far as it is pleasant for me) interests me" (G 4:413n). If Kant believes that it is in virtue of its association with pleasure that we desire an object, then it only makes sense that he would also believe that it is in virtue of pleasure that we are interested in (i.e., rationally desire) an object as well.[7] This seems to be precisely what Kant is expressing here.

But Kant goes beyond suggesting that all desires are ultimately desires for pleasure when he indicates that it is the anticipation of this pleasure that causes these desires in the first place. For example, in the second Critique, Kant refers to an anticipation of pleasure when he writes, "When one inquires into the determining grounds of desire . . . [one] finds them in an expected agreeableness [erwarteten Annehmlichkeit] resulting from something or other" (Pr. R 5:23). He also says that "the determining ground of choice consists in the conception of an object and its relation to the subject, whereby the faculty of desire is determined to seek its realization. Such a relation to the subject is called pleasure in the reality of an object" (Pr. R 5:21). Kant is suggesting here that the relation between subject and object that consists of pleasure in the reality or existence of an object determines the faculty of desire producing desire. Thus, the faculty of desire is determined by the prospect of taking pleasure in an object that does not yet exist. Finally, later in the same text, Kant writes, "If the concept of the good is not derived from a practical law but rather serves as the ground of the latter, it can only be the concept of something whose existence promises pleasure [dessen Existenz Lust verheißt] and thus determines the causality of the subject (the faculty of desire) to produce it" (Pr. R 5:58). Kant's point is that when the good determines our practical laws (i.e., in cases of nonmoral action), then the good is a *promised* pleasure.[8] In saying this Kant also suggests that it is the anticipation of a pleasure associated with a particular end that determines the faculty of desire causing a desire.

The Problem of Three Accounts, and Some Responses to This Problem

Thus, Kant tells us in different places that two distinct experiences of pleasure, as well as anticipation of pleasure, cause desire. Now, I claimed in the previous chapter that Kant's understanding of pleasure seems to change sometime around 1790. Does this development (which I will explore in more detail in section III) influence Kant's account of desire formation?

The only of Kant's three views that does not get expression prior to the third *Critique* is the one according to which it is the experience of pleasure at an object that causes a desire. However, it does not seem that this view *replaces* the other two accounts since these latter are referred to both before and after 1790. Indeed, there is evidence that the presence of multiple accounts is not simply a matter of Kant changing his mind from one text to another, given the fact that he presents the anticipation of pleasure account and the anticipatory pleasure account in the very same passage in the second *Critique*. He writes, "*Pleasure from the conception of the existence of a thing*, in so far as it is a determining ground of the desire for this thing, is based upon the susceptibility of the subject because it depends upon the actual presence of an object. Thus it belongs to sense (feeling) and not to the understanding, which expresses a relation of a conception to an object by concepts and not the relation of an idea to the subject by feelings. It is only in so far as the faculty of desire is determined by the sensation of agreeableness which the subject *expects from the actual existence* of the object" (Pr. R 5:22). I will return to this passage below, but for now it is worth noting that Kant shifts here between talking of an *expected* pleasure and a pleasure just from the *conception* of the existence of something, while explicitly referring to both as *providing the determining ground for the faculty of desire*. Is Kant simply being careless or does he leave undeveloped a more comprehensive underlying theory of desire formation according to which pleasure determines the faculty of desire in both of these ways as well as in the other way outlined above?

As far as I know, commentators have responded to the presence of three distinct accounts of the relation of pleasure and desire by either passing over the issue blindly, or simply noting that Kant maintains different views and giving no further explanation.[9] Either way, there has been virtually nothing written on the subject. Falling into the first category is T. H. Green, when he writes, "Kant's error lies in supposing that there is no alternative between the determination of desire by the anticipation of pleasure and its determination by the conception of a moral law" (Green 1888, 119). Green just assumes that Kant subscribes to the traditional understanding of hedonism. Other well-known Kant scholars such as Irwin, Beck, and Meerbote also argue that for Kant all desires are grounded in an anticipation of pleasure, and thus ignore the role of any experience of pleasure in the formation of desires.[10] For example, Ralf Meerbote writes:

> In an overwhelming number of passages, Kant says that [heteronomous] desires take the form of anticipations of future pleasures by the agent (or self-awareness of the agent's present pleasures). At the same time, other heteronomous desires will be generated on the strength of rationalization connections between actions. Kant believes that in the end such extended heteronomous desires can be traced back to initially given desires. . . . If Kant believes that in the end all heteronomous desires concern present or future pleasure of the agent, then apparently all heteronomous imperatives are in the end instructions concerning how to achieve such pleasure. (Meerbote 1984, 66–67)

The implication of the second sentence in this passage is that the set of heteronomous desires referred to in the first sentence are generated by the agent's anticipation of future pleasure.[11]

So, the traditional interpretation of Kant's thinking on pleasure seems to assume that an *anticipation* of pleasure is the only relevant factor in the determination of the faculty of desire. This may be a result of the fact that (in spite of what Reath says) Kant refers *most frequently* in this context to the anticipation of pleasure. It also appears, however, that the traditional reading does not take any pains to distinguish between an anticipation of pleasure causing a *desire* and an anticipation of pleasure causing an *action*. In truth, of course, it is only the latter that necessarily involves a commitment to hedonism. The failure to distinguish between these two things is perhaps understandable, in that Kant often seems to use the expression "determination of the faculty of desire" to refer to both the causing of a desire and the causing of an action.[12] But, as Reath points out, the distinction is crucial, since the causal relationship between pleasure and desire tells us nothing about the causal relationship between pleasure and action. That is to say, one can hold that an anticipation of pleasure is the cause of a desire without holding that it is necessarily the object of that desire, and thus the cause of any action that follows from the desire.

II. RECONCILING KANT'S DISTINCT ACCOUNTS OF DESIRE FORMATION

In what follows, I will argue that Kant's references to two *experiences* of pleasure as well as to an *anticipation* of pleasure can be brought together to form a single, coherent, and hedonistic account of desire formation. I will make my argument in three steps. First, I contend that it is possible to argue that an anticipatory pleasure is grounded in an anticipation of pleasure. (I will postpone discussing the need for the presence of an anticipatory pleasure until section III.) Second, I argue that an experience of pleasure at an object or action, when it is taken on its own, does not provide a sufficient explanation of desire formation. This allows us to see why Kant might have understood that such an account must be supplemented in order to explain desire formation. Third, I contend that supplementing this account with the remaining two explanations of the role of pleasure in desire formation results in a coherent theory.

I am not arguing here that this is the *right* theory of desire formation, or, indeed, that this is the theory that Kant presents in any complete or comprehensive way. I am just arguing that it is a plausible theory that consistently unifies all of the partial accounts that Kant presents. It is a viable theory of desire formation that Kant leaves undeveloped and implicit in his thinking. My main intention, then, is to remove the suggestion that

Kant is confused or incoherent by gathering his various comments into a single, coherent, plausible, and ultimately hedonistic theory of desire formation. With this last point in mind I will conclude this section by returning to, and responding to, Reath's antihedonistic claims about desire formation in Kant. More specifically, I will finish my account by providing direct evidence against Reath's challenge to a hedonistic interpretation of Kant's theory of nonmoral motivation.

Anticipatory Pleasure and the Anticipation of Pleasure

The first thing to sort out is the relationship between an anticipatory experience of pleasure and an anticipation of pleasure. An anticipatory feeling of pleasure at the thought of an object can be grounded in an anticipation of pleasure in the existence of this object. This happens, for example, when one thinks of a cold drink, expects it to bring pleasure, and, as a result, experiences (anticipatory) pleasure at the thought of this drink. Kant appears to support the notion that this feeling is grounded in an anticipation of pleasure in the following passage (already quoted above):

> *Pleasure from the conception of the existence of a thing,* in so far as it is a determining ground of the desire for this thing, is based upon the susceptibility of the subject because it depends upon the actual presence of an object. Thus it belongs to sense (feeling) and not to the understanding, which expresses a relation of a conception to an object by concepts and not the relation of an idea to the subject by feelings. It is only in so far as the faculty of desire is determined by the sensation of agreeableness which the subject *expects from the actual existence* of the object. (Pr. R 5:22)

Since both the feeling of pleasure from the conception of the existence of something and the feeling of agreeableness that the subject expects from the existence of the object determine the faculty of desire, some relation between these two is established here (assuming, of course, that Kant thinks that there is structurally only one way in which the faculty of desire is determined). The anticipation of pleasure and the anticipatory pleasure are somehow connected such that both can be said to determine the faculty of desire. It seems that the most reasonable way of reading this is to say that the former is the ground of the latter in the way explained above.

Now, it should be noted that even though an anticipation of pleasure can ground an anticipatory feeling of pleasure, it is not, strictly speaking, necessary for one to expect pleasure in the future in order to experience an anticipatory pleasure. It is possible, for example, to experience an anticipatory feeling of pleasure upon thinking of something that will take place (or exist) after one's death. Imagine a writer who feels a glow of satisfaction at the thought of certain works of his being published posthumously. Of course, he is not actually going to derive any pleasure from this in the future. Examples such as this make it clear that an anticipation of pleasure is not necessary in order for there to be an anticipatory pleasure.[13] All that is necessary in order to experience pleasure upon thinking of something is that there be some association of pleasure with the end in question. In our example, it is necessary that the writer's posthumous works be somehow linked with pleasure in his mind, but not necessary that he anticipates pleasure upon seeing them published. He might imagine the pleasure of those who will get a chance to read new works of his after he is gone. Now, the possibility that an anticipatory pleasure can exist without a grounding anticipation of pleasure means that the anticipatory pleasure at the thought of some end can cause a desire for this end without one aiming to receive pleasure from the same end. I will return to this point in section III below, and it will be a central issue in my discussion of respect in the final chapter.

At the same time, however, there is overwhelming evidence to indicate that Kant does think that all nonmoral desires *are*, in fact, aimed at some future pleasure. It does not appear that Kant considers examples such as the publishing one in his account of desire formation. As we saw above, Kant tells us repeatedly that all nonmoral desires are aimed at pleasure, and insofar as he holds this to be the case, he seems to be committed to the idea that all anticipatory pleasures are grounded in an anticipation of pleasure. So, for Kant, we expect pleasure from every nonmoral end upon thinking of which we experience pleasure.

The Causal Sufficiency of an Experience of Pleasure at Some Object

According to Reath, Kant thinks that an experience of pleasure at a particular object or action is sufficient to cause a desire. Now, if this is so, then Kant's discussions of anticipatory pleasure and the anticipation of pleasure in this context are entirely superfluous. Reath presents the following example to illustrate his point: "Consider an attachment to baseball. Perhaps your interest is initially sparked when you find playing or watching the sport exciting, or engaging, and *these enjoyable experiences motivate you to continue playing or watching,* etc." (Reath 1989a, 48; emphasis added). Notice here that Reath passes quickly from the presence of the satisfactions to the formation of a desire. He does the same in the second example he lays out: "The formation of a friendship may follow a similar pattern. You begin to like someone because you enjoy the person's company or conversation, and these experiences create a desire for further association" (Reath 1989a, 48). But is this a sufficient account, or is there more to the story of desire formation? Reath says that "These examples suggest plausible patterns by which desires are formed" (Reath 1989a, 49), but he does not give us the details of these "patterns." How, precisely, do we get from the experiences of pleasure to the formations of desires?

Reath's omission here is extremely significant if an anticipation of pleasure is required in order to fill in this gap. Indeed, there is good reason to believe that any account of desire formation that moves directly from the experience of a pleasurable action or object to the presence of a desire is incomplete—and thus that Kant's references to an anticipation of pleasure and an anticipatory pleasure are not superfluous. The central question here is whether it makes sense to say that we go *immediately* from enjoying something to desiring more of it in the future, or whether something else must happen between these two things. In order to show that something else must happen, consider a case in which the enjoyment of something does not immediately result in a desire to repeat the experience of this thing. Suppose, for example, that you are eating in a foreign country and your host offers you an unfamiliar appetizer. You politely and unquestioningly accept and enjoy the dish. You are then told that it is, in fact, monkey. You do not agree with eating monkeys and so even though you ate and enjoyed the appetizer, you do not form a desire to eat it again. It might be objected that a desire is not formed in this example because an aversion already exists. But this objection misses the point of the argument, which is just that there is a gap of some sort between pleasure and any desire formed. If there were no gap, the aversion would have no space in which to operate—that is to say, no space in which to block the desire. If this gap is filled with information of a certain kind then no desire is formed.

Now, of course, this case must be distinguished from the case in which you are conflicted or torn about repeating the pleasant experience. Suppose you drink and enjoy alcohol, but are then told that alcohol is bad for your congenitally damaged liver. In this case, the desire for alcohol might already have been formed and now be in conflict with the desire to stay healthy. In the monkey-appetizer case, we can conclude that there is no desire formed if the news that the appetizer was monkey does not result in a conflict between your monkey-eating principles and any new desire. I see no reason why we cannot imagine such a case. Life seems to offer many pleasures that we enjoy once (and, perhaps, fondly remember), but for one reason or another do not provide a basis or foundation for the formation of any further desire. Consider, for example, going to a particular play, or film, or art exhibition. Or consider "once in a lifetime" pleasures such as bungee jumping, or hang gliding, or traveling the world. There are surely countless such pleasures that we enjoy once but do not immediately form a desire to repeat. Such cases illustrate the point that pleasure at an object or action is not immediately followed by a desire for this object or action in the future. This suggests that something else must happen, between the experience of pleasure and the formation of the desire, to allow for this formation.

In order to discover what this something else is, we must look more closely at what happens when you find out that it is monkey that you have eaten. One way of putting it is that you do not *imagine ever getting pleasure* from the appetizer again (or, if we accept that an anticipation of pleasure is not needed in order to experience an anticipatory pleasure, then we might say that you do not experience an anticipatory pleasure upon thinking of the appetizer). You might recall with horror your eating of the dish and think, "Never again." Had you been told that the appetizer was an abundant and extremely nutritious local vegetable you might have *thought that eating it again would be pleasant,* and in this case a desire would have been formed. Or, had you been told nothing at all you might have *thought that eating the appetizer was pleasant and that you must remember to order it again should you ever return.* We can see from this example that the thought of the object or action in the future goes in the gap between the experienced pleasure and the desire. In order to form a desire, then, you must at least have some conception of experiencing the object again in the future. Finding out that you just ate monkey results in your not anticipating that you would feel pleasure if you were to eat the same dish again. You might even imagine experiencing an unpleasant feeling of disgust at the prospect, and in this case an aversion would be formed. Thus, the reason that finding out what you ate results in no desire being formed is that as a consequence of this knowledge you do not anticipate getting pleasure from (or experience anticipatory pleasure at the thought of) eating this dish again. The key notion, then, is that you must have some conception of what it is for which you are forming a desire in order to form this desire. If you did not somehow believe that you were going to get pleasure from something you would not desire it.

I am not claiming that any of these thoughts or beliefs must be self-consciously present to the agent as the desire is being formed. The danger in proposing a kind of *process* of desire formation, in the way that I have, is that the account might suggest that we form desires in a rational and self-reflective way. But, of course, it is not plausible to think that when we experience new pleasures we reflect, evaluate these pleasures, and *decide* whether or not to form desires. Admittedly, this is certainly possible: we saw in the previous chapter that in the case of passions Kant seems to think that their formation involves some rational reflection. But it is clear that for Kant at least some desires are formed without any rational reflection on the part of the agent. In these cases, the agent is somewhat passively susceptible to the experience of pleasure and the subsequent formation of desires.[14] At the same time, it seems equally unsatisfying to believe that the experience of pleasure at an object is immediately and inexplicably followed by the formation of a desire. I think that there is some middle ground between these positions. On my understanding, the thought of the object or action in the future can take the form of a relatively explicit reflection (the monkey case), or it can simply be a fleeting representation that we take no time to ponder self-consciously. Imagine riding a roller coaster and screaming and having all the usual fun. The roller coaster jolts to a stop and one thinks, "One more go," and rushes to the end of the line. It seems that on some level the thought of going again must occur before one's desire for "one more go" can come about.

Reconciling the Three Accounts

It appears, then, that there is good reason to believe that the experience of pleasure at an object or action must be supplemented by an anticipation of pleasure (or at least an anticipatory pleasure) in order for a desire to come into existence. But is there any reason—apart from the presence in his thinking of two further accounts with which to fill the gap between pleasure at the experience of an object and the presence of a desire—to think that Kant would have agreed with this point? Actually, Kant's definition of desire$_1$ (discussed in the previous chapter) is helpful here. Kant says that "The faculty of desire is the faculty such a being has of causing, *through its ideas, the reality of the objects of these ideas*" (Pr. R 5:9n; emphasis added). An obvious implication of this definition is that a desire$_1$ orients us to production *out of the ideas* that we have. So, for Kant, our desires$_1$ are deeply connected to the ideas that we have of certain objects or actions.[15] This seems to suggest that Kant would agree that the immediate experience of pleasure at something is not sufficient to cause a desire without the mediation of some future-oriented idea of what is desired.

Kant's three accounts of the role of pleasure in desire formation can be brought together, then, in the following way. An anticipation of pleasure at the prospect of experiencing an object or action grounds an anticipatory experience of pleasure at the thought of this object or action. But the condition for the possibility of anticipating pleasure is a feeling of pleasure at a previous experience of some object or action. We would not anticipate pleasure at some object or action if a previous experience (our own, or someone else's reported to us) did not link this object or action with pleasure.[16] Taking Kant's own example of developing a desire for alcohol, we can outline the sequence as follows. One experiences pleasure in drinking a new drink. This experience of pleasure leads one to associate pleasure with this drink and thus to anticipate pleasure upon drinking this drink in the future. This anticipation of pleasure leads to an experience of pleasure at the thought of the drink and it is this experience of pleasure that actually determines the faculty of desire causing a desire. Again, these stages can be present without one's having to go self-consciously through each of them. So, Kant's three accounts of desire formation can be brought together to form a single coherent account.

Now, again, it is not clear that Kant ever had this larger unified account explicitly in mind. There is no direct evidence for this. But what is clear is that whether he intended it or not, Kant's various statements on the formation of desires can be plausibly brought together in this way.

A Response to the Antihedonistic Argument

At this point, Reath's arguments might be raised as an objection to my account. Reath contends that just because pleasure plays a role in the origin of a desire, it does not follow that pleasure is, at the same time, the object of desire. This is undoubtedly true; there is no *necessary* connection between pleasure as an origin of desire and pleasure as an object of desire. So far in this chapter I have tried to supply evidence to show, first, that Kant does *in fact* hold that desires are aimed at pleasure, and, second, that the anticipation of this pleasure plays a role in causing desires that is both compatible with and, indeed, *required by* the role played by an experience of pleasure at an object or action (i.e., the account of desire formation to which Reath subscribes). Thus, aside from the direct evidence presented in section I above, I have argued that there is a hedonistic theory of desire in Kant by showing that there is more to the Kantian story of desire formation than Reath has considered.

In concluding this section, I want to point to even more direct evidence against Reath's argument that Kant does *not* see pleasure as both object and origin of desire. This evidence can be found if we look more closely at the desire formation passage from the *Religion*. The first line of this passage reads, "A propensity is really only the predisposition to crave a delight which, when once experienced, arouses in the subject an *inclination* to it" [*Hang ist eigentlich nur die Prädisposition zum Begehren eines Genusses, der, wenn das Subjekt die Erfahrung davon gemacht haben wird, Neigung dazu hervorbringt*] (Rel 6:29n). We saw in section I that this account seems to help Reath's argument, since Kant is indicating that an experience of pleasure at something plays a key role in the origins of an inclination. But, upon closer inspection, we can see that the propensity of which Kant speaks is a propensity to desire (*Begehren*) a "delight" (*Genusses*), and that the desire/inclination formed is toward that very delight (*dazu*, "to it"). Kant might be using "delight" as a synonym for the object itself here, but it is more natural to read him as referring to the object via the *effect* of delight that it has on us. Thus, what we are inclined to is the delight/pleasure that the object brings.[17] Kant's example in the same passage bears out this reading, since the inclination of the "savages" is toward the delightful state of intoxication (*Rausch*) caused by the alcohol, and not toward the alcohol as such. Thus, the pleasure that is at the origin of inclination is for Kant *also* the object of the inclination formed, and his most explicit treatment of desire formation makes this clear.

III. ANTICIPATORY PLEASURE AND THE FACULTY OF DESIRE

The final stage in the account of desire formation just presented involves the determination of the faculty of desire by an anticipatory pleasure at the thought of some object or action. But, one might ask, why is it necessary to have an experience of pleasure do this work? Why does Kant not simply (or only) say that the *thought* of pleasure associated with a certain thing causes a desire for this thing? In other words, is adding an anticipatory experience of pleasure to the already complicated causal story not just adding a superfluous stage?[18] This stage would only be necessary if Kant somehow believed that it takes an actual experience of pleasure to determine the faculty of desire. That is to say, an anticipatory pleasure would only be necessary if Kant proposed that an experience of pleasure is needed as the immediate cause of a desire. Fortunately, Kant's mature definitions of pleasure provide support for just such a proposal insofar as they express the idea that pleasure is the subjective dimension of a representation that tends to maintain itself.

In the previous chapter, I claimed that Kant's understanding of the nature of pleasure develops sometime around the writing of the second and third *Critiques*. This development sees him move from treating pleasure as a brute sensation to considering it to be part of a state of mind with a kind of causality for maintaining itself. What exactly is involved in this shift? In her article, "A New Look at Kant's Theory of Pleasure," Rachel Zuckert explains that "it was a consideration of *aesthetic* pleasure that led Kant to reformulate his views as to the nature of pleasure. Indeed, Kant signals the paradigmatic nature of aesthetic pleasure by claiming that the principle of purposiveness without a purpose is 'constitutive' of aesthetic pleasure" (Zuckert 2002, 245). So, in the third *Critique* 5:220, when Kant says that pleasure is the "consciousness of the causality of a representation with respect to the state of the subject, for maintaining it in that state [*es in demselben zu erhalten*]," it is his account of aesthetic pleasure that has provided him with this new formulation. Aside from the aesthetic considerations that inform this development (which I will not get into here), Zuckert argues that Kant's new formulation solves some problems for his theory of moral motivation. She argues, quite correctly, I think, that Kant's earlier view of pleasure as a sensation did not allow him to distinguish between moral pleasure and other kinds of pleasure. Kant's new conception, insofar as it is intentional, allows for such a distinction. We will elaborate on this distinction in chapter 5 when we focus on the question of moral motivation, but for now let us a take a more detailed look at this new notion of pleasure itself.

Kant's definition of pleasure in the third *Critique* (quoted above) is coupled with an account of displeasure. He says that displeasure "is that representation that contains the ground for determining the state of the representations to their own opposite" (CJ 5:220). Meanwhile, in the First Introduction to the third *Critique,* Kant says, "Pleasure is a state of mind [*Zustand des Gemüts*] in which a representation is in agreement with itself, as a ground, either merely for preserving this state itself . . . or for producing its object" (CJ 20:231). Later on, in the *Anthropology,* Kant puts the same point in the following way: "Whatever incites me directly (through my senses) to abandon (to depart from) my condition is unpleasant to me, it gives me pain; and whatever drives me to maintain (to remain in) my condition is pleasant to me, it gratifies me" (A 7:231). Kant presents what appears to be the same understanding of pleasure in a variety of different (and difficult) ways across these accounts.

In the first two definitions quoted above, Kant says that pleasure is the *consciousness* of a representation, but that displeasure is an actual representation. Which is it? The first thing to note is that Kant maintains an intentional understanding of pleasure. Pleasure is always pleasure *in,* or *at,* some idea—it is not just a brute sensation but is always attached to some idea. It is for this reason that Kant says that it is the "consciousness" (*Bewußtsein*) of a representation. But for Kant a representation can include this consciousness of itself. So, a representation involves an idea and the pleasure or displeasure taken in or at this idea. On this reading, pleasure is a feature or dimension of a representation and not an actual representation. In Kant's own language, pleasure and displeasure are the "subjective aspects" of our representations. Kant tells us this when he writes, "One can characterize sensibility as the subjective aspect of our representations in general. . . . What is subjective in our representations cannot become *an element in our cognition* because it involves *only* a relation of the representation to the *subject*" (MM 6:212n). So, for example, "enjoying an ice cream" is a representation—it involves the idea of the ice cream and the pleasure taken in it. Recall from chapter 1 that in the *Metaphysics* Kant says that the feeling of love is "pleasure joined immediately to the representation of an object's existence" (MM 6:402). Loving someone is a representation made up of the idea of that person and pleasure immediately taken in this idea as such. The object of the representation can be present and causing the idea in which pleasure is taken, or it may simply be the idea of a future object in which we take pleasure. In the latter case, the pleasure taken is what I have been calling an anticipatory pleasure—it is a pleasure at the mere thought of something. So, the subjective aspect or dimension of a representation may be an anticipatory pleasure.

Now, in the definitions quoted above, Kant also identifies pleasure with a "state of mind." The agent's state of mind seems to be the way in which she feels upon having a representation. A state of mind just *is* the having of a representation. We can say, then, that a state of mind is a representation, except that the emphasis in this term is on the subjective or feeling dimension of this representation and not on the object represented. According to Kant's definitions, this state of mind maintains itself through (or on the basis of) the causality of a representation. To feel pleasure, then, is to be in a state of mind that tends to maintain itself. In short, pleasurable representations cause us to maintain the state of mind that accompanies them. In the case of nonaesthetic pleasurable representations, they do this by causing desires. Now, for Kant, desires can maintain a pleasurable state of mind in a couple of ways: most obviously, insofar as the object desired and achieved is itself pleasurable (and thus the representation of it will allow the agent to stay in a pleasant state of mind), or, less obviously, insofar as the mere satisfaction of the desire is itself pleasurable (and the state of mind associated with the satisfaction of the desire maintains itself). Kant points to the latter kind of case when he writes, "The attainment of every aim is combined with the feeling of pleasure" (CJ 5:187). The mere satisfaction of a desire for some end is pleasant, regardless of the nature of the end attained. It follows from this that causing a desire can maintain a pleasurable state of mind just insofar as the satisfaction of desires is a pleasant experience.

Kant's definitions of pleasure seem to involve a deeper analysis of just what it means to have such a pleasurable representation. According to this deeper analysis, to experience pleasure is to be conscious of a causality directed at staying in the state of mind that accompanies a representation. To experience a pleasurable representation, then, is to feel something with a causality directed at keeping us feeling this feeling. Notice, this is a function-based or effect-based account of pleasure, and thus must be understood in conjunction with Kant's definition of the faculty of desire (looked at in the previous chapter).[19] The feeling of pleasure is defined here in terms of the effects of pleasurable representations. The effects of these representations draw the faculty of desire into the account. Remember, the faculty of desire is that by which objects are produced out of the ideas of these objects. We can say that the faculty of pleasure or displeasure is that which *causes* these objects to be produced by determining the faculty of desire. So, the causal function of a feeling of pleasure brings us immediately to the faculty of desire because it is this faculty that is determined to do the causal work prompted by pleasure. Desires are the vehicle for a causality that tends to maintain a particular state of mind.

In light of this account of pleasure, we can begin to see more clearly why an anticipatory feeling of pleasure (i.e., a pleasurable representation of some future object or action) is present as a final stage in determining the faculty of desire.[20] On the face of it, for Kant, an agent desires something because it is associated with pleasure. But Kant's function-based account brings out that, on a deeper level, we want pleasure because pleasure is the subjective aspect of representations that tend to maintain themselves. Thus, we always experience pleasure in desiring anything. An anticipation of pleasure is effective when it gives rise to an experience of (anticipatory) pleasure at the thought of something that causes a desire for this thing. It is this anticipatory pleasure at the thought of an object that determines the faculty of desire, causing the experience of pleasure to be maintained through a desire for the actual object. On my account, then, a new desire is created when pleasure tends toward maintenance by determining the faculty of desire.

We are in a better position now to understand just how this anticipatory feeling of pleasure can be a part of moving the agent *without* the presence of an actual anticipation of pleasure. By way of setting up the problem, let us return to the example of the writer who forms a desire on the basis of pleasure at the thought of his posthumous publications. This agent does not anticipate getting pleasure from the reception of these works. Moreover, we can easily imagine that he writes and prepares them (in accordance with his desire) without being moved by any pleasure anticipated from these acts themselves. According to Kant's account, these acts come about in view of a pleasurable representation of the posthumous works, with a causality directed at maintaining itself. But how can pleasure move us in this way without the expectation that it will actually be maintained? And if there is an expectation that it will be maintained, then are we not moved by the expectation (or anticipation) of pleasure after all?

The key here is that Kant's characterization of pleasure does not commit him to the idea that pleasurable representations maintain themselves by *aiming* at the pleasure associated with a represented end or action. If Kant were saying this, it would follow that there is no difference between a desire and a pleasure. A pleasurable representation would just be a desire for more of such representations. Clearly, such an identification would break down Kant's fundamental division between the faculty of desire and the faculty of pleasure and displeasure. However, the somewhat difficult language that Kant uses in defining pleasure points us away from the idea that pleasurable representations somehow *want* or *desire* to maintain themselves by *aiming* for more pleasure. Kant speaks of representations having a "causality . . . for maintaining" the subject in a certain state. Even though I have glossed this definition by saying that a pleasurable representation is a "causality *directed* at maintaining" a certain state, Kant does not use this kind of explicitly intentional language. Instead, Kant's function-based account focuses on what pleasurable representations *do* or *tend to do*: they tend to cause (through the creation of desires in nonmoral cases) behaviors that result in the maintenance of pleasurable states of mind. Even if the desire in question does not aim at pleasure, pleasure can still be maintained through the gratification received from merely satisfying the desire. All that Kant's characterization of pleasure commits him to, then, is the idea that pleasure at the thought of something tends to cause us to act toward the object of this thought (through the generation of a desire for this object). The satisfaction of this desire is pleasurable and thus maintains that state of mind. So, pleasurable representations tend to allow us to maintain a pleasurable state of mind just insofar as they cause desires. Applying this to our example, we can conclude that the writer's pleasure at the thought of his posthumous works tends to maintain itself by causing a desire. This desire maintains pleasure just insofar as its satisfaction (through the processes of writing) produces further pleasurable representations. Note again, however, that it is not necessary that the agent expect pleasure from these actions or from the end result.

Of course, if our pleasure at the thought of something is grounded in an anticipation of pleasure at achieving some end, then this first pleasure will cause desires aimed at the end and its associated pleasure. In other words, if one already anticipates pleasure from an end, then any desire for this end that is caused (by an anticipatory pleasure) is going to involve aiming at the pleasure that is connected with the end. Again, it is worth emphasizing that insofar as Kant thinks that all nonmoral desires are aimed at pleasure, he seems committed to the idea that these desires do indeed involve this combination of an anticipation of pleasure and an anticipatory pleasure.

Let us take a look now at some passages that will help to fill out and support some of what I have argued above. In the *Anthropology*, Kant suggests that we are always experiencing some kind of feeling. This suggestion is implicit when Kant says,

> But we are incessantly moved by the stream of time, and the change of sensations resultant from it. Even if the abandonment of one instant, and the occurring of another is one and the same act (of change), it is, nevertheless, in our thought and our awareness of change, a temporal sequence conforming to the relation of cause and effect. Now the question arises whether the awareness of leaving the present state, or the prospect of entering a future state, awakens in us the sensation of gratification. In the first instance the gratification is nothing more than ending the pain and therefore something negative; whereas in the second instance the presentiment of pleasantness, that is an expected intensification of the state of pleasure, would be some-

thing positive. . . . But the life (of the animal) is, as physicians have also noticed, a continuing play [*kontinuierliches Spiel*] of the antagonism between these two feelings (pleasure and pain). (A 7:231)

Kant explicitly discusses an anticipatory feeling of pleasure here, though not exactly in these terms. He tells us that the expectation of an intensification of pleasure is itself a positive feeling of gratification. In saying this, he puts an anticipation of pleasure at the ground of anticipatory pleasure. Kant seems to indicate that the mind is permanently immersed in a flux of pleasure and pain. We are incessantly moving through time and this movement constantly registers with us as feeling or sensing beings. That is to say, as our sensations and representations change through time, so do our feelings. But if all feeling is pleasure or pain, then the constant movement through time is accompanied by continual, even if slight, fluctuations in our experiences of pleasure or pain.[21] It is on the basis of this insight that Kant tells us that an ordinary life of mixed fortunes is a "continuing" (*kontinuierliches*) play of pleasure and pain. The functional role of pleasure in this play is to cause desire for those objects the representations of which are accompanied by pleasure.

Elsewhere in the *Anthropology*, Kant reiterates the idea that desire formation must be understood against the background of a play of pleasure or pain.[22]

Pain must precede every gratification; pain always comes first. What else but a quick death from joy would follow a steady advancement of vitality, which cannot be increased beyond a certain point anyway? Also, no gratification can immediately follow another; but between one and another there must occur pain. Actually small checks on our vital power, with interspersed advancements, constitute the state of health which we erroneously take for a continuously felt condition of well-being, since it always consists only of erratic sequences of pleasant feelings (constantly interspersed with pain). (A 7:231)

Thus, in actual fact, feelings of both pleasure and pain are required in order to cause a desire. It is not simply that pleasurable representations determine the faculty of desire; instead, painful and pleasurable representations together do. The basic engine (and direction) of desire comes from the possession of a pleasurable representation with a causality directed at maintaining itself in the face of a continual slipping into pain.[23] It is against the threat of this slipping into pain that anticipatory feelings of pleasure determine the faculty of desire.

In this chapter we have seen that Kant's apparently conflicting comments on desire formation can be reconciled in a coherent theory. According to this theory, an anticipatory pleasure (i.e., a pleasurable representation of some future object or action) determines the faculty of desire and causes a desire for this thing. This anticipatory pleasure can be based on a past association of pleasure with an object, an anticipation of pleasure, or both. When it comes to causing nonmoral desires, Kant seems to think that it is both, insofar as he maintains that all such desires aim at pleasure. I have stressed, however, that this is not a position that Kant *must* hold, since in view of his account of pleasure he could argue that an anticipatory pleasure determines the faculty of desire without an anticipation of pleasure.

Of course, this is not all that there is to say about Kant's theory of action. After all, we have not even raised the question of the rationality of actions, or the role that reason plays in our choices. For Kant, all actions are performed on the basis of maxims and not directly out of our desires$_1$. In order to develop our account of his theory of nonmoral action, we must look at the relationship between desires$_1$ and maxims. More specifically, we must look at how maxims are formed out of desires$_1$. Before turning to this question, however, the first thing to sort out is the possibility of freedom in the nonmoral realm.

. . . .

CHAPTER THREE

NONMORAL FREEDOM IN KANT

Kant's understanding of the nature and origin of pathological desire$_1$ is only the first of two dimensions (i.e., the pathological and the rational) that make up his theory of nonmoral action. Over the next two chapters I will shift my focus to the rational dimension, completing my account of Kant's theory of nonmoral action by looking at how he thinks these actions are free, principled, and yet sensuously affected. In chapters 1 and 2, I laid the groundwork for an analysis of the ways in which actions are sensuously affected by presenting an account of Kant's understanding of sensibility—that is, his treatment of desires$_1$ and pleasure, and the relationship between the two. The task now is to see how this sensibility is reconciled with the free and principled nature of action. I will start in this chapter by looking at the question of freedom in the nonmoral context. The central issue here is the kind of freedom that is attached to the sensuously affected actions of a human agent.

Some scholars maintain that Kant has a deterministic theory of nonmoral action.[1] Now, if it is true that Kant does not have a concept of freedom in the nonmoral realm, then any attempt to explicate his theory of moral motivation in light of his account of nonmoral action is fundamentally misguided. Thus, in order to justify my methodological approach, it is at the least necessary to establish that Kant thinks that nonmoral actions are free.

I will develop my argument for the freedom of nonmoral actions in Kant's system in three main steps. I will give voice in section I to the position according to which Kant does *not* have a concept of nonmoral freedom. On this view, Kant has only one concept of freedom: moral freedom. Some critics argue that, as a result, only moral and immoral actions are free, while choices between nonmoral actions are not. I will conclude this section by presenting evidence to indicate that this reading might not represent Kant's position. In section II, I will present Henry Allison's well-known attempt to articulate the grounds for a theory of nonmoral freedom in Kant, in which he uses the Incorporation Thesis to argue that nonmoral choices are free. I will contend, however, that Allison's reading does not do enough to establish nonmoral freedom. In section III, finally, I will provide my own argument for the presence of a concept of nonmoral freedom in Kant's system, maintaining that this concept can be grounded in his notion of moral freedom.

I. NONMORAL DETERMINISM

According to a popular recent interpretation, Kant employs only one concept of freedom—the "power [*Vermögen*] of pure reason to be of itself practical" (MM 6:213)—and grounds this concept in the "fact" of moral obligation. On this view, a free choice is a choice made in accordance with the moral law, and our freedom is a moral freedom to defy our natural impulses in acting morally. Immoral choices, however, are also free insofar as we have a *power* or *capacity* (*Vermögen*) to act morally, and, thus, are responsible for not doing so.[2] But it follows from this account that Kant has no concept of freedom in the nonmoral realm. In a choice between two nonmoral ends, where the capacity to act morally is irrelevant, there is no freedom. Hannah Ginsborg presents this position quite clearly when she writes that for Kant we have the freedom "*not* to satisfy any given desire if it conflicts with our duty. In other words, the freedom under the idea of which we act is not the freedom to act on any one desire in preference to any other, but rather the freedom to refrain from acting on any one of our desires: specifically when duty commands us to do so" (Ginsborg 1998, 14). So, freedom is really only a moral freedom *from* our pathological desires$_1$. Morality provides a capacity to act contrary to these desires$_1$ (in choosing for the sake of our duty), and we are responsible when we fail to exercise this capacity.

In order to understand this position more clearly, let us take a brief look at the nature of the freedom that Kant associates with moral choices.

For Kant, there are two dimensions to every moral choice: the presence of a governing principle that one necessarily gives to oneself (i.e., the moral law), and the specific choice of a subjective principle of action (i.e., a maxim) based on this governing principle.[3] The first dimension ensures that moral choices are causally and motivationally independent of all pathological desires$_1$. That is to say, it ensures that moral choices are neither mechanically (i.e., efficiently) *caused* by preceding desires$_1$, nor *motivated* by desires$_1$ that we see as reasons drawing us into action. With this causal and motivational independence in mind, Kant writes that freedom is that "property of [rational] causality by which it can be effective independent of foreign causes determining it" (G 4:446). This notion of freedom is transcendental freedom, and in the second *Critique* Kant maintains that it is "independence from everything empirical and hence from nature generally" (Pr. R 5:97). In the first *Critique,* Kant specifies that transcendental freedom allows one "the power of beginning a state spontaneously [*von selbst*]" (A 533/B 561). To begin a state spontaneously is to bring something about without being caused or motivated by anything external in doing so. Now, the spontaneity of a moral choice is made possible by the (transcendental) independence of the moral law from nature. But notice that, while the spontaneity of a moral choice is rooted in its association with the moral law, there must be a *specific choice* that instantiates this spontaneity in the world. This specific choice is referred to above as the second dimension of moral choice.

These considerations help to clarify the sense in which nonmoral choices are not free (on this first interpretation of Kantian freedom). For Kant, the principle of happiness governs nonmoral choices. For now, let us just take happiness (on Kant's account) to be the maximal pleasure that we get from the satisfaction of a coherent set of our desires$_1$.[4] So, nonmoral choices are not free (on this interpretation) because the principle governing these choices is imported from our pathological nature. Thus, a specific choice is only free if it is spontaneous, and it is only spontaneous insofar as it borrows this spontaneity from its grounding principle (i.e., the first dimension outlined above). Nonmoral choices cannot borrow the spontaneity of the moral law, and thus are not free in this sense. If this is the only concept of freedom in Kant (as many argue), then nonmoral choices are, indeed, not free at all.

Yet this reading flies in the face of quite a bit of evidence to suggest that Kant thinks that nonmoral choices are free. I will briefly present three such pieces of evidence. In the *Groundwork,* Kant explores the difficulty that an agent has in trying to understand what will bring him happiness.

> If he wills riches, how much anxiety, envy, and intrigues might be not thereby drawn upon his shoulders! If he wills much knowledge and vision, perhaps it might become only an eye that much sharper to show him as more dreadful the evils which are now hidden from him and which are yet unavoidable; or it might be to burden his desires—which already sufficiently engage him— with even more needs! If he wills long life, who guarantees that it will not be long misery. . . . In short, he is not capable, on any principle and with complete certainty, of ascertaining what would make him truly happy; omniscience would be needed for this. . . . The imperatives of prudence . . . are to be taken as counsels rather than as commands of reason. (G 4:418)

In this passage, Kant seems to think that there are free choices between nonmoral ends: knowledge or ignorance, a long life or a short life. It might be argued that the agent's lack of knowledge makes it appear this way, but that, in fact, were he to know, he could not but act toward that end that promotes his happiness.[5] However, Kant presents the agent as being genuinely *torn* between various options and thus forced to choose. He refers to the (admittedly uncertain) principles that the agent chooses in aiming at happiness as counsels, or imperatives, of prudence. So, Kant posits the governing principle of happiness and a number of imperatives of prudence under it, and suggests that it is in the *choice* of these subordinate imperatives that the agent is uncertain. The agent chooses these imperatives in a way that initially seems similar to the way in which moral maxims are chosen (i.e., on the basis of some governing principle). Now, even though it is true that these nonmoral choices lack the spontaneity of moral choices (because they lack a connection to any transcendental law), they appear to be spontaneous in some sense.

Kant's views on the concept of an "end" also suggest that he thinks that there is some notion of freedom in the nonmoral realm. In the *Metaphysics,* he writes, "An end [*Zweck*] is an object of free choice, the representation of which determines it to an action (by which the object is brought about). Every action, therefore, has its end; and since no one can have an end without himself making the object of his choice into an end, to have any [*irgendeinen*] end of action whatsoever is an act of freedom on the part of the acting subject, not an effect of *nature*" (MM 6:385). Kant speaks of "every" action having an end, and then says that to have "any" end is the result of an act of freedom. The clear implication here is that nonmoral actions have ends and that these ends are freely chosen in some significant sense.[6] Kant echoes this point elsewhere in the *Metaphysics* when he tells us that "an *end* is an object of the choice (of a rational being)" and that only "I myself can *make* something my end" (MM 6:381). A little later he writes, "To have an end that I have not made an end is self-contradictory, an act of freedom which is not yet free" (MM 6:381). Finally, he also says, "What end anyone wants to set for his action is left to his free choice" (MM 6:382). Now, there is no *prima facie* reason to think that Kant is not also thinking of nonmoral ends when he makes these assertions.

The third piece of evidence to indicate that Kant thinks that nonmoral choices are free is his account of *practical* freedom.[7] As we saw in the Introduction, Kant thinks of practical freedom as the independence of the human will from sensuous necessitation—though not from sensuous affection. This notion is defined in the first *Critique* as the "will's independence of coercion through sensuous impulses" (A 534/B 562). In the second *Critique,* Kant evokes this idea of practical freedom when he refers to our will as "pathologically affected (though not pathologically determined—and thus still free)" (Pr. R 5:32). Later, in the *Metaphysics,* Kant employs the same concept immediately before his definition of freedom as the capacity of pure reason to be practical (quoted above). "That which can be determined only by inclination (sensible impulse, stimulus) would be animal choice. Human choice, however, is a choice that can indeed be affected but not determined by impulses, and is therefore of itself (apart from an acquired proficiency of reason) not pure but can still be determined to actions by pure will" (MM 6:213). I will return below to the question of the relation between this notion of freedom and the concept of moral freedom that is defined directly after it. For now, it is important to note that this concept of practical freedom suggests that human choices are *never* entirely determined by our sensibility (though they are affected by this sensibility). Thus, the idea of independence from sensible necessitation seems to afford us a concept of freedom that operates in the nonmoral realm. But what exactly is the nature of the freedom that this idea of being pathologically affected, but not necessitated, affords us?

II. ALLISON AND THE INCORPORATION THESIS

Henry Allison attempts to answer this question in what is probably the most well-known interpretation of Kant's theory of freedom in the English-language literature.[8] I have referred to Allison in passing numerous times in this study but I want to pause now to take a more detailed look at his central interpretive claim: the Incorporation Thesis. The Incorporation Thesis is at the heart of Allison's argument for the existence of a concept of free nonmoral choice in Kant. According to this thesis, an action is free because a pathological desire$_1$ does not determine the will unless an agent lets it. Kant tells us that "Freedom of the will is of a wholly unique nature in that an incentive can determine the will to an action *only so far as the individual has incorporated it into his maxim* . . . ; only thus can an incentive, whatever it may be, co-exist with the absolute spontaneity [*absoluten Spontaneität*] of the will" (Rel 6:24).[9] An agent lets a desire$_1$ determine the will by incorporating it into a maxim. Allison argues that the act of incorporating a desire$_1$ is a *spontaneous,* and thus free, act. In making this argument, Allison posits a concept of spontaneity that is distinct from the spontaneity discussed in section I (above) in that it is not grounded in the transcendental freedom of the moral law. This critical move *seems* to be supported by Kant's claim that only incorporation allows incentive-based actions to coexist with spontaneity. Allison takes Kant to be saying that the incorporation of incentives involves a spontaneous choice—"a genuine, albeit limited, spontaneity" that is distinct from the spontaneity associated with moral choice (Allison 1990, 207). However, it should be pointed out that Kant refers to the reconciliation of incentives with the "*absolute* spontaneity" of the will, and thus (in spite of what Allison says) he does not seem to be allowing for a new limited spontaneity. Instead, Kant seems to be talking about the *absolute* spontaneity associated with the transcendental freedom of morality. Let us take a closer look at what Allison is saying before we return to this issue.

For Allison, a nonmoral action is not *as* free as a moral one in that it is not governed by the principle of pure reason. The desires$_1$ that provide motives for nonmoral choices are pathological and are governed by a pathological principle. Allison insists, however, that the motivational dependence of these choices on pathological grounds (i.e., the principle of happiness and pathological desires$_1$) still allows for a genuine kind of freedom. He writes, "An agent would be free in the practical (but not transcendental) sense if that agent's choices were ultimately governed by some fundamental drive or natural impulse, for example, self-preservation or maximization of pleasure, which might be acted upon in any number of ways but could not be contravened. Such an agent would be practically free, even in an incompatibilist sense, because the drive or impulse serves to limit the agent's options rather than to necessitate causally a given choice" (Allison 1990, 207). On this view, desire$_1$-based choices are practically, but not transcendentally, free. Allison thinks that practical freedom, though distinct from transcendental freedom, is still a genuinely incompatibilist notion residing somewhere between a compatibilist (or nonspontaneous) concept of freedom and a full-fledged transcendental freedom. Practical freedom is an independence from antecedent sensible causes, and thus allows for choices that are spontaneous in a distinct nonmoral sense. Allison writes that in the case of nonmoral choices, "a rational agent is not regarded as being determined in a quasi-mechanistic fashion by the strongest desire. . . . On the contrary, to the extent to which such actions are taken as genuine expressions of agency and, therefore, as imputable, they are thought to involve an *act of spontaneity* on the part of the agent, through which the inclination or desire is deemed or taken as an appropriate basis of action" (Allison 1990, 39; emphasis added). Elsewhere, Allison tells us a little more about this act of spontaneity: "It is the value placed on a desire or inclination by an agent that gives it its 'motivational force,' its status as a reason to act" (Allison 1996, 113). So, the spontaneous act of incorporation is, at least in part, an act of giving value to a desire$_1$. This kind of spontaneity means that though nonmoral choices are restricted to that which brings us pleasure, they are entirely spontaneous within the limits laid down by this general trajectory. The act of incorporation allows for this nonmoral spontaneity by providing a wedge of sorts between our desires$_1$ and our choices.

Without pretending to offer a full analysis of Allison's larger position, I want to point to a problem with this interpretation of nonmoral freedom in Kant. For Allison, the act of incorporation is a spontaneous act of *taking* a desire$_1$ as a basis (or reason) for acting. So, again, this act is crucial since it is responsible for introducing spontaneity into nonmoral actions. Allison says that Kant assumes that "to conceive of oneself (or someone else) as a rational agent is to adopt a model of deliberative rationality in terms of which choice involves both a taking as and a framing or positing" (Allison 1990, 38). Allison suggests here and elsewhere that the act of incorporation or "taking as" is an act of value positing: the agent values a desire$_1$ as a *good* reason for action and is not determined (but merely affected) by her sensibility in doing so. But upon what basis is a desire$_1$ *valued* as a reason for action? As indicated above, the answer for Kant (in the nonmoral context) is the principle of happiness. It is on the basis of our concept of happiness that we incorporate incentives into nonmoral maxims. Allison seems to recognize this when he tells us that our drive for the "maximization of pleasure" (which is surely Allison's shorthand for happiness) "limits" our options. But in what sense can a drive for happiness simply "limit" options? What is the precise sense of the term "limit" here?

Now, if the only basis for the incorporation of nonmoral incentives is happiness and our interest in happiness is, at bottom, a second-order desire$_1$ for *maximal* pleasure, then Allison has a problem. If we are moved by the desire$_1$ to maximize pleasure, and that which constitutes our maximal pleasure is determined by feeling (*Gefühl*), then we are entirely determined by feeling. Remember, feeling for Kant is a susceptibility to feelings of pleasure or pain.[10] Any given experience of pleasure or pain is contingent upon our susceptibility to feelings, and this susceptibility is just an empirical fact about each of us. We do not choose what it is that we find pleasure in, and it follows that we do not choose what it is that we find maximal pleasure in either. Consequently, our concept of happiness (i.e., maximal pleasure) is not something that we can posit in any old fashion. Instead, our susceptibility to pleasure determines our concept of maximal pleasure or happiness, and in any given case of nonmoral choice this concept determines our choice.[11]

Allison might respond here, as he does to a similar objection from Stephen Engstrom, that "The Incorporation Thesis of itself entails that desires do not come with preassigned weights" (Allison 1996, 113).[12] He goes on to explain that, "On the contrary, it is the value placed on a desire or inclination by an agent that gives it its 'motivational force'" (Allison 1996, 113). The problem, again, is that this valuing process must be grounded in *something*, and, unless we have reason to think otherwise, that something is the agent's sensibility—which does in fact provide a weighting of sorts. The Incorporation Thesis (on its own) does provide independence from causal necessitation by our desires$_1$, but it does not (on its own) seem to provide independence from motivational necessitation. Thus, there is no reason not to think that the agent, as Allison conceives her, would simply choose to incorporate (and thus be motivated by) that end which promises most pleasure. It is worth noting in this context that Allison distinguishes between practical freedom and transcendental freedom (and its successor concept *autonomy*) by saying that the spontaneity associated with practical freedom "involves causal independence or, in Kantian terms, 'independence of the causality of nature.'" By contrast, autonomy involves what I have called 'motivational independence,' by which I mean the capacity to determine oneself to act on the basis of considerations that are completely independent of one's needs as a sensuous being" (Allison 1996, 111).

But even though he says this much, Allison does not seem to realize that, unless practical freedom also involves some kind of motivational independence from nature, it simply slides back into a kind of delayed pathological determination. In a sense, without any further account the act of incorporation that Allison describes simply puts off or delays sensible necessitation.

It is just not clear, then, that Allison's reading of the Incorporation Thesis does enough to show that Kant thinks that nonmoral choices are free. In reflecting on his 1990 work, Allison tells us that he "distinguished between practical freedom and transcendental freedom and claimed that the Incorporation Thesis required only the former" (Allison 1996, 109). As we saw above, Allison uses the Incorporation Thesis to argue that practical freedom is an incompatibilist notion of freedom. At the same time, we see here that in the order of reality he argues that the Incorporation Thesis is grounded in practical freedom. We will see below that it is Allison's failure to draw out all of the implications of the notion of practical freedom (as a grounding notion) that prevents him from seeing how the act of incorporation can resist motivational dependence upon our sensibility. The incorporation of incentives is not grounded in a concept of genuinely spontaneous (practical) freedom if this incorporation simply falls back on our sensibility, and Allison gives us no compelling reason to see the "genuine, albeit limited, spontaneity" that he associates with practical freedom as a kind of spontaneity at all.[13] The result is that Allison's interpretation of the crucial incorporation passage from the *Religion* does not establish the presence of a concept of nonmoral freedom in Kant's system. Moreover, as I noted above, when Kant says in this passage that incorporation reconciles incentives with *absolute* spontaneity, it seems that he is not thinking of a distinct ("limited" and nonmoral) kind of spontaneity at all. The clear suggestion is that there is only one notion of spontaneity in Kant's account.

III. THE CONCEPT OF NONMORAL FREEDOM

But Allison's flawed attempt to establish a concept of nonmoral freedom is well motivated, since (as we saw above) Kant *does* seem to treat nonmoral choices as though they were free. In what follows, I will construct a Kantian account of nonmoral freedom by starting with the immediate condition for the possibility of such a freedom and working back toward some ultimate ground.

Freedom of Indifference Grounded in Practical Freedom

At the very least, Kant requires a notion of the freedom of indifference in order to conceive of nonmoral choice as free. On this concept of freedom, nonmoral choices are free just insofar as one could always do otherwise. Thus, a choice between a blue car and a red car is a free choice if one could have chosen that which, in the actual event, one did not choose. We might ask first, then, whether we can ground such a notion of freedom in Kant's conceptual system.

In fact, Kant's concept of practical freedom grounds the notion that one could always do otherwise (i.e., a freedom of indifference). To claim that we are necessitated by our sensibility is just to deny that we have the ability to do other than that which our sensibility demands. To deny necessitation (as Kant's notion of practical freedom does) is, therefore, to allow for a capacity to do otherwise. Kant explicitly draws this link between practical freedom and the freedom of indifference in a lecture from 1785: "Can I really conceive of a pathological compulsion in man as well? Truly, I cannot, for freedom consists in this, that he can be without compulsion in the pathological sense; nor should he be compelled in that way. Even if a man is so constrained, *he can nevertheless act otherwise*" (LM 29:617; emphasis added). In this passage, Kant connects our not being pathologically necessitated with our capacity to act otherwise. Thus, for Kant, the concept of practical freedom includes the notion of a capacity to do otherwise. To be sensuously *affected* (the other dimension of the concept of practical freedom) is to act on a sensuous motive, but to be able to refuse to act on any one such motive in particular. The concept of practical freedom allows us the idea that we just *typically* choose means to that end which our sensibility demands (i.e., happiness), but that we can always do otherwise.[14]

Kant himself speaks of agents doing other than pursuing happiness in the nonmoral context. For example, in the *Groundwork* he writes, "It is not to be wondered at . . . that a single inclination, definite as to what it promises and as to the time at which it can be satisfied, can outweigh a fluctuating idea and that, for example, a man with the gout can choose [*wählen*] to enjoy what he likes and to suffer what he may, because according to his calculations at least on this occasion he has not sacrificed the enjoyment of the present moment to a perhaps groundless expectation of a happiness supposed to lie in health" (G 4:399). The more immediate desire for certain foods overcomes the gouty agent's desire for happiness. He chooses an action that he knows is contrary to his happiness.

I will postpone a full discussion of weakness of the will and Kant's concept of happiness until the next chapter, but for now it is worth briefly considering an obvious objection to this example. It might be argued that for Kant the gouty agent's action is not really a *free* choice at all, since it is not a principled action, and Kant thinks that all properly free choices involve maxims. The conclusion that the gouty agent's action is not principled follows from the consideration that it is a nonmoral action that is not governed by the principle of happiness. Without presenting a full response to this argument here, it can be shown quite easily that Kant does in fact think that there are some principled actions that are contrary to happiness.

Kant's treatment of passions (*Leidenschaften*) makes it clear that he thinks there are freely chosen nonmoral maxims that oppose happiness. Recall from chapter 1 that Kant conceives of passions as inclinations that are "hardly" controlled by reason. We saw there that this means that passionate maxims are not chosen on the basis of our concept of happiness. Kant writes, "Inclination, which hinders the use of reason to compare, at a particular moment of choice, a specific inclination against the sum of all inclinations, is passion" (A 7:265). Passions are powerful and stubborn such that they try to prevent us comparing them to other inclinations and ranking them in the system of pleasures that, for Kant, makes up our happiness.[15] But, at the same time, passionate action is maxim-governed, and, thus, minimally rational. "Passion always presupposes a maxim of the subject, namely, to act according to a purpose prescribed for him by his inclination" (A 7:266). The clear implication, then, is that the free choice of a passionate maxim is an instance of doing other than what happiness dictates.

And so, Kant's concept of practical freedom grounds a notion of freedom in the nonmoral realm insofar as it entails a concept of doing other than what happiness dictates (or acting otherwise). But how can one explain how it is that practical freedom grounds the ability to do otherwise without somehow relying (as Allison appears to do) upon an ungrounded notion of nonmoral spontaneity? This question can be rephrased in terms of the essential nature of practical freedom. We might ask, How do we know that we are free from sensible necessitation (though not affection) such that we can always do otherwise? Or, How is the notion of practical freedom itself grounded?

Practical Freedom Grounded in Moral Freedom

In order to answer this question we must return to Kant's understanding of moral freedom. In the second *Critique*, Kant maintains that it is a "Fact of Reason" that we can act morally. He derives the concept of moral freedom from this fact.[16] Morality (or the fact of our acting morally) is the "*ratio cognoscendi*" of our freedom (Pr. R 5:4n). In other words, without morality there would be no basis for the concept of moral freedom. Now, as Kant conceives it, moral freedom—the "power of pure reason to be of itself practical" (MM 6:213)—is essentially a capacity to act independently of our sensibility, and in complete accordance with our rationality. It is a capacity to deny the determined course of natural events and express our essential nature as rational beings. Notice, there are two distinct dimensions to this concept of moral freedom: separation from our sensibility and unification with our rationality.[17] In what follows, I will argue that, for Kant, the first dimension of this concept provides the ground for the notion of practical freedom, which in turn allows for a concept of the freedom of indifference. In other words, I will contend that Kant derives his notion of nonmoral freedom from morality.

In saying that morality is the *ratio cognoscendi* of moral freedom, Kant specifically does not mean to say that moral freedom itself relies upon morality, but just that our knowledge of it (i.e., the concept of it) does. So, for Kant, the fact of morality does not introduce freedom into the world. If Kant believed that it did, then the search for a concept of nonmoral freedom in Kant's system would obviously be futile. Now, it follows from the epistemological priority of morality that our concept of ourselves as separate from nature is given to us through morality. But notice, this separation, or independence, from pathological (i.e., natural) necessitation is at the heart of our concept of practical freedom. Thus, our concept of practical freedom is also given to us through morality as a part of the larger concept of moral freedom. In other words, the concept of practical freedom is a *part* of the concept of moral freedom—it is a *dimension* of the concept of the capacity to act morally. It follows, of course, that the freedom of indifference implied by practical freedom is also grounded in morality.[18] Let me explain more precisely how these concepts relate.

Kant juxtaposes practical freedom and moral freedom in the *Metaphysics* and presents the former as the negative concept of the latter. This passage was quoted and briefly discussed above, but it is time now to give it more detailed consideration. Kant writes, "Human choice . . . is a choice that can indeed be affected but not determined by impulses, and is therefore of itself . . . not pure but can still be determined to actions by pure will. Freedom of choice is this independence from being determined by sensible impulses; this is the negative concept of freedom. The positive concept of freedom is that of the ability of pure reason to be of itself practical" (MM 6:213). The relation between negative and positive concepts of freedom described here can be seen as a part-to-whole relation in which the whole is the ground of the part. When Kant defines something negatively he says what it is not—he draws the limits of a concept and excludes what is outside of these limits. Negatively conceived, freedom is a kind of independence from sensible necessitation (though not sensible affection)—it is *not* being dependent on sensibility for determination. For Kant, the positive concept of freedom adds to, but also *includes,* the account given through this negative concept. It adds an account of what there is a freedom to do (i.e., there is a freedom to act morally). But it also *includes* the account presented in the negative concept in the sense that a part of the positive account of being able to act on the moral law is the capacity to act independently of our pathological determination. Thus, for Kant, being able to act morally— the "ability of pure reason to be of itself practical"—includes within itself an independence from pathological necessitation. The concept of moral freedom includes the essence of the concept of practical freedom.

Now, this relation between part and whole is also evident in the positive and negative formulations of freedom that Kant presents in the *Groundwork.* "As will is a kind of causality of living beings so far as they are rational, freedom would be that property of this causality by which it can be effective independent of foreign causes determining it. . . . The preceding definition of freedom is negative and therefore affords no insight into its essence. But a positive concept of freedom flows [*fließt*] from it which is so *much the richer and more fruitful.* . . . What else, then, can the freedom of the will be but autonomy (i.e., the property of the will to be law to itself)?" (G 4:446–47). In this passage, oddly enough, the "richer and more fruitful" positive concept of being a law to oneself "flows from" the concept of independence from foreign causes. Thus, the positive concept is derived from the negative in the *Groundwork,* and vice versa in the *Metaphysics.* The direction of derivation in the earlier text is a result of the fact that Kant was deducing morality from freedom at this stage. On this argument, the capacity to reason points to our membership in a merely intelligible world, which gives us independence from natural causality, which, in turn, points to our autonomy (i.e., our capacity to act morally). Kant famously rejects this argument starting in the second *Critique* when he contends that the fact of morality grounds our conception of moral freedom (i.e., autonomy). The result is that in the *Metaphysics* he can argue (with more intuitive plausibility) that the "richer and more fruitful" positive concept of freedom (i.e., autonomy) precedes and includes within itself the notion of independence from pathological determination. The implication of this latter position is that if a will (i.e., practical reason) is capable of determining itself, then it is by definition capable of determining itself independently of foreign (i.e., nonrational) causes.

It is important to note that the *Groundwork* distinction between positive and negative concepts of freedom is different from the aforementioned distinction made in the *Metaphysics* in another respect. Leaving aside the issue of derivational direction, these distinctions still do not map precisely onto each other. The negative concept of freedom in the *Groundwork* passage is just independence from nature—it is not exactly the same as *practical* freedom because it says nothing about being pathologically *affected*. As we saw above, Kant conceives of transcendental freedom in the first *Critique* as a complete causal independence from nature that grounds our notion of an ability to act spontaneously. In the *Groundwork* passage just quoted, this transcendental freedom shows up as the negative concept of freedom, and is coupled with the positive concept of autonomy (i.e., moral freedom). So, in the *Metaphysics,* practical freedom is the negative concept of freedom, while in the *Groundwork,* transcendental freedom is the negative concept of freedom. It seems to follow, then, that the concepts of transcendental freedom and practical freedom are closely linked. In fact, for Kant the concept of practical freedom is derived from the concept of transcendental freedom. Kant says just this in the first *Critique* when he writes that the "practical concept of freedom is based on [the] transcendental idea" such that the "denial of transcendental freedom must, therefore, involve the elimination of all practical freedom" (A 534/B 562). Kant's point is that the denial of the concept of transcendental freedom cuts the ground from under the concept of practical freedom.[19]

The concept of transcendental freedom grounds the notion of practical freedom in the sense that the former is identical to the independence from pathological necessity that is at the heart of this latter notion. It is in this sense that the concept of practical freedom is that "mainly

empirical" (A 448/B 476) concept that is made up of both the concept
of transcendental freedom (i.e., the intelligible part) and the concept of
sensibility (i.e., the empirical part). In the second *Critique,* Kant has the
same mixed concept in mind when he says that practical freedom involves
"a transcendental predicate of the causality of a being that belongs to
the sensible world" (Pr. R 5:94). The notion of practical freedom occu-
pies, as Bernard Carnois puts it, an "intermediate position . . . between
nature, into which it is in some manner inserted, and transcendental freedom, on which it is grounded" (Carnois 1987, 29). In the first *Critique,*
Kant understands the notion of being sensuously affected that characterizes practical freedom in terms of a kind of partial causality, when he
explains that our sensibility is not "so determining that it excludes a
causality of our will" (A 534/B 562). Along the same lines, he tells us
elsewhere that actions are "instigated [*veranlasst*] but not entirely determined by sensibility; for reason must provide a complement of sufficiency"
(R 5611 18:252). So, practical freedom is a hybrid concept representing
a hybrid kind of causality. This practical concept allows us to conceive
of our independence from being necessitated, though not affected, by
sensibility—and this essentially implies a freedom of indifference. The
fact of morality gives us the concept of moral freedom, and from this
concept we can derive the notion of transcendental freedom. From this
latter notion we get practical freedom, which in turn grounds the concept of a freedom of indifference.

    I do not mean to suggest here that when we act morally we exercise
moral freedom, but that when we act nonmorally we exercise practical
freedom as a distinct kind of freedom. Again, moral freedom is *prior* to,
and thus (in a sense) distinct from, practical freedom just in the conceptual order. In the order of reality, *all* human choices are practically free.
That is to say, for Kant all of our actions—moral and nonmoral—are
sensuously affected though not sensuously necessitated. Moral actions
are those practically free actions that *also* express moral freedom; they
are sensuously affected choices that express our essentially rational self
(and our causal freedom from nature).[20] But, at the same time, if it were
not for morality there would be no *concept* of practical freedom—that
is to say, there would be no understanding that we have a capacity to
choose independently of sensuous determinism. It is with this in mind
that Kant, in discussing freedom and the moral law, says that "the two

concepts are so inseparably connected that one could even define practical freedom through independence of the will from anything other than the moral law alone" (Pr. R 5:94). What does Kant mean in this rarely discussed passage? On the face of it, our practical freedom *does* seem to demonstrate an "independence" from the moral law insofar as we often act immorally through (practically) free choices. Kant's point must be (just as he, in fact, says) that our *concept* of practical freedom is inseparable from, or dependent upon, the moral law. It is inseparable from, or dependent upon, the moral law insofar as the latter is its *ground*. Morality allows us to conceive of practical freedom as independence from everything except itself, since it is morality itself that permits us to conceive of practical freedom through the concept of moral freedom.

Of course, the fact that morality grounds our concept of freedom does not mean that we can only know that *moral* choices are free choices, since the concept of moral freedom brings with it a *distinguishable* concept of the capacity to act independently of sensible necessitation. The distinction of this capacity within the larger concept of the capacity to act morally means that we can understand that, even though we often choose ends in a way that does not involve any separation from nature (i.e., in a way that nature determines), we could always do otherwise. An immoral choice should be considered a failure to exercise that dimension of the capacity to act morally that allows us to separate from our sensibility. It follows that an immoral action is only understood to be free in the sense that it could have been otherwise.[21]

Now, when it comes to choices between nonmoral options, we can employ the same conceptual dimension of the larger capacity to act morally (i.e., the concept of the capacity to act contrary to sensible necessitation) in order to understand the possibility of acting in a way that is other than what nature—in the guise of happiness—determines. Clearly, on this account, it is true that we *still* act on a sensible motive when we choose between nonmoral ends, and thus that we do not *fully* exercise the capacity to separate from our sensibility.[22] However, we do exercise this capacity insofar as we can choose independently of the sensible *determination* of happiness. This account helps us make better sense of the aforementioned incorporation passage in the *Religion*, where Kant says that the act of incorporation reconciles incentives of *all* kinds with "absolute spontaneity." Thus, the act of incorporating any incentive somehow relates to our absolute spontaneity, the capacity to act without any preceding causes in nature. Obviously, it is not fully possible to reconcile absolute spontaneity with incentives in the nonmoral context, since our motives for acting in this context are drawn from nature. Yet, whenever we incorporate a nonmoral incentive, we can understand this as a demonstration of our independence from nature (and thus of our absolute spontaneity) insofar as we might not incorporate in accordance with pathological necessity (i.e., happiness). The concept of this degree of independence is only possible in view of morality. Thus, incorporation reconciles incentives with absolute spontaneity in the sense that the act of incorporation can be understood as availing of absolute spontaneity in allowing us an independence from the necessitation of incentives. In other words, the concept of moral freedom (and absolute spontaneity) permits us to conceive of the possibility of choosing other than what our sensibility demands, even when we are sensibly motivated.

Kant directly connects the concept of moral freedom and the concept of a *general* capacity to do otherwise (or a freedom of indifference) in an important footnote in the *Religion*. This footnote provides good evidence for my argument, so I will quote it at length.

> The concept of the freedom of the will does not precede the consciousness of the moral law in us but is deduced from the determinability of our will by this law as an unconditional command. Of this we can soon be convinced by asking ourselves whether we are certainly and immediately conscious of power to *overcome*, by a firm resolve, every incentive, however great, to transgression. . . . Everyone will have to admit that he does not know whether, were such a situation to arise, he would not be shaken in his resolution. Still, duty commands him unconditionally: he ought to remain true to his resolve; and thence he rightly concludes that he must be able to do so, and that his will is therefore free. Those who fallaciously represent this inscrutable property as quite comprehensible create an illusion by means of the word determinism (the thesis that the will is determined by inner self-sufficient grounds) as though the difficulty consisted in reconciling this with freedom—which after all never occurs to one; whereas what we wish to understand, and never shall un-

derstand, is how predeterminism, according to which voluntary actions, as events, have their determining grounds in antecedent time (which, with what happened in it, is no longer within our power), *can be consistent with freedom, according to which that act as well as its opposite must be within the power of the subject at the moment of its taking place.* (Rel 6:49n; emphases added)

Kant starts here with the familiar post-second-*Critique* claim that the basis for positing a concept of freedom is our capacity to act morally. This capacity affords us the awareness that we can do something that goes against all of our natural desires$_1$. On this concept of freedom, to be free means to be able to act independently of all sensuous determination by acting morally. Kant further articulates this concept of freedom by suggesting that morality grants us a *capacity to do other than* (or "overcome") that which sensibility dictates. He then says that reconciling this freedom with predeterminism is an inscrutable problem. But, in claiming this, Kant makes an unannounced move and identifies freedom with a general (i.e., moral and nonmoral) ability to do otherwise. He explains this notion of freedom as the ability to do x or the opposite of x. Now, the shift from the specifically moral capacity to do other than that which our sensibility dictates to the general capacity to do otherwise only makes sense if Kant thinks that the concept of freedom, granted us by the moral law, includes a nonmoral ability to do otherwise. If this is not the case, then Kant simply makes a careless and confusing mistake in moving from a moral capacity to do otherwise to a general capacity.

It might be objected, in response to my argument, that Kant explicitly undermines the notion of a freedom of indifference in the *Metaphysics*, and, consequently, that all talk of this notion in his system is misguided. The relevant passage from the *Metaphysics* is worth taking a look at in some detail. Kant writes, "But freedom of choice cannot be defined—as some have tried to define it—as the ability to make a choice for or against the law (*libertas indifferentiae*), even though choice as a phenomenon provides frequent examples of this in experience. . . . We can also see that freedom can never be located in a rational subject's being able to choose in opposition to his (lawgiving) reason, even though experience proves often enough that this happens" (MM 6:226–27).

Kant's point here is that freedom is not *defined* by the ability to choose between the moral and immoral, nor is it *defined* by the ability to defy morality and act immorally. In making these assertions, Kant never denies that there is, in our experience, a freedom of indifference or a freedom to be immoral—he just denies that these kinds of freedom are definitive. Indeed, Kant states clearly a little earlier in the same book that *Willkür* is the "faculty to do or not do what pleases . . . joined with one's consciousness of the ability to bring about its object by one's action" (MM 6:213). Kant thinks that *Willkür does* have this power to act otherwise, but ultimately he does not think that this power is definitive of the freedom of *Willkür.*

Kant explains in more detail what he means, in saying that the freedom of indifference and the freedom to defy morality are not definitive, when he tells us that "it is one thing to accept a proposition (on the basis of experience) and another thing to make it the expository principle (of the concept of free choice) and the universal feature for distinguishing it (from *arbitrio bruto s. servo*); for the first does not maintain that the feature belongs necessarily to the concept, but the second requires this" (MM 6:226). So, neither kind of freedom mentioned above (i.e., the freedom of indifference or the freedom to defy morality) belongs to the concept of freedom necessarily. This is what it means to say that these notions do not *define* our concept of freedom. Acting on the moral law is, however, *definitive* of the concept of free choice. In other words, acting on the moral law does belong to the concept of freedom *necessarily.* For Kant, it is a *contingent* fact of human nature that our concept of freedom (or absolute self-determination) includes within it the notion of separating from nature. It is just in view of the fact of our partly sensible natures that this is so. As a result, the concept of the freedom of indifference (which relies upon the notion of separating from our pathological natures) is only *contingently* contained in the notion of freedom. In purely rational creatures the concept of freedom does not include the freedom of indifference, because for these creatures there is no pathological nature to escape. It is with this in mind that Kant says that the freedom of indifference and the freedom to act immorally are not bases for distinguishing human from animal choice (*"arbitrio bruto s. servo"*). Although animals do not have these freedoms, and thus *are* different from humans in this respect, Kant's point is that this difference is only a *consequence* of the fact that animals do not have the capacity to act morally. It is this latter capacity, then, that is the definitive difference (and thus the basis for distinguishing) between animals and humans. Kant's key thought, again, is that the freedom of indifference (i.e., nonmoral freedom) and the ability to act immorally *follow* from the moral notion of freedom.

Thus we see that both moral and nonmoral choices are free in the minimal sense that in both cases we could have done otherwise. They differ, however, in that the former *also* express our most essentially rational nature. But this should not be taken to mean that the concept of moral freedom is somehow an addition, or supplement, to a morally neutral idea of freedom. In fact, for Kant, it is only in view of moral freedom that we have the derivative concept of a freedom to act otherwise. This is the sense in which moral choice is definitive of human freedom.

In the end, it will turn out that for Kant moral choices differ from their nonmoral counterparts in view of a distinction between the origins and natures of the incentives that move the sensuously affected agent, and the ends toward which this agent acts. Before we turn to examine these differences in greater depth (in chapter 5), let us first continue our inquiry by looking more closely at exactly how Kant thinks rational yet sensuously affected agents choose nonmoral maxims.

· ·

CHAPTER FOUR

RATIONAL ACTION

Interests and Maxims

Having addressed the issue of whether Kant does in fact have a concept of nonmoral freedom, let me turn now more directly to his understanding of the structure of nonmoral choices. Generally speaking, Kant thinks that desires$_1$ provide incentives, or driving springs (*Triebfedern*), to action, and that these incentives only determine action if we let them. We let them when we incorporate them into maxims. As Kant writes in the *Religion*, "An incentive can determine the will to an action *only insofar as the person has incorporated* [*aufgenommen*] *it into his maxim* (has made it a general rule according to which he intends to act)" (Rel 6:24). For Kant, then, we act directly on the basis of maxims and not desires$_1$. A maxim is a chosen principle that provides the immediate basis for the actions of a rational agent, and as such it is the central concept in Kant's theory of rational action. We might think of maxims as guiding principles to which we are committed in some way. Here are some examples drawn from everyday life: "Clean the house once a week"; "Go grocery shopping every Wednesday and Friday"; "Eat three times a day."[1] The main question that I want to ask in this chapter is how Kant thinks nonmoral maxims are formed. What, on the Kantian model, does choosing a nonmoral maxim involve?

Kant's understanding of practical freedom suggests that incorporated incentives still "partially cause," by pathologically affecting, maxim-governed action. But if maxim-based actions are pathologically affected, it follows that our maxims must somehow still be connected to our pathology—they must carry some pathological weight. This suggests that the act of incorporation cannot simply be a cognitive matter of abstracting a purpose or end from a desire$_1$ and devising a principle of action around it. Instead, it seems that both the choice of a maxim and the subsequent choice of an action based on this maxim are affected by our pathological natures. The main focus of my investigation in this chapter will be on proposing an account of how it is that Kantian maxims are formed such that they govern *pathologically affected* actions. In other words, I will be looking at how maxims are chosen such that they carry some pathological weight.

I will, however, postpone focusing exclusively on the formation of nonmoral maxims until section II of this chapter. I begin in section I by skipping ahead and presenting an account of how these maxims actually function to justify action in Kant's system. This account will allow us to see the different kinds of nonmoral maxims possible within this system, and will thereby prepare the ground for an analysis of how these maxims are formed. This might seem like an unusual methodological approach, so let me take a moment here to say more about it. In view of my discussions of Kant's psychology in chapter 1 and theory of desire formation in chapter 2, it might be reasonable to expect that the next step in my account would be to look at how maxims are formed out of desires$_1$ and feelings. This approach would lead us naturally to Kant's treatment of rational action out of these maxims. In this way, I would address (perhaps construct) the bridge from Kant's psychology to his theory of rational action before discussing this theory itself. However, I am to a large extent going to leave the bridging question of how incentives are incorporated (and maxims formed) until section II, and in section I go straight to Kant's understanding of the nature of rational, maxim-based action. The virtue of this method is that it allows for a detailed introduction to the concepts central to Kant's theory of rational action: incentives, interests, and maxims. This usefully prepares the ground for a closer look into how the various nonmoral interests and maxims possible in Kant's system are grounded.

I. THE INCORPORATION THESIS AND WEAKNESS OF THE WILL

In order to present an interpretation of Kant's theory of maxim-governed rational action in a way that is more than merely expositional, I am going to build my account around a specific problem mentioned, but not dwelled upon, in the previous chapter. While investigating the freedom of nonmoral action, I argued that Kant seems to allow for the possibility of nonmoral choices that are contrary to our happiness. Both Kant's treatment of the gout-sufferer's inclinations and his account of the passions indicate that he believes in the possibility of such choices, and thus in a nonmoral freedom to do other than that which our happiness demands. But still, we might question whether Kant is *consistent* in allowing for the possibility of this nonmoral weakness of the will.

Terms of the Debate: Weakness of the Will and Maxims

After the publication of Allison's *Kant's Theory of Freedom,* questions were raised about the compatibility of the Incorporation Thesis and weakness of the will in Kant's theory of rational agency.[2] If all actions are based on maxims, and maxims involve the incorporation of an incentive into a subjective principle of action, then it seems that a weak action must also involve the incorporation of an incentive into such a principle. But can a weak action be a principled action? Typically, weakness of the will is understood as the phenomenon whereby an agent is somehow overcome by a desire$_1$ upon which she knows she should not act. But such an occurrence does not seem possible when all desires$_1$ must be incorporated into maxims before they can be acted upon. In short, Kant's insistence on maxim-governed action seems to undermine the existence of weak actions. Kant must somehow claim that an agent chooses against happiness (i.e., in a weak fashion) and yet in a principled way. Now, it should be noted that Kant himself never even raises the issue of the compatibility of weakness of the will and the ubiquity of principled action.[3] In this section, I will argue that, given Kant's understanding of rational agency and the nature of maxims, his lack of concern over the "problem" of reconciling the ubiquity of principled action and the existence of nonmoral weakness of the will is, in fact, well founded.

The phenomenon of weakness of the will seems to point to the presence of unmaximed or unprincipled action. But is this really so? If an agent always acts on a maxim, then she has somehow committed to all of her actions. Now, on one account, to be committed to an action is to regard that action as justified or good (in some sense). So, the problem for Kant, on this account, is that maxims seem to make actions good (in some sense), and, since we always act out of maxims, it follows that we always act with the belief that what we are doing is good (in some sense).

But this seems to rule out the possibility of weakness of the will. Kant can solve this problem by claiming that having a maxim (i.e., committing to a course of action) is not exactly identical to regarding an action as justified or good (in some sense). That is to say, he can reconcile the ubiquity of principled action and the existence of weakness of the will by modifying the notion of principled action, such that there is principled (i.e., maximed), and yet weak, action. In what follows, I will argue that Kant's treatment of rational agency actually allows for just such a concept of principled action. In other words, I will show that there is a sense in which Kant thinks that some acts are not justified by their maxims.

Before turning to this we must first settle on a working (and, of course, Kantian) conception of maxims. What are the elements common to each and every maxim? In the *Groundwork*, Kant gives the following example of a maxim: "When I believe myself to be in need of money I will borrow money and promise to repay it, although I know I shall never be able to do so" (G 4:422). This example allows us to articulate all of the elements of a Kantian maxim. Such a maxim includes an action (i.e., borrowing money and falsely promising to repay it), a situation in which this action is called for (i.e., being in need of money), and—as Kant indicates earlier in the same passage—the end, or object, of the action (i.e., relieving distress or need [*Not*]). (Notice, an end is the object or aim of a $desire_1$ insofar as the agent chooses this object for pursuit; we will return to this below when we look at the notion of an interest.[4]) It is relatively uncontroversial, then, to say that a Kantian maxim consists of a statement about performing a type of action, in a certain situation, and for a particular end.[5]

What is required to reconcile Kant's account of rational action with the existence of nonmoral weakness of the will is an account of maxims that prompt weak actions. These maxims are going to have to call for actions that the agent thinks are not good (in some sense). Now, on Kant's understanding of rational action, there are such nonjustifying maxims. Indeed, Kant makes just this point in the *Groundwork* when he comments on our failure to abide by imperatives:

All imperatives command either *hypothetically* or *categorically*. . . . Since every practical law presents a possible action as good and thus as necessary for a subject practically determinable by

reason, all imperatives are formulas of the determination of action which is necessary by the principle of a will which is in any
way good. If the action is good only as a means to something
else, the imperative is hypothetical; but if it is thought of as good
in itself . . . the imperative is categorical. The imperative thus
says what action possible for me would be good, and it presents
the practical rule in relation to a will which does not forthwith
perform an action simply because it is good, in part because the
subject does not always know that the action is good, and in
part (when he does know it) because his maxims can still be
opposed to the objective principles of a practical reason. The
hypothetical imperative, therefore, says only that the action is
good to some purpose, possible or actual. (G 4:414)

The hypothetical imperative, then, is one of Kant's "objective principles
of a practical reason." It is the general rational principle of choosing the
means if one chooses the end. The categorical imperative is the other objective principle, and in one version states that we must act in such a way
that the maxim of our action can be a universal law. For Kant, maxims
can be posited in accordance with the hypothetical imperative or the
categorical imperative. So, maxims *can* be devised with the end of some
desire$_1$, or with morality, in mind.[6] In the former case, the maxim makes
any action falling under it "good for" reaching the end of the desire$_1$—
it has a hypothetical imperative built into it. This, then, is one sense in
which maxims make actions good or justify them. In the latter case, the
maxim makes the action morally "good." This is the other sense in which
maxims justify actions or make them good. Kant's point in this passage
is that even when we know what course of action is good (in either sense),
our maxims can still suggest that we act along different lines. In other
words, maxim-governed actions can be both *not* "good for" something
and *not* morally "good." Now, what is the nature of these unjustified actions to which Kant refers?

Outline of the Argument

I will argue that we can understand the nature and possibility of these unjustified yet maxim-governed actions as follows. For the agent, all nonmoral maxims minimally justify their actions as good for the immediate

end contained in the maxim (e.g., relieving distress). But, at the same time, Kant thinks that there are two basic kinds of nonmoral maxims, and so two ways that nonmoral maxims justify.[7] Some maxims provide a double justification for actions falling under them—they justify actions in terms of both the immediate end contained in the maxim and happiness (as a more removed end). Other maxims *only* justify actions in terms of the immediate end contained in the maxim (i.e., minimal justification). It follows, then, that these latter maxims might be nonjustifying for the agent in the sense that they might *not* be "good for" happiness. On this Kantian account, a weak action in the nonmoral sphere is an action that does not aim at happiness. The agent knows that she should not do the action because it is not good for happiness, but, at the same time, the action is justified by the maxim that it falls under because she thinks that it is good for reaching the immediate end contained in this maxim. Let me take a look at each of the main premises of this argument in turn.

Minimal Justification

The first thing to establish, then, is the claim that for the agent all maxims minimally justify her actions. In one of his clearest accounts of maxims, Kant writes, "A maxim is the subjective principle of acting and must be distinguished from the objective principle (i.e., the practical law). The former contains the practical rule which reason determines according to the conditions of the subject (often his ignorance or inclinations) and is thus the principle according to which the subject acts [*nach welchem das Subjekt handelt*]. The law, on the other hand, is the objective principle valid for every rational being, and the principle by which it ought to act, i.e., an imperative" (G 4:420n). On this account, maxims are those principles upon which we actually act and are distinct from objective principles of reason, which are those principles upon which we ought to act.[8] For Kant, the hypothetical imperative (one of his "objective principles of a practical reason" [G 4:414]) can provide the basis for *objectively valid* subjective principles or maxims.[9] Thus, nonmoral maxims are (objectively) justifying standards of action if they abide by the hypothetical imperative, and they are not if they do not so abide. All maxims have hypothetical imperatives built into them in the sense that all maxims contain an immediate end to which the action recommended by the maxim is supposed to be a means. For example, borrowing money is supposed to be a means to relieving distress. But, for Kant, only some maxims actually abide by the hypothetical imperative. As we saw in the *Groundwork* 4:414 passage above, Kant thinks that we can make mistakes about how to achieve our ends and posit maxims that are not rational and do not, in fact, justify our actions. Thus, borrowing money that you have no intention of paying back from the Mafia is *not* a good means to the immediate end of relieving distress. A maxim recommending this action as a means to the end of relieving distress is not a rational maxim. It appears, then, that such a maxim does not (objectively) justify the action that falls under it at all.

Yet, in spite of this, it is true that every agent, insofar as she posits her maxim with an end in mind, *thinks* that she is positing a means to this end. Thus, every agent *regards* her actions as justified by the immediate ends contained in her maxims. We can conclude from this that there is a sense in which she thinks of every maxim-based action as justified or good as a means to the immediate end contained in the maxim. This is the sense in which all maxims minimally (or, we might say, subjectively) justify actions.[10] Now, since the question of weakness of the will concerns how an agent acts given that she has certain beliefs about the relative value of her choices, it is only this apparent justification that is relevant to the issue at hand. That is to say, in discussing cases of weakness of the will we are only interested in actions that the agent considers, or perceives as, justified. What is relevant for the issue of weakness is that there is a sense in which an agent regards every maxim-governed action as good or justified.

Introduction to Maxim Formation: Two Kinds of Interests/Maxims

Now, if Kant has two conceptions of nonmoral maxims—double justifying in terms of the immediate end contained in the maxim and the end of happiness, and single (or minimally) justifying in terms of the immediate end alone—then it should follow that he has two distinct accounts of how these maxims are formed.[11] And, indeed, there is evidence for two such accounts of maxim formation in Kant's works. The two models are, broadly speaking, as follows: maxims that provide double justification are formed on the basis of incentives, interests, and happiness; single justifying maxims are formed simply on the basis of incentives and interests (i.e., without any consideration of happiness). Before I sketch out

these two distinct accounts, let me first take a brief detour in order to introduce the issue of maxim formation more generally. This detour will
bring the crucial ideas of incentives (*Triebfedern*) and interests (*Interessen*)
into the discussion.

Kant writes of maxim formation in two key places in his published
works. In the now familiar incorporation passage from the *Religion,* he
says, "An incentive can determine the will to an action *only insofar as
the person has incorporated [aufgenommen] it into his maxim* (has made
it a general rule according to which he intends to act); only thus can
an incentive, whatever it may be, co-exist with the absolute spontaneity
of the will (i.e., freedom)" (Rel 6:24). This passage does not commit
Kant to either account of maxims mentioned above (double or single
justifying), but it does indicate that if anything is going to be a maxim it
must involve the incorporation of an incentive into a general rule governing action.

For Kant, an incentive is the driving spring of action; it is that dimension of a desire$_1$ that moves us. "The subjective ground of desire is the
incentive [*Triebfeder*] while the objective ground of volition is the motive [*Bewegungsgrund*]. Thus arises the distinction between subjective
purposes, which rest on incentives, and objective purposes, which depend on motives valid for every rational being" (G 4:427). The common
distinction to which Kant refers here is between what we want to do (i.e.,
subjective purposes) and what we ought to do (i.e., objective purposes).
What we want to do is given us by incentives and what we ought to do
is given us by motives. The subjective ground of desire$_1$ is the executive
determination of the faculty of desire and the objective ground of volition is the legislative determination of this faculty. The subjective ground
of our desires$_1$ (i.e., incentives) creates these desires$_1$, and, at the same
time, provides them with the force that moves us to some object, while
the objective ground tells us what we ought to do in response to these
desires$_1$. And so, again, an incentive is that dimension of a desire$_1$ that
moves or drives us. For example, in the desire$_1$ (or, in this case, passion)
to acquire great amounts of wealth, greed might be the incentive. Now,
it is in virtue of something like greed that we get pleasure in pursuing
wealth as an object. So, an incentive is that dimension of a desire$_1$ that at-
tracts us to the pleasure of the object desired. At the same time, however,
Kant often uses the term "incentive" to refer to the pleasure desired. For

example, in the third *Critique* he writes, "In relation to the feeling of pleasure an object is to be counted either among the agreeable or the beautiful. . . . The agreeable, as an incentive for the desires, is of the same kind throughout, no matter where it comes from and how specifically different the representation may be. Hence in judging of its influence on the mind it is only a matter of the number of the charms (simultaneous and successive), and as it were only of the mass of the agreeable sensation" (CJ 5:266). Incentives are directly linked here to agreeable sensations. Kant, then, seems to use the notion of an incentive such that it has these two dimensions: a subjective dimension (e.g., greed) and an objective dimension (e.g., pleasure in the object of greed).[12] In other words, Kant's concept of an incentive can refer to a subjective feature of $desire_1$ (i.e., its moving force) or an objective feature (i.e., the pleasure we are moved toward)—these are two poles of a $desire_1$. Now, $desires_1$ are the concrete psychological bases of maxims. $Desires_1$ are converted into maxims when the incentives associated with these $desires_1$ are somehow taken up into principles of action.

In the second *Critique,* while focusing on the feeling of respect as the moral incentive, Kant says the following general things about maxim formation: "From the concept of an incentive there comes that of an interest which can never be attributed to a being which does not have reason; it indicates an incentive of the will so far as it is presented by reason. . . . Now on the concept of an interest [*Interesse*] rests that of a maxim" (Pr. R 5:79–80). Kant indicates here that interests provide a bridge between incentives/$desires_1$ and maxims. Thus, the incorporation of an incentive into a maxim involves at least two dimensions: the transformation of an incentive/$desire_1$ into an interest, and the positing of a maxim based on this interest. We will see now that, broadly speaking, interests come about in two ways and that this is the source of the two kinds of maxims (single and double justifying) referred to above.

Kant gives us a clue as to the nature of this first dimension of maxim formation (forming an interest out of an incentive/$desire_1$) when he says in this passage from the second *Critique* that an interest is an incentive so far as this incentive is "presented by reason." Thus, interests are rational incentives—they are incentives that have somehow been subjected to our rationality. How might we understand this? Kant defines an interest in the *Groundwork* as the "dependence of a contingently determinable will on principles of reason" (G 4:413n). In this same footnote he contrasts interests and desires$_1$, characterizing desires$_1$ (or, more specifically, inclinations) as the "dependence of the faculty of desire on sensations." According to this account, sensations are to desires$_1$ (or inclinations) as principles of reason are to interests. Now, in chapter 2, we saw that for Kant sensations of pleasure or displeasure determine the faculty of desire and cause desires$_1$. Is Kant saying, then, that interests are produced, or caused, when "principles of reason" determine the will? The principles of reason to which Kant refers in this and the surrounding sections of the *Groundwork* are the categorical imperative and the hypothetical imperative. It would follow, then, that for Kant nonmoral interests are produced when the hypothetical imperative determines the will.[13]

But why would Kant say this? How does the principle of choosing the means if one chooses the end produce an interest? It is not immediately obvious that having an interest in some end entails figuring out the means to this end. I might be interested in going to Japan without having even tried to figure out how I will be able to afford to get there. Of course, it is true that positing a *maxim based on this interest* involves the hypothetical imperative. For example, I might say to myself, "Save as much money as possible for the next four months in order to take a trip to Japan." Clearly, saving money is a good means to the end of affording a trip to Japan. The question that concerns me here, however, is how the hypothetical imperative might be involved in *producing the interest* upon which such a maxim is based.

Kant seems to present a slightly different account of the ground of interest in the *Metaphysics* 6:212. In this passage, Kant revisits the desire$_1$/interest dichotomy, this time focusing on the closeness of their relation. He writes that an interest is "a connection of pleasure with the faculty of desire that the understanding judges to hold as a general rule [*allgemeinen Regel*]" (MM 6:212). As we saw in chapter 2, Kant's focus in this section of the *Metaphysics* is on the causal relation between pleasure and the faculty of desire. Thus, the "connection of pleasure with the faculty of desire" determines this faculty causing a desire$_1$. Kant is noting, then, that this determining connection between pleasure and the faculty of desire is called an interest under certain circumstances. It seems to follow from this that an interest is a kind of desire$_1$ (which connects with Kant's claim that interests are incentives "presented by reason").

More precisely, it is a desire$_1$ that the understanding brings to the level of my rational, deliberative life by judging it to "hold as a general rule." Kant's point seems to be that my understanding, in judging that "x is (as a general rule) pleasurable for me," affirms my desire$_1$ for x in such a way that I may be said to have an interest in x, instead of a mere pathological desire$_1$ for it. If my understanding does not make this judgment, then my desire$_1$ for x might be something that I never act upon again, or something that I regard as a product of a unique set of circumstances such that it does not hold as a rule. So, there is clearly a difference between randomly taking pleasure in, for example, driving fast, and forming a desire$_1$ to do this again (along the lines of what I discussed in chapter 2), and experiencing pleasure in taking a long drive in the country, judging that this is something I typically (or as a general rule) enjoy and taking this pleasure (and the desire$_1$ it grounds) into my life (as an interest). The former is an unreflective pathological desire$_1$ for an object that has never been subjected to a rational judgment, while the latter is an interest in an end that has been formed from such a desire$_1$. Kant refers to such interests as "interests of inclination" (MM 6:213). Thus, to say that an interest is an incentive "presented by reason" is to say that an interest involves presenting the pleasure we associate with an end as a basis, or reason, for action in our lives.

Although Kant seems to be talking about interests in different ways across these two passages—the *Groundwork* 4:413n and the *Metaphysics* 6:212—there is a way of bringing these accounts together. In the *Groundwork* passage, Kant appears to be suggesting that an interest is formed when the hypothetical imperative determines the will. Given that the hypothetical imperative is an objective principle of reason, this clearly gives us one sense in which an interest is rational. The other sense in which an interest is rational is that it involves transforming an unreflective desire$_1$ into a rational desire$_1$ for an end through the judgment that this end is pleasurable as a general rule and is thus the kind of end that we will include in our lives. Now, it seems that this second kind of judgment is a minimal requirement for the transformation of desires$_1$ into interests. In other words, the judgment that we find pleasure in an end as a general rule is required in order to speak of "incentives presented by reason" at all. But if the end in which we are interested is also sought after according to the hypothetical imperative (in a way that I have left a question mark over), then this interest is *more* rational. Thus, on this account, there are (broadly speaking) two ways in which nonmoral interests (and the maxims connected to them) are formed out of incentives. Some interests (and maxims) are formed through the minimally rational judgment that we typically find pleasure in a certain end. Other interests (and maxims) are formed when this judgment is combined with a judgment that is somehow grounded in the hypothetical imperative. We will take a look at the nature of this latter judgment now.

Happiness-Related Interests/Maxims

For Kant, one kind of rational judgment that we can make concerning a desire$_1$ in the nonmoral sphere is a judgment about how (or whether) this desire$_1$ can be reconciled with other desires$_1$. Some interests (and the maxims that they ground) come about through this kind of rational judgment, and it is these interests/maxims that are a product of the implementation of the hypothetical imperative. Suppose an agent desires$_1$ to eat a lot of chocolate, but also desires$_1$ to lose weight. It is unlikely that she can satisfy both of these desires$_1$ at the same time, so the agent may have to select only one end in which to be interested: enjoying chocolate or losing weight. This selection is made by judging one desire$_1$ to be more important than the other (i.e., somehow ranking it higher). Now, Kant thinks that the standard on the basis of which one desire$_1$ is ranked higher than another—such that we form an interest in its end—is happiness. Thus, one basis for the formation of nonmoral interests (and the maxims that are grounded in these interests) is the agent's conception of happiness. The will is determined, then, by the hypothetical imperative in producing interests, in the sense that we form interests in those ends that are a means to the larger end of happiness. Kant writes, "Man is a being of needs, so far as he belongs to the world of sense, and to this extent his reason certainly has an inescapable responsibility from the side of his sensuous nature to attend to its interest and to form practical maxims with a view to the happiness of this and, where possible, of a future life" (Pr. R 5:61). Kant explicitly relates the formation of nonmoral maxims to happiness here. (Notice, the connection between nonmoral interests and happiness is left implicit.)

Kant also tells us that forming maxims with a view to our happiness is not something that we arbitrarily decide to do—it is a part of our very nature. "There is one end, however, which we may presuppose as actual in all rational beings so far as imperatives apply to them, that is, so far as they are dependent beings. There is one purpose which they not only can have but which we can presuppose they all do have by a necessity of nature. This purpose is happiness" (G 4:415). In the *Metaphysics*, Kant puts this same point in the following way: "It is unavoidable for human nature to wish for and seek happiness" (MM 6:388). In the previous chapter I maintained that, in spite of passages such as these, Kant could not mean that we *necessarily* pursue happiness as an end.[14] So, what exactly is necessary about the concept of happiness and how does this necessity impact our nonmoral freedom?

Taking a closer look at Kant's notion of happiness can help us answer this question. Broadly speaking, Kant presents what appear to be three distinct accounts of happiness. In some places, he tells us that happiness is the satisfaction of *all* of our inclinations (e.g., G 4:399). At other times, he says that happiness is the satisfaction of a tolerably coherent subset of our inclinations (e.g., Pr. R 5:73; Rel 6:58). And, finally, he also writes that happiness is the consciousness of an uninterrupted agreeableness accompanying our whole existence (e.g., Pr. R 5:22).[15] It is possible to reconcile these accounts in the following way. When Kant says that happiness is the satisfaction of all inclinations, he may be thinking of happiness as the satisfaction of each and every desire$_1$ as it arises, such that a maximal or (as close as possible to an) uninterrupted pleasure is experienced. Kant seems to modify this view in light of the consideration that, since many of our desires$_1$ conflict with each other, maximal satisfaction can only really come from satisfying *some* of these desires$_1$. Maximal pleasure, then, comes from satisfying a system or ordered set of desires$_1$. Notice, happiness is not the *same* as the system of desires$_1$, but is, rather, the pleasure that arises from the satisfaction of such a system. All things going well, the satisfaction of this system will give us close to an "uninterrupted agreeableness."

Kant thinks that this notion of happiness plays the role of a regulative ideal of sorts. So, in the *Groundwork*, he refers to the "*Idea* of happiness" and tells us that this Idea involves "an absolute whole, a maximum of well-being . . . in my present and in every future condition" (G 4:418).[16] Now, insofar as the desires$_1$ included in our Idea of happiness are only those that can be brought into a tolerably coherent system, it follows that happiness provides us with a kind of second-order desire$_1$ to satisfy a privileged subset of our desires$_1$. The ends in which we are interested are a *means* to the larger end (or Idea) of happiness in the sense that forming these ends into a "fairly tolerable system" (Pr. R 5:73) is a means to fulfilling the second-order desire$_1$ for maximal pleasure (i.e., happiness). Happiness, then, is a necessary end insofar as all agents have, by their nature, a conception (or Idea) of happiness in terms of which they can form their interests and maxims (as means). It is not entailed in this, however, that all interests and maxims are *necessarily* formed in view of this Idea of happiness.

In our example, then, the agent will—with various means-ends possibilities in mind—try to reconcile her conflicting desires$_1$ in terms of an overarching conception of happiness. She may, for example, decide to sacrifice her desire$_1$ for chocolate in order to lose weight. Losing weight would then become an interest of hers upon which she would base maxims directing her behavior toward her Idea of happiness. Or, she might maintain some level of interest in chocolate by modifying her interest in losing weight such that she accepts that she will eat a certain amount of chocolate, and, therefore, take longer to lose weight. In either case, the important point is that desires$_1$ are rationally juxtaposed and compared, in terms of the second-order desire$_1$ for the end of happiness, before interests are formed and ends are incorporated into maxims. Maxims, then, can be formed in view of a conception of happiness, and as such they are justifying. They justify any action that they prompt insofar as this action is "good for" happiness.

Of course, this does not mean that all interests formed in this way are, in actual fact, good for our happiness. Kant is quite clear that when it comes to happiness we can be thoroughly mistaken about what actions are good. He refers to the kinds of hypothetical imperatives that are built into maxims aimed at happiness as assertorical imperatives: "The hypothetical imperative which represents the practical necessity of an action as means to the promotion of happiness is an assertorical imperative" (G 4:415). Now, because every person's conception of happiness is so vague, it is not entirely clear that we are rationally necessitated by assertorical imperatives at all. "If it were only easy to give a definite concept of happiness, the imperatives of prudence would perfectly correspond to those of skill and would likewise be analytical. For it could then be said in this case as well as in the former that whoever wills the end wills also (necessarily according to reason) the only means to it which are in his power" (G 4:417). If the goal were clear, then the means to this goal would be rationally (or objectively) necessitated for all rational beings. But the goal is not clear. Our Idea of happiness as an end is vague, and as a result the means to it are also unclear. This is the first of three closely related problems linked to the notion of happiness as an end. The second difficulty is that our finite natures are such that we might change our conception of happiness over time. In other words, our idea of what a life of maximal pleasure involves may change as we have new experiences. This may, in turn, result in further confusion over the means to happiness as we reshuffle our desires$_1$ to meet our new conception of happiness. And lastly, as Kant puts it, "it is impossible for even a most clear-sighted and most capable but finite being to form here a definite concept of that which he wills. If he wills riches, how much anxiety, envy, and intrigues might he thereby draw upon his shoulders!" (G 4:418). In other words, it is impossible to tell whether acting on a particular maxim will, ultimately, result in something that conflicts with another interest, the end of which we consider a means to our happiness. Even if we have a clear and stable idea of happiness, we cannot be certain that acting on a given maxim will realize this end, because it is impossible to predict how acting on this maxim will affect the ends of other maxims. Our limited natures entail that we rarely know the best means to the end of happiness with any certainty.

And yet, in spite of the fact that happiness might not rationally necessitate maxims in the full sense (i.e., objectively), it does not follow that these maxims do not justify actions. These maxims do still justify actions *for the agent* insofar as she *thinks* that following a maxim will be good (in this case) as a means to happiness. It is in this limited sense that the hypothetical imperative determines the will in the case of happiness-directed interests and maxims.

So, forming an interest in view of our conception of happiness provides the basis for the incorporation of an incentive into a maxim that is ultimately aimed at happiness. But, notice here, these maxims actually justify the actions that fall under them twice over, in terms of the immediate end contained in the maxim, and in terms of the end of happiness. So, in the example considered above, the agent might posit a maxim that contains the end of losing weight. She proposes, "I will go to the gym four times a week." Going to the gym is justified in terms of both the end of losing weight and the end of happiness. It is "good for" two related ends. If she posits a chocolate-eating maxim like "Only eat chocolate twice a week," then the same applies concerning the justifying power of this maxim. That is to say, maintaining this maxim means that eating chocolate twice weekly will be good for her end of enjoying chocolate *and* her happiness.

But, though they may appear to be similar, there is a deep distinction between the two examples of happiness-related maxims just mentioned. Let me explain what I mean by first saying more about the continuing role of pleasure in Kant's account of action. I argued in chapter 2 that, in spite of recent interpretations, Kant does in fact think that every nonmoral desire$_1$ involves the anticipation of a pleasure that is associated with the object of this desire$_1$. It is crucial to note that Kant extends this position to the interests and maxims that are formed out of desires$_1$. In other words, for Kant the connection of a desired end with pleasure is not broken when this desire$_1$ is transformed (through a judgment) into an interest (and, finally, a maxim). Thus, Kant thinks that all nonmoral interests and all nonmoral maxims are aimed at pleasure. In the *Groundwork* 4:413n he writes that the "object of the action (so far [*sofern*] as it is pleasant for me) *interests* me" (emphasis added). In other words, it is only insofar as an object is pleasant that I am interested in it. Very much along the same lines, Kant writes (*after* the development of his thinking on pleasure) in the third *Critique*, "But to will something and to have satisfaction [*Wohlgefallen*] in its existence, i.e., *to take an interest in it, are identical*" (CJ 5:209; emphasis added). Similarly, in a lecture from 1794–95, Kant says, "What gratifies us is also agreeable to us, and we take an interest in that existence each and every time because this [interest] and the gratification with it take place only to the degree that and as long as the existence of the object pleases us" (LM 29:1009). So, when we consider a certain end it provokes an anticipation of either pleasure or displeasure that is equivalent to our taking an interest or a (positive) disinterest in the end in question. It follows, then, that to desire$_1$ something and to have an interest in it (though these are distinct in the ways discussed above) are not really distinct in their respective relations with pleasure.

Now, to incorporate an incentive into a maxim is to take the feeling of pleasure that is associated with some end in which we are interested into a subjective principle that governs the actions that are aimed at this end and its associated pleasure. Thus, Kant characterizes the nature of the relation between a maxim and pleasure by saying, "The material of a practical principle is the object of the will. This object either is the determining ground of the will or it is not. If it is, the rule of the will is subject to an empirical condition (to the relation of the determining notion to feelings of pleasure or displeasure), and therefore it is not a practical law" (Pr. R 5:27). Kant's point here is that if the end, or object, contained in a maxim determines choice, then this determination is contingent upon the empirical fact of whether or not the agent associates pleasure with this end or object. In saying this, Kant implies that it is the anticipation of a pleasure that is associated with an end contained in a maxim that determines choice (according to the maxim). Thus, for Kant, the end in which we are interested is associated with pleasure, and this association is not broken when the end is incorporated into a maxim. Maxims are not merely cognitive principles. Instead, they represent the meeting ground of our rationality and our pathology. I will return to this point at greater length in section II below.

To get back to the main line of the argument, in our examples of a chocolate-eating maxim and a weight-loss maxim, both of these principles contained two separable ends—the immediate end and the end of happiness. But Kant draws a significant distinction between the *ways* in which pleasure is associated with the ends that are contained in our maxims. This distinction accounts for an important difference between the chocolate-eating maxim and the weight-loss maxim. The immediate end of the chocolate-eating maxim is enjoying a certain amount of chocolate, while the immediate end of the weight-loss maxim is losing weight. For Kant, the difference between these two ends is that the former is *pleasant in itself*, while the latter is only *pleasant as a means* to some other end. Kant discusses this distinction in the third *Critique* when he writes, "That is good which pleases by means of reason alone, through the mere concept. We call something good for something (the useful) that pleases only as a means; however, another thing is called good in itself that pleases for itself. Both always involve the concept of an end, hence the relation of reason to (at least possible) willing, and consequently a satisfaction in the existence of an object or of an action, i.e., some sort of interest" (CJ 5:207). That end which is good in itself pleases for itself, while that end which is good as a means is pleasant as a means. We are interested in both sorts of ends. Kant goes on stipulate that the *agreeable* end is pleasant in itself, and the *good* end only pleases insofar as it is a means to something else.[17]

How, then, does this distinction between the ways in which pleasure is associated with particular ends affect the argument concerning the reconciliation of principled action and weakness of the will? In the case of the agent's weight-loss maxim, there is a double justification in terms of the immediate end contained in the maxim and happiness. The weight-loss maxim makes working out *good for* losing weight and *good for* happiness. But this immediate end of losing weight is itself *only* good for happiness. That is to say, it is only pleasant insofar as it is a means to the end of happiness. In the case of the chocolate-eating maxim, there is also double justification in terms of the immediate end contained in the maxim and happiness, but the immediate end (i.e., eating a certain amount of chocolate) is good for happiness *and* good in itself—that is to say, it pleases "as a means" and it "pleases for itself." But, notice, this distinction between the ways in which ends please also opens up the possibility that for Kant an agent might be interested in an immediate end that *just* pleases for itself and does not also please as a means to happiness. Such an interest would not be determined by the hypothetical imperative at all. Yet it would still meet the minimal rational requirement of an interest, as discussed above, in that it would involve the judgment that x is pleasant for me as a general rule.

So, on this account, there are two basic kinds of ends and three types of interests built around these ends: (a) there are interests in ends that please just as a means to happiness; (b) there are interests in ends that please in themselves and as a means to happiness; and (c) there are interests in ends that please for themselves but not as a means to happiness. Interests falling under category (a) only *appear* to justify the actions they prompt in terms of two ends; in fact, the immediate end is only really an end in view of its relation to happiness. Interests falling under category (b) are legitimately double justifying, while those included in category (c) are single justifying. We will see now that the presence of interests in ends that just please for themselves and not also as a means to happiness removes any potential incompatibility between the existence of weakness of the will and the ubiquity of principled action in Kant's account.

Pleasure-Related Interests/Maxims

As we saw in the previous chapter, Kant's famous gout-sufferer knowingly acts in opposition to his conception of happiness. "It is not to be wondered at . . . that a single inclination, definite as to what it promises and as to the time at which it can be satisfied, can outweigh a fluctuating idea and that, for example, a man with the gout can choose to enjoy what he likes and to suffer what he may, because according to his calculations at least on this occasion he has not sacrificed the enjoyment of the present moment to a perhaps groundless expectation of a happiness supposed to lie in health" (G 4:399). The gout-sufferer acts weakly but his action is still governed by a maxim. The more immediate interest in eating that which pleases overcomes the justifying weight of a maxim integral to the gout-sufferer's vague conception of happiness (i.e., a health maxim). The gout-sufferer's maxim-governed action is good for the pleasure associated with the immediate end of eating, but not good for happiness, and therefore not justified in terms of happiness.

Kant makes this same point for passionate action. In chapter 1, we saw Kant present the following example illustrating just how passions can lead us to ignore other inclinations: "The ambition of a person may always be an inclination whose direction is sanctioned by reason; but the ambitious person desires, nevertheless, to be loved by others also; he needs pleasant relations with others, maintenance of his assets, and so forth. But if he is, however, passionately ambitious, then he is blind to those other purposes which his inclinations also offer to him. Consequently he ignores completely that he is hated by others or that he runs the risk of impoverishing himself through his extravagant expenses" (A 7:266). Again, at the heart of the distinction between passions and inclinations is the view that the former do not allow for the consideration of other inclinations. But, of course, it is precisely in view of such consideration that our Idea of happiness is formed. It is with this in mind that Kant writes in the third *Critique* that passions "belong to the faculty of desire, and are inclinations that make all determinability of the faculty of desire by means of principles difficult or impossible" (CJ 5:272n). Leaving morality aside, Kant may be referring here to the hypothetical imperative, or the principle of happiness, or both. Thus, passions make it "difficult or impossible" to form nonmoral interests in view of the Idea of happiness and the hypothetical imperative. The passionately ambitious person—unlike a more normally ambitious person—sacrifices his other inclinations, and consequently his happiness, in the dogged pursuit of this one passion.

It cannot be objected here that Kant does not see passionate action as maxim-governed action, since (as we saw in chapter 1) he draws an explicit link between passions and maxims when he writes, "Passion always presupposes a maxim of the subject, namely, to act according to a purpose prescribed for him by his inclination" (A 7:266). Kant also connects passions and maxims, saying, "A passion is a sensible desire that has become a lasting inclination (e.g., hatred, as opposed to anger). The calm with which one gives oneself up to it permits reflection and allows the mind to form principles upon it" (MM 6:408). So, maxims of a certain kind are formed out of passions. Consequently, we can see that for Kant reason has *some* connection with our passions. This is reflected in Kant's claim that reason "hardly" controls the passions. There must be enough rational control for interests to be formed and maxims posited on the basis of these interests. Passionate interests are minimally rational in the sense discussed above, in that they involve a judgment about the end of the passion being pleasurable for the agent. Thus, the agent forms an interest in the end of the passion, making this end one she is going to pursue. She can then form maxims designed to satisfy her passion based on this interest. Thus, even though reason "hardly" controls the passions, it has enough control to regulate the satisfaction of these passions in some way. Reason does not function to compare desires$_1$ to each other here, but just to establish regularity and stability in the satisfaction of passions through the positing of maxims.

On Kant's account, then, weak action is chosen and *somewhat* rational. It is somewhat rational insofar as weak actions involve a compartmentalization of choice. We act weakly when we focus on the immediate end of our choice and ignore the sense in which this choice is "not good" for happiness. In short, Kant can reconcile principled action with weakness of the will insofar as there can be, on his account, a difference between being motivated by happiness and by pleasure.

II. INCORPORATION OF INCENTIVES: A CLOSER LOOK AT THE FORMATION OF NONMORAL INTERESTS AND MAXIMS

This account of principled nonmoral action has provided us with a substantial background for a more detailed analysis of how incorporation takes place and thus how nonmoral maxims are formed. It must be kept in mind, however, that any reconstruction of Kant's thought on the specifics of interest and maxim formation is hampered by the fact that he says very little on either of these subjects. In what follows, I will to a large extent be relying on and extrapolating from central principles of motivation and choice in Kant's system with which we are already familiar. Kant thinks that the act of incorporating an incentive is necessary before a desire$_1$ can express itself in the actions of a rational agent. The act of incorporation is therefore the point of contact between our psychology and our rationality.[18] But what exactly is involved when a sensuously affected agent incorporates an incentive into a nonmoral maxim? We have seen that this process involves two distinct dimensions: taking an interest in something, and forming a maxim based on this interest.[19] We will see now that for Kant both of these dimensions involve *choices* that could have been otherwise. Furthermore, these choices are always affected by pleasure at the thought of an object of desire$_1$ (i.e., the subjective aspect of a representation of an object of desire$_1$).

For Kant, all interests are formed when an agent brings the pleasure that is associated with a particular object or state of affairs into her deliberative life. What, in more precise terms, does this mean? Recall that Kant tells us in the second *Critique* that an interest is an incentive "presented by reason" (Pr. R 5:79). To present an incentive by reason is to present an *object* associated with this incentive as an *end* that one is going to pursue rationally and deliberately. It follows from this that to take an interest in something is to form an end out of an object of desire$_1$ by presenting or taking this object as a reason or basis for action. We take or present an object as an end by making a judgment about this object, or, more precisely, about the pleasure associated with this object (i.e., the pleasurable dimension of our representation of that object). This transformative judgment involves a choice insofar as we could always do otherwise than present any given object as an end. For Kant, this judgment transforms relatively passive desires$_1$ into bases for activity.

A desire$_1$ is thereby transformed from something that we passively have, and may never act upon, into something that we include in our active and intentional thinking about our lives—that is to say, something we are going to consider a reason for action.[20]

As we saw in section I, Kant's system allows for three possible kinds of nonmoral interests. Let us take a look at these before focusing more closely on the role of pleasure in the choice of interests.

1. There are interests in ends that please just as a means to happiness. Interests of this kind are posited on the basis of the hypothetical imperative. For example, one might take an interest in eating raw vegetables even though one takes no pleasure at all in these vegetables except insofar as one considers them good for one's happiness. One might even find raw vegetables positively unpleasant and yet still form such an interest in them. So, the end of eating raw vegetables is pleasant, and this pleasure is a reason for action, just in view of one's conception of happiness.

2. There are interests in ends that please both in themselves and as a means to happiness.[21] Having an interest in practicing philosophy might be such an interest. So, an agent might derive pleasure from doing philosophy, both for itself and as a means to her happiness. That is to say, she might not only enjoy the actual practice of the subject (i.e., reading, discussing, and writing), but also think of a happy life as a life of understanding, knowledge, and reflection. In this case, she takes the end of doing philosophy as a reason for reading and discussing certain kinds of books, both insofar as she finds these things pleasing for themselves and insofar as they are a means to living what she considers a fully realized life of human happiness.

Notice, here, these kinds of interests are only *typically* grounded in sensible desires$_1$ that we subsequently regard as essential means to happiness. It does not *have* to be the case that interests in ends that are good in themselves and good as a means to happiness are grounded in sensible desires$_1$. In fact, it is also possible for a merely sensible desire$_1$ for (and connected interest in) something to develop out of an interest in something as a means. One might think that doing law is good for one's happiness because of the earning potential associated with corporate law, and then, while practicing this law, develop a sensible desire$_1$ for law-related work based on an enjoyment of depositions, trials, etc.

3. There are interests in ends that just please for themselves and not also as a means to happiness.[22] These interests express themselves in weak actions. For example, an agent might have a self-destructive interest such as in taking harmful drugs. He might be interested in the end of taking these drugs, and at the same time know that they are bad for his happiness.[23] All of the actions that are based on interests that just please for themselves are weak in the sense that the agent knows that they are not good for happiness and yet performs them. But this does not mean that they are unusual kinds of interests. Kant's primary examples of such interests are those based on the passions. As we saw in previous chapters, the passions are rather commonplace desires$_1$, such as sexual desires$_1$ and competitive social desires$_1$.

So, though it may initially appear that the explanatory burden that Kant places on his notion of happiness is enormous, his treatment of the passions lightens this load. The suggestion that Kant thinks that *all* of the nonmoral actions of a rational agent are related to happiness must be balanced against his treatment of the passions. This treatment makes it clear that, for Kant, humans are not always reasonable and prudential calculators of their own happiness. In general (and this is a point upon which I focused in chapter 1), Kant's insistence on maximed action does not necessarily commit him to a naive overestimation of human rationality. Instead, Kant treats nonmoral actions as more or less rational, with the less rational ones being by no means exceptional. They are just actions that are performed without any real regard for the larger picture of someone's life. They are still governed by maxims, and thus chosen, but the horizons of the choice are very limited.

Taking an Interest

Broadly speaking, these are the three basic kinds of nonmoral interests that exist on the Kantian model. At the heart of the formation of an interest is the choice of an end. Again, this choice converts the object of a desire$_1$ into the end of an interest. Each choice of interest involves a judgment in which the pleasure associated with an object—whether it is associated with this object in view of a connection to happiness or simply in itself—is taken as a basis for action. Thus, to form an interest in some end is to take a position regarding the pleasure that is associated with that end. Each judgment is a freely made choice in the sense that we could always do otherwise than judge the associated pleasure in the way that we do. The choice of an interest is a practically free choice.

But to say that a practically free choice is sensibly affected is to say more than that pleasure is associated with the object of this choice (or, indeed, that pleasure plays a role in causing the desire$_1$ that grounds the choice). We saw in chapter 2 that, for Kant, pleasure affects us not merely insofar as it is aimed at, but more importantly through its presence at the *thought* or *idea* of an object. This was the case in the formation of certain desires$_1$ and I think that this is also the case when it comes to the choice of interests.[24] Kant's intentional understanding of pleasure means that pleasure is taken in or at the idea of an object. We saw that this is the same as saying that pleasure is the subjective dimension of a representation. If this pleasure is at the prospect of an object or action in the future then it is an anticipatory pleasure. Now, since Kant thinks that these pleasurable representations are causal, and that choices are affected by our sensibility, he is implicitly committed to the idea that pleasure plays a role in the choice of objects (i.e., ends).

So, again, when Kant speaks of choices being sensibly affected, this does not just mean that we are affected by the pleasure connected to the ends of sensible desires$_1$ that we choose. It also means that the way in which we actively pursue the objects of our desires$_1$ is through having feelings of pleasure at the thought of these objects that affect our choices. The initial association of pleasure with a particular object means that the thought of this object is accompanied by pleasure. Along these lines, Kant tells us in the *Metaphysics* that "In every determination of choice we go *from* the thought of the possible action to the action by way of feeling pleasure or pain and taking an interest in the action or its effect" (MM 6:399).[25] So, some pleasure or pain is present and affecting, or influencing, every choice of an interest that we make. In his lectures, Kant speaks of the existence of something that pleases us and says that "we take an interest in that existence each and every time because this [interest] *and the gratification with it* take place only to the degree that and as long as the existence of the object pleases us" (LM 29:1009; emphasis added). Again, the idea here is that the pleasure that affects a choice is felt as we make the choice. This is the deepest implication of Kant's notion of practical freedom. Of course, this should not be surprising if we reflect on one of Kant's basic claims about our sensibility (looked at in chapter 2). For Kant, we are never in a pleasure-neutral state—we are always feeling some pleasure or pain. It follows from this that every choice that we make is made in the presence of pleasure or pain; every choice is conditioned by this presence.

Let me start, then, with the choice of interests in ends that are pleasant as a means to happiness. How are these interests formed through a sensibly affected choice? In his lectures Kant refers to this first kind of interest as an intellectual desire$_1$ and thinks of these desires$_1$ as determinations of the higher faculty of desire.[26] He explains the origins of these intellectual desires$_1$ by telling us that the recognition of the usefulness of a certain object produces a feeling of pleasure. Intellectual desires$_1$ come from "representations of satisfaction or dissatisfaction which . . . depend on the manner in which we cognize the objects through concepts" (LM 28:254). It is clear from the context that one of the "concepts" to which Kant is referring here is the concept of a means-ends relation (i.e., the hypothetical imperative). A representation that includes a kind of pleasure or pain arises when we conceive of objects as useful for our ends. In the same lectures on empirical psychology, Kant refers to the pleasant feelings that are produced by the thought of rational principles as intellectual pleasures, and the feelings of pleasure produced by our sensible receptivity to objects and the ideas of these objects as sensible pleasures (LM 29:891). This is the basis upon which Kant refers to the desires$_1$ produced by these different feelings of pleasure as intellectual and sensible, respectively (LM 29:894).[27] So, again, Kant holds not just that the objects that are a means to some end are pleasant (as we saw in section I above), but also that the thought of these objects includes a feeling of pleasure as a subjective dimension.

For Kant, then, the hypothetical imperative produces interests in ends that are a means to some greater end. It does this by associating pleasure with this end and thereby producing a feeling of pleasure at the thought of some object—it is this pleasure that affects us in the choice of an interest. The choice of an end that is a means to the greater end of happiness is a choice affected by the feeling of pleasure accompanying the thought of some object. This feeling of pleasure affects such a choice because (as we saw in chapter 2) it is in the nature of pleasurable representations to tend to maintain themselves. The choice of an interest can maintain the pleasurable representation in a couple of ways: through the mere satisfaction that we get upon acting on the interest, or through attaining the pleasure that is associated with the end in which we are interested. Insofar as Kant is a hedonist, he commits to the idea that the latter is always involved in the choice of nonmoral interests. Now, the pleasure at the thought of an object only *affects* the choice of this object as an end because we can always do otherwise than pursue that which is urged by the strongest feeling of pleasure.

Earlier, I said that to choose an interest is to choose an object as an end. I explained that to decide that something is an end is to decide that it is a good reason for action. This recently popular way of talking about the formation of interests in Kant can be reconciled with what I have just argued about the sensible conditions under which a choice is made. In the case at which we have been looking, the basis for the choice of an end is the usefulness of the end for happiness. The end provides a good reason for action because it is a means to happiness. In other words, to choose this interest is to judge that the connection between the end of this interest and happiness is a good reason for action. But, as we saw above, Kant tells us in the third *Critique* that this end is associated with pleasure insofar as it is a means to happiness—that is, it is "pleasant as a means." Kant also thinks that the fact that such an end is associated with pleasure causes pleasure at the very thought of this end. It is this latter pleasure that immediately affects the choice of the interest insofar as pleasurable representations tend to maintain themselves. Now, it might appear from this that an interest is formed for two distinct reasons. On the one hand, it seems that an interest in a particular end is formed because the end in question is a means to happiness. On the other hand, it seems that we choose an interest because doing so tends to maintain a feeling of pleasure that accompanies the thought of the end. But, on Kant's system (and this is what I am trying to bring to light), these reasons are intrinsically linked, because it is only in view of its instrumental connection to happiness that there is pleasure at the thought of some object. The fact that feelings of pleasure move us insofar as they tend to maintain themselves serves to explain just *how* the connection of an object to happiness functions as a basis for the choice of an interest in this object. In other words, the account of pleasure maintaining itself does not provide a separate explanation for the choice of an end so much as it articulates *the way in which* the explanation in terms of happiness actually works.

Let us take the example of health to illustrate the point. When we consider health a means to happiness, we associate this object with a feeling of pleasure. This association grounds a feeling of pleasure at the thought of health. If we have a feeling of pleasure upon thinking of health then we can choose to be interested in health or not (i.e., we can always do otherwise). The pleasurable representation of health affects us in the choice of health since all pleasurable representations tend to maintain themselves. If we choose to be interested in our health, then pleasure is maintained because there is a positive pleasure associated with the performance of healthy acts. So, the basis upon which we choose to be interested in health is the consideration that it is good for our happiness, but the mechanism by which this choice is made involves the effect, or influence, of pleasure.

Again, the anticipatory pleasure at the thought of health (i.e., the subjective dimension of this representation) does not determine anything, since we are sensuously *affected* but not *determined* by any pleasures that we experience. We are not compelled to take an interest in an object based solely on the feeling of pleasure—even in the case of an intellectual feeling of pleasure arising through the hypothetical imperative and our conception of happiness. We must, instead, choose to take an interest in any given end. Now, there is no doubt but that the stronger the feeling of pleasure at the thought of health, the greater the affect on the action. Consequently, the decision to be healthy is also affected by our conception of happiness, since the strength of the feeling of pleasure that accompanies the choice is contingent upon the extent to which the object in question (i.e., health) is seen as a means to happiness. The more our happiness is seen to be contingent upon health, the more pleasure we feel at the thought of health.

Let us turn now briefly to the formation of the other two kinds of nonmoral interests. We can be brief here because the structure of the formation of these interests is identical to the structure of the formation of interests in ends that are a means to happiness. The difference between the formation of these interests and the first kind of interest discussed above lies in the basis upon which pleasure is associated with the relevant object. In the case of interests in ends that are good in themselves and good as a means to happiness, pleasure is linked with an object both for itself and because it is a means to happiness. Obviously, this kind of object is heavily favored by our sensibility. In the case of interests in ends that are just good in themselves and not good for happiness, there is both a pleasure and a displeasure associated with this object. Our sensibility throws up conflicting feelings about what to do in the case of these weak desires$_1$. A weak person will choose an interest in an end that is not good for her happiness.

Choosing a Maxim

For Kant, we choose maxims on the basis of our interests. He writes that choice begins with "the ends that a human being may set for himself and [continues] in accordance with them [when he] prescribe[s] the maxims he is to adopt" (MM 6:382). Maxims provide us with principled instruction on how our interests will be pursued in the world. We saw in section I that a fully articulated maxim contains an action, a set of conditions under which this action is to be performed, and an end at which the action is directed. Now, the end of a maxim is given through the choice of an interest, so forming a maxim involves *choosing an action* (aimed at this end) *that is to be performed under certain circumstances.* In other words, positing a maxim on the basis of an interest involves figuring out the means to achieving an end in which one is interested. Now, some ends are not states of affairs but rather actions. For example, the end of "going to the gym" is an action. In these cases, it seems that choosing a maxim is about choosing a specific action that realizes the "end" of the more generally described action. One might posit a maxim such as "Go to the gym first thing in the morning at least three times a week."

Let me illustrate how maxims are formed on Kant's system by taking another example. In the case of the money-borrowing maxim presented at the start of this chapter, the end in which the agent is interested is relieving financial distress. She posits a maxim containing this end by choosing among the means that are at her disposal for relieving distress. Suppose she recognizes that one means to this end involves a significant tightening of her budget. Now, the representation of such a life change will include either a feeling of pleasure or a feeling of displeasure. Given that the action is good for relieving distress, it is pleasant as a means, and thus she will experience some pleasure. This pleasure influences her in the direction of choosing an interest in the action that is a means to relieving financial distress. If she so chooses, then she chooses a maxim.

Notice here that the formation of a maxim is primarily about the choice of an *interest* in a specific action. We can see, then, that for Kant the choice of a maxim is also a rational but sensuously affected choice. In positing a maxim we consider an action as an end, and make a decision about this action that is affected by the pleasure associated with the thought of this action. The tendency to maintain this latter pleasure calls for the choice of the relevant maxim.[28]

Let us suppose, however, that the thought of tightening her budget also produces a feeling of displeasure in our agent, since this action does not fit with her materialistic conception of happiness. In this case, her choice is affected in conflicting ways. This possibility illustrates the point that the choice of a maxim involves the choice of an action that is instrumentally relevant not only to the end in which she is interested but also to happiness. That is, the rational bases upon which we choose nonmoral maxims must include the hypothetical imperative, but, as an extension of this, can also include our rational conception of happiness. All of the viable possibilities that we consider in choosing a maxim are pleasant as a means to the end in question, but they might also be pleasant as a means to happiness. The decisive issue in the choice of a maxim, then, can often be whether a given action is pleasant as a means to happiness as well, or whether this kind of action fundamentally conflicts with our conception of happiness.

It might be objected here that my understanding of maxim formation contains a worrying kind of regress. If, in choosing a maxim, we take an interest in a certain kind of action that is a means to the end contained in the maxim, do we then have to choose another maxim on the basis of this interest? This second maxim would be chosen as part of the larger process of forming the first maxim. If the same thing happens regarding the choice of the second maxim, then there will be a third and fourth maxim, and so on. A closer look at what it means to form an interest in the context of choosing a maxim shows us that this difficulty can be avoided. The interest that we have in a particular course of action is an interest in this action as a means to the attainment of a certain end. Now, typically, an action is not the kind of thing for which we require a maxim dictating a means to it as an end, since actions do not require the positing of means toward their accomplishment. Instead, actions just require doing; they are the kinds of things that we simply do, and so we do not require means toward them. Thus, there is no further maxim chosen unless we must choose a course of action that is a means to another course of action. Of course, in the case of actions generally described (such as "going to the gym"), we might posit a maxim specifying a more particular action as a means toward this general action.

So far, I have explained how an incentive is incorporated into a maxim by describing how we form an interest in an end and an interest in means to that end.[29] On this account, the choosing of a maxim involves selecting a course of action on the basis of its relation to a presupposed end and its acceptability in terms of our conception of happiness. An end is "incorporated" into a maxim, then, insofar as a principle governing action is built around it. But this process seems to give us a merely cognitive principle—a rational rule that we can call to mind. Where is the pathological weight associated with maxims to which I referred at the start of this chapter? Kant's notion of practical freedom certainly seems to indicate that our actions on the basis of maxims are pathologically affected actions. It surely follows from this that maxims have some pathological dimension.

Indeed, in support of this consideration Kant tells us that *incentives* (not *ends*) are incorporated into maxims. "An incentive can determine the will to an action *only insofar as the person has incorporated [aufgenommen] it into his maxim* (has made it a general rule according to which he intends to act); only thus can an incentive, whatever it may be, coexist with the absolute spontaneity of the will (i.e., freedom)" (Rel 6:24). The point here is that incorporation does not just involve the cognitive act of *recognizing* or *seeing* an *end* as a basis for (the selection of an) action. Instead, it involves taking a *felt* incentive, associated with some end, into a rational principle that will govern some dimension of our life. Thus, it involves infusing one's feelings into one's rationally considered plans for action. The result is a rational principle that packs some affective punch. I think that it is with this in mind that Kant writes in the second *Critique*, "All three concepts—of incentive, interest and maxim—can, however, be applied only to finite beings. For without exception they presuppose a limitation of the nature of the being, in that the subjective character of its choice does not of itself agree with the objective law of a practical reason; they presuppose that the being must be impelled [angetrieben] in some manner to action, since an internal obstacle stands against it" (Pr. R 5:79). Kant's point is that, owing to our sensibility, the "subjective character" or execution of our choice does not always coincide with the legislation of this choice. In other words, we do not always do what we ought to do because there are sensible forces affecting our choices. To say that the concepts of interest and maxim *presuppose* this disagreement between legislation and execution is to say that these concepts must be understood in light of the fact that all human action is sensibly conditioned. Kant goes on to suggest explicitly that this is the same as presupposing that humans must be driven or impelled to act. Acting on the basis of a maxim, though it is a principled kind of action, does involve being driven in some way by an affective force. Kant's assumption seems to be, then, that maxims carry some sensible force. Maxims get this sensible force when incentives—or, more precisely, incentives considered as the feeling of pleasure or pain associated with an end—are incorporated into them. How, then, does this infusion of sensibility into rational principles happen?

When we choose an interest, we choose to make an end out of an object with which there is some pleasure associated. But this associated pleasure grounds a feeling of pleasure in the thought of the object, and this pleasure affects the choice of the end. So, when we choose to be interested in some end, we are choosing in the presence of an anticipatory feeling of pleasure. This end carries the sensible force of this pleasure into any maxim that is formed around it. The same applies in the case of the choice of objects or actions that provide a means to some end (i.e., the choice of a maxim). The choice of a maxim on the basis of an interest in an end is also a sensibly affected choice. Remember, this latter choice is basically the choice of an action. When we choose this action—the conception of which is experienced as pleasant—we also incorporate pleasure into our maxim. Pleasure, then, is incorporated into and present in a maxim in the sense that the thought of the maxim will include a feeling of pleasure that tends to maintain itself. In other words, the representation of a maxim includes pleasure as a subjective aspect or dimension. In short, the incorporated incentive is an anticipatory feeling of pleasure at the thought of the maxim.[30] This feeling gives the maxim sensible force in affecting specific choices.

CHAPTER FIVE

RESPECT AS AN INCENTIVE TO MORAL ACTION

Kant's theory of moral motivation has been a focal point of disagreement among many moral philosophers since the late eighteenth century, specifically regarding the role that Kant thinks respect (*Achtung*) plays in moral action. Kant tells us in many places that there is no antecedent feeling tending to morality but that reason directly determines the will in the case of moral choice.[1] But, at times, he also says that respect is an incentive to moral action, and that it is a moral feeling. It appears from this that there is in fact an antecedent feeling that tends to morality. Now, Kant seems to affirm both of these positions in a number of places, and thus to hold that there both is and is not a feeling that plays a role in moral motivation. I argued in my Introduction that, in the face of this evidential standoff, a new approach must be taken to understanding Kant's notion of respect. The approach that I have adopted in this study has been to frame the issue in terms of a juxtaposition of moral and nonmoral motivation. Over the course of the first four chapters, I have prepared for an analysis of *how* respect motivates by looking closely at nonmoral action. My argument is that even though Kant distinguishes between moral and nonmoral motivation, he also draws the two together by insisting on the motivational need for a moral feeling, and by giving this feeling a role in moral action that corresponds in essential ways to the role that nonmoral feelings play in nonmoral action. This correspondence illuminates Kant's comments on the feeling of respect, and allows us to see them as part of a systematic understanding of how moral action works.

In this final chapter, I will justify my methodological approach by arguing that there are a number of things both explicit and implicit in Kant's thought which indicate that he thinks that moral and nonmoral actions are analogous in some significant way (section II).[2] I will go on to present an account of Kant's conception of the structure of moral motivation, one which draws upon his nonmoral account for clarity, and defend this account with evidence from the texts (section III). Before any of this, however, let me focus the discussion by turning briefly to a few of the interpretations of Kantian moral motivation with which I disagree.

I. SOME READINGS OF KANT ON MORAL MOTIVATION

Most scholars have tried to maintain a strong distinction between moral and nonmoral motivation by interpreting Kant's comments on respect in such a way as to avoid understanding this notion as a feeling that motivates. Broadly speaking, there are three main positions taken along these lines.[3] According to one such view—held by commentators such as Paul Guyer and Karl Ameriks—respect is not a motive at all but is rather the phenomenal effect of having *already* (noumenally) chosen to act morally.[4] On this view, when an agent acts morally it is the moral law that directly determines choice, and this determination registers phenomenally as a feeling of respect.

Andrews Reath and Nancy Sherman argue for a similar position, claiming that the *feeling* dimension of respect is an effect of a moral choice.[5] They develop this interpretation by contending that, for Kant, moral choice is actually motivated by the *cognitive* dimension of respect. This dimension involves the purely intellectual recognition that the moral law is a sufficient reason for acting. Thus, respect has both affective and intellectual dimensions, but only the intellectual dimension plays a role in motivating moral action.

On a third reading, Kant is confused, or inconsistent, insofar as he presents respect as a feeling that motivates. So, for example, A. Murray MacBeath writes of Kant's treatment of the feeling of respect, "This feeling is a fiction conjured up out of a defective view of rational action" (MacBeath 1973, 313). MacBeath contends that Kant's view of rational action is defective because he is under the influence of the Humean doctrine that some kind of intermediary feeling is required in order to move the rational agent. A variation on this interpretation (primarily defended by Ralph Walker) holds that Kant abandons the notion of respect as an incentive to moral action in his mature moral writings.[6] On this account, the feeling of respect is just a stubborn leftover from a period in Kant's thinking during which he was influenced by the British moral sense theorists.

We might say, then, that in spite of a handful of recent articles by scholars such as Larry Herrera, Richard McCarty, Josefine Nauckhoff, and A. T. Nuyen—who argue forcibly to the contrary—the view that the feeling of respect plays no motivational role in moral action is still dominant in Kant studies.[7] Now, these four commentators focus their efforts on offering arguments against the antimotivational interpretation of respect by marshalling what they see as direct textual evidence in favor of reading respect as a feeling that motivates. Their reading of these texts seems right, but as I argued in the Introduction, the evidence is not conclusive either way—and so, in this study, I have not gone directly to the relevant evidence but instead have tried to lend support to the argument for the motivational efficacy of respect by juxtaposing this notion with Kant's theory of nonmoral action. My account differs from that offered by commentators who essentially agree with my position, insofar as I find evidence for the motivational role of respect not simply (or only) in what Kant says about it directly, but in the light thrown onto Kant's comments on moral action by the parallels that exist between these comments and his general theory of action. The essential point that I will argue along these lines is that Kant's theory of action commits him to the view that reason guides human action (moral and nonmoral) by allowing for the incorporation of feelings of pleasure and pain into maxims. These feelings are experienced at the thought of certain ends or actions, and their incorporation into principles of action is essential in giving these principles motivational efficacy.

II. EVIDENCE FOR A STRUCTURAL PARALLEL BETWEEN MORAL AND NONMORAL ACTION

Parallel Determinations of the Faculty of Desire

The first issue that requires attention, then, is whether it is valid to argue for a parallel between Kant's conceptions of moral and nonmoral agency.

What is the evidence to support the idea that Kant thinks that these two are similar in some relevant way? It might be objected here that it misrepresents Kant's position even to speak of moral and nonmoral action at the same time. Some critics maintain that Kant's distinction between the higher and lower faculties of desire institutes a divide between moral and nonmoral action that cannot be overcome. Kant defines the faculty of desire as the power to bring things into existence out of our ideas of these things. We saw in chapter 1 that this functional definition allows Kant to shift between saying that there are different faculties of desire (i.e., different powers of production), and that there is a single faculty with different ways of being determined (i.e., different ways of producing through the same power). Now, on either of the ways of understanding the faculty of desire, there is no doubt but that Kant sees the higher faculty of desire and lower faculty of desire as significantly distinct. But to what exactly does this distinction amount?

For Kant, the higher faculty of desire is the capacity to have desires$_1$ without our receptivity to the sensuous impact of external objects playing a causal role in the formation of these desires$_1$. Kant tells us in a lecture from the mid-1770s, "The faculty of desire is either a higher or a lower faculty of desire. The lower faculty of desire is a power to desire something so far as we are affected by objects. The higher faculty of desire is a power to desire something from ourselves independently of objects" (LM 28:228). The desires$_1$ produced by the higher faculty of desire are produced independently of our sensuous receptivity to external objects, while the desires$_1$ that are produced in view of this receptivity belong to the lower faculty of desire. On this account, the distinction between the higher and lower faculties of desire primarily refers to the cause or origin of the desire$_1$ in question: every desire$_1$ has either a higher (nonsensuous) or a lower (sensuous) cause.

We saw in chapter 2 that the lower faculty of desire produces desires$_1$ through the intercession of a feeling of pleasure at the thought of some sensible object. Kant thinks that in the case of the higher faculty of desire, reason itself (or, more specifically, the categorical imperative) produces some kind of feeling of pleasure that determines this faculty, causing what he calls an "intellectual desire."[8] Kant writes that intellectual desires come from "representations of satisfaction [*Wohlgefallens*] or dissatisfaction which . . . depend on the manner in which we cognize the objects through concepts" (LM 28:254). This passage suggests that the higher faculty of desire is determined in essentially the same way as the lower faculty, except that the cause of the determining feelings is a rational principle or concept and not our susceptibility to a sensible object. In the case of the categorical imperative, we cognize objects through the concept of duty. So, depending upon whether or not an object (or, in this case, action) falls under the concept of our duty, its representation will include a feeling of satisfaction. Now, is there any published evidence to support this line of thinking reported in Kant's lectures? Or, to ask the question more generally, does Kant say anything in his published works to indicate that he thinks that the higher faculty of desire (i.e., the categorical imperative) produces desires₁ in a way that is analogous to the way in which the lower faculty of desire produces desires₁ (i.e., through a feeling of pleasure)?

Kant appears to draw a link between the higher and lower faculties of desire in the second *Critique* when he writes, "Respect, and not the gratification or enjoyment of happiness, is thus something for which there can be no feeling antecedent to reason and underlying it (for this would always be aesthetic and pathological): respect as consciousness of direct necessitation of the will by the law is hardly [*kaum*] an analogue of the feeling of pleasure, *although in relation to the faculty of desire it does the same thing* but from different sources [*indem es im Verhältnisse zum Begehrungsvermögen gerade eben dasselbe, aber aus andern Quellen tut*]" (Pr. R 5:117; emphasis added).⁹ Kant is clearly wrestling with the issue of the place or role of the feeling of respect here. He argues that respect differs from pathological feelings of pleasure, and is hardly analogous to them, but yet, "in relation to the faculty of desire it does the same thing." What does Kant mean by this? If the moral law determines us to action directly, without any mediating feelings of any kind, then it only "does the same thing" in relation to the faculty of desire insofar as it actually *determines* this faculty. But surely Kant means more than that. And, in fact, closer inspection reveals that Kant says that respect, and not the moral law, "does the same thing" in relation to the faculty of desire. So, the feeling of respect "does the same thing" as a nonmoral feeling of pleasure, "but from different sources." Though Kant is reluctant to say that respect is simply a feeling of pleasure, he seems to be drawn to denying the implication (suggested by the parallel that he sees between the ways in which moral and nonmoral feelings determine the faculty of desire) that it is. After all, why would he deny that respect is just like a pathological feeling of pleasure if something were not suggesting that it is? The sense in which the feeling of respect is "hardly an analogue" of pleasure lies in the fact that the cognitive dimension of the representation that is respect is a consciousness of the moral law (as it applies in any given situation). Remember, for Kant, all feelings have an intentional dimension, and it is this dimension plus the feeling aspect that make up a representation. My claim, then, is that Kant draws a radical distinction between respect and other feelings of pleasure on the basis of this consciousness, and not on the basis of the impact that both have as feelings on the faculty of desire.[10]

Kant's concept of practical freedom gives us further reason to draw moral and nonmoral action together. According to Kant, all human actions are practically free. We saw in chapter 3 that to be practically free is to be independent of sensible necessitation, though not of sensible affection. This does not mean that sensible affection in any given choice is optional; instead, Kant thinks that all human actions are *necessarily* sensibly affected. The fact that we are not purely rational beings means that we *must* have some sensible incentive to act morally. The moral law *must* appeal to us in view of the kind of creatures that we are. Thus Kant writes, "Now as an act from duty wholly excludes the influence of inclination and therewith every object of the will, nothing remains which can determine the will objectively except law and subjectively except pure respect for this practical law" (G 4:400). The will must be both "objectively" and "subjectively" determined. Kant explains what this means in a footnote to this passage, saying, "A maxim is the subjective principle of volition. The objective principle (i.e., that which would serve all rational beings also subjectively as a practical principle if reason had full control over the faculty of desire) is the practical law" (G 4:400n). Notice here that a maxim is a "subjective" principle not just in the sense that it is a principle adopted by, and valid for, the individual agent (only), but, primarily, in the sense that it carries executive (and not necessarily legislative) power. Kant is always careful to make sure that the executive role of the feeling of respect is not confused with any legislative role. "Moral feeling has been erroneously construed by some as the standard for our moral judgment, whereas it must be regarded rather as the subjective effect which the law has upon the will to which reason alone gives objective grounds" (G 4:460). By "subjective effect" here, Kant clearly means executive effect (or the effect that will carry the motivational power to execute the law), and not simply the effect of compliance to the moral law on feeling (as Guyer and Ameriks claim).

Now, Kant suggests in the *Groundwork* 4:400n, quoted above, that the very existence of maxims is, by definition, a product of our partly sensible natures. If we were fully rational we would not have any need for maxims, since we would always act on the basis of practical laws. Only beings that are partly sensible require maxims. The implication here (argued for in a different way at the end of the previous chapter) is that maxims carry sensible weight, since it is only as such that they are required for partly sensible creatures like us. This interpretation is confirmed in the second *Critique* when Kant says (in the passage quoted in the previous chapter), "All three concepts—of incentive, interest and maxim—can, however, be applied only to finite beings. For without exception they presuppose a limitation of the nature of the being, in that the subjective character of its choice does not of itself agree with the objective law of a practical reason; they presuppose that the being must be impelled [*angetrieben*] in some manner to action, since an internal obstacle stands against it" (Pr. R 5:79). Kant's point is that it is only in view of our sensibility (i.e., our "limitation") that we have incentives, interests, and maxims. As a result, these concepts reflect the requirements associated with our sensibility. To form a maxim, then, is to form something that must register with us as sensible creatures. It is to posit something that must impel us with its sensible weight.

Kant does not think that moral actions provide an exception to this requirement. He tells us that the objective principle would act as a subjective (i.e., executive) principle for human beings if reason had full control over the faculty of desire. But reason does not have full control over the faculty of desire. Consequently, we *need* the objective or rational (universal) principle to produce a feeling that will have subjective (i.e., executive) impact through a maxim, and thereby combat nonmoral interests on a sensible level.[11] The full significance of Kant's notion of practical freedom is that, given our nature, sensible factors *must* play a role in our choices. *All* of our choices are, necessarily, sensibly affected, though not sensibly necessitated.[12] Again, this includes our choices of moral interests and maxims.

Now, as we saw in chapter 4, there is more than one way in which a choice can be sensibly affected. If the feeling that determines the faculty of desire and causes a desire$_1$ (that is part of the ground of a choice) is sensible, then the choice that follows is sensibly affected. Thus, a choice can be sensibly affected just insofar as our sensibility plays a causal role in the desire$_1$ that we choose to make a reason for action (i.e., to take an interest in). A choice can also be sensibly affected if we choose an end in view of its association with pleasure. But Kant does not think that moral choices have either sensible feelings at their ground, or pleasure associated with their ends (in view of which they are made). These are *not* the kinds of sensible influence that are relevant to moral choice.

However, the most important sense in which a choice is sensibly affected is that there is a pleasure present influencing the agent in making the choice. For Kant, this kind of sensible affect is relevant even if the affecting feelings are only *conditioned* by sensible factors. In the second *Critique,* Kant refers to the way in which the moral *feeling* of respect is conditioned by our sensibility when he says, "sensuous feeling which is the basis of all our inclinations, is the condition [*Bedingung*] of the particular feeling we call respect, but the cause that determines this feeling lies in the pure practical reason" (Pr. R 5:75). Kant clearly distinguishes between the cause of the moral feeling of respect and its condition. So, even though the feeling of respect is not caused by our sensible susceptibility to objects, sensible feelings are the condition for (or are required for the existence of) this moral feeling. Our sensibility is a condition for moral feeling insofar as this sensibility provides a medium that is necessary for the existence of feelings associated with the moral law. In other words, were we not sensible creatures we would not be capable of moral feeling. For Kant, the fact that the moral feeling of respect is conditioned by sensible feeling ultimately means that moral feelings play (in some respects) the same kind of role in the choice of moral actions as nonmoral feelings do in the choice of nonmoral actions. In other words, Kant thinks that because moral feeling is conditioned by sensible feeling, moral choices are affected in a way that parallels (in some respects) the way in which nonmoral choices are affected. In the previous chapter, we saw that nonmoral choices are sensibly affected insofar as pleasurable representations of nonmoral objects or actions with a causality directed at maintaining themselves are present during choice. Kant thinks that moral choice is also affected by a kind of pleasure at the thought of the object in question. That is to say, Kant maintains that the subjective dimension of our representation of a prospective moral action affects our moral choice.

Kant affirms just this kind of sensible influence in the following passage from the *Metaphysics:*

> Moral Feeling: This is the susceptibility to feel pleasure or displeasure merely from being aware [*dem Bewußtsein*] that our actions are consistent with or contrary to the law of duty. Every determination of choice proceeds *from* the representation of a possible action *to* the deed through the feeling of pleasure or displeasure, taking an interest in the action or its effect. The state of *feeling* here (the way in which inner sense is affected) is either *pathological* or *moral.*—The former is that feeling which precedes the representation of the law; the latter, that which can only follow upon it. (MM 6:399)

Kant asserts in this passage that *every* determination of *Willkür* (i.e., every choice) proceeds in the same way: there is the thought of the action, followed by a feeling of pleasure, and then an interest (and presumably a maxim), and finally the action. Both moral and nonmoral actions come to be through this medium of sensibility (i.e., the feeling of pleasure). So, both moral and nonmoral actions are sensibly affected in this way. Notice, Kant omits any mention of an anticipation of pleasure associated with the thought of the action, signifying that this is not part of his conception of what moral and nonmoral actions share in common. Toward the end of this passage Kant distinguishes between moral and nonmoral choice, not in terms of this process of determination, but in terms of the order in which the feeling and thought of the law occur: the moral feeling follows the thought of the law, whereas the nonmoral feeling precedes it.[13] In spite of this difference, however, the overall sense of the passage is that moral and nonmoral feelings determine the faculty of desire in much the same way. Before turning to look in more detail at the structure of moral motivation, let me briefly pause here to elaborate on the distinctions between moral and nonmoral action that Kant explicitly draws.

Differences between Moral and Nonmoral Action

Now, as we have seen on a few occasions, Kant thinks that the primary difference between moral and nonmoral action is that moral feeling has its source in (and therefore succeeds) reason, while pathological feeling precedes reason. Kant repeatedly refers to this distinction in the second *Critique* and the *Metaphysics*. He also points to this difference in the origin of moral and nonmoral feelings in the *Groundwork* when he writes, "It might be objected that I seek refuge in an obscure feeling behind the word 'respect,' instead of clearly resolving the question with a concept of reason. *But though respect is a feeling, it is not one received through any [outer] influence but is self-wrought by a rational concept;* thus it differs specifically from all feelings of the former kind which may be referred to inclination or fear" (G 4:401n; emphasis added). After the development of Kant's thinking on pleasure around 1790, this distinction between the origins of moral and pathological feelings is reinforced by the notion that feelings can be differentiated on the basis of their intentional objects. Pleasure is always pleasure in, or at, some idea, and so Kant can differentiate pathological feelings and moral feelings in terms of their very makeup: pathological feelings have nonmoral intentional objects and moral feelings have moral intentional objects. Thus, on Kant's mature account it is not the case that all feelings are essentially the same, except that some have moral parents and others do not. Instead, the parentage of the respective feelings translates into a concrete distinction between the feelings themselves. We will see throughout the remainder of this chapter that the development of Kant's thinking on pleasure after the second *Critique* allows him to flesh out his thinking on respect as the moral incentive.[14]

The third critical distinction that Kant draws between moral and nonmoral action is that the feeling of respect determines moral choice without any consideration of an expected pleasure. Kant tells us that "the preeminent good can consist only in the conception of law itself (which can be present only in a rational being) so far as this conception and not the hoped-for effect is the determining ground of the will" (G 4:401). The conception of the law gives us our duty and a moral action must be done "from duty" alone (G 4:399). So, we do not choose moral maxims because we expect to get pleasure from acting morally. This is a standard feature of Kant's ethics and I will return to it a number of times below. Now, in the absence of any other differences between moral and nonmoral action beyond the origins of the relevant feelings, the intentional objects of these feelings, and the aim of the relevant choices, we should take Kant quite literally when he says that moral and nonmoral feelings "do the same thing" in relation to the faculty of desire. That is to say, we should take Kant to mean that moral feelings lead to moral choices in much the same way as nonmoral feelings lead to nonmoral choices.

III. THE STRUCTURE OF MORAL MOTIVATION

For Kant, moral agency is structured in essentially the same way as nonmoral agency. This shared structure allows us to see Kant's comments on moral motivation in a clarifying light. In broad outline, I will argue as follows: respect, for Kant, is the moral incentive or driving force (*Triebfeder*). It drives or moves us to moral action, and does so insofar as it is a moral feeling made up of a kind of pleasure and pain. Now, just as nonmoral feelings of pleasure and pain are made possible by feeling, so respect is made possible by moral feeling. Kant thinks that, in virtue of moral feeling, the representation of a moral action includes as a subjective dimension feelings of pleasure and pain (i.e., the feeling of respect) that affect us in the choice of an interest in this action. Respect is a kind of pleasure and pain that we get upon thinking of the demands of the moral law, and this feeling grounds moral interest insofar as it determines the higher faculty of desire. Finally, this interest grounds a subjective principle governing moral action when the feeling of respect is incorporated into a maxim. So, the choice of one's duty essentially involves the incorporation of a moral feeling into a dutiful maxim (though, as I will explain, this does not mean that one chooses one's duty for the sake of pleasure). I will proceed by breaking this argument into a number of specific claims concerning moral motivation.

Moral Feeling and Respect

In the *Metaphysics*, Kant defines moral feeling as "our susceptibility to feel pleasure or pain merely from being aware [*dem Bewußtsein*] that our actions are consistent with or contrary to the law of duty" (MM 6:399).

Given that respect is a feeling that arises at the thought that one can be "determined . . . solely by the law" (Pr. R 5:81), we can conclude that moral feeling is a susceptibility to the feeling of respect. Very much along these lines, Kant says that "the capacity of . . . having respect for the moral law . . . is really moral feeling" (Pr. R 5:80). Thus, moral feeling is to respect as nonmoral feeling is to pathological feelings of pleasure and pain. This, then, is the first parallel between the structure of moral and nonmoral action. Notice here that Kant often uses the term "moral feeling" when he is actually speaking about respect. That is to say, he often refers to the concrete feeling via the deeper susceptibility to this feeling (a habit of which we also see evidence in the nonmoral context).

Respect and Moral Interest (or Intellectual Desire$_1$)

In the same passage from the second *Critique* in which Kant connects moral feeling and respect, he also refers to the relationship between respect and moral *interest*. He writes that "the capacity of taking . . . an interest in the law (or of having respect for the moral law) is really moral feeling" (Pr. R 5:80). The implication here is that taking an interest in the moral law is *equivalent* to feeling respect. At the very least, these two are connected, insofar as moral feeling is the condition for the possibility of both. But Kant specifies later in the second *Critique* that the relation between respect and moral interest is a grounding relation, when he tells us that this feeling of respect "produces [*hervorbringt*] an interest in obedience to the law, and this we call the moral interest" (Pr. R 5:80). Kant makes the same point in the *Groundwork* when he comments that, although it is impossible to explain theoretically the interest that man takes in moral laws, "he does actually take an interest in them, and the foundation of this interest in us we will call the moral feeling" (G 4:460). In this passage, the context indicates that by moral feeling Kant means respect. These passages provide published support for the point that Kant makes in his lectures, when he says that intellectual desires$_1$ are grounded in "representations of satisfaction or dissatisfaction which . . . depend on the manner in which we cognize the objects through concepts" (LM 28:254). Respect, then, is an intellectual feeling of satisfaction that arises through the concept of duty, and this feeling grounds an intellectual desire$_1$ (i.e., a moral interest). Now, Kant tells us that "Respect [*Achtung*] for the moral law is . . . the sole and undoubted moral incentive [*Triebfeder*]" (Pr. R 5:78). In the *Religion* he puts it this way: "This capacity for simple respect for the moral law within us would thus be moral feeling, which in and through itself does not constitute an end of the natural predisposition except so far as it is the motivating force of the will" (Rel 6:29). So, as an incentive or motivating force, respect brings forth moral interest just as nonmoral incentives of pleasure and pain bring forth nonmoral interests. This is the second helpful parallel that we can draw between the structure of moral and nonmoral action: in both cases feelings provide the ground for our choice of interests.

To recap: Kant posits feeling, respect, and interest as the basic concepts in his account of moral motivation, and orders them such that feeling allows for respect, which in turn produces or, more literally, *brings forth* moral interest. The broad outlines of a structural parallel are clearly evident here. Before I turn to the parallel between Kant's thinking on moral and nonmoral maxim formation, let me first look more closely at this grounding relation between respect and moral interest. What does the parallel between moral and nonmoral action tell us about the relation between respect and moral interest? We saw in chapter 4 that nonmoral interests are formed when an agent chooses to make a particular pleasure an end in her life. We also saw that, according to Kant's later thinking on pleasure, this choice comes about through a pleasurable representation that tends to maintain itself in an action. Of course, insofar as moral interests are not about making pleasure an end in one's life, Kant does not think that they are formed in precisely the same way as nonmoral interests. But can we conclude that Kant maintains that the feeling of respect brings forth moral interests in a way that parallels the way in which nonmoral feelings bring forth nonmoral interests? Or, more specifically, is there any reason to believe that for Kant respect involves (a) feelings of pleasure of some kind that (b) maintain themselves by affecting the choice of an interest in moral actions?

Kant elaborates on the complex nature of the feeling of respect in the second *Critique*.

> Now everything in self-love belongs to inclination, and all inclination rests on feelings; therefore, whatever checks all inclinations in self-love necessarily has, by that fact, an influence on feeling. Thus we conceive how it is possible to understand a priori that

the moral law can exercise an effect on feeling, since it blocks the inclinations and the propensity to make them the supreme practical condition (i.e., self-love) from all participation in supreme legislation. This effect is on the one side merely negative, but on the other, in respect to the restrictive practical ground of pure practical reason, it is positive. And to the latter, no kind of feeling, even under the name of a practical or moral feeling, may be assumed as prior to the moral law and as its basis. The negative effect on feeling (unpleasantness) is, like all influences on feeling and every feeling itself, pathological. *As the effect of the consciousness of the moral law . . . this feeling of a rational subject affected with inclinations is called humiliation. But in relation to its positive ground, the law, it is at the same time respect for the law;* for this law there is no feeling, but, as it removes a resistance, this dislodgment of an obstacle is, in the judgment of reason, equally esteemed as a positive assistance to its causality. (Pr. R 5:74–75; emphasis added)[15]

Respect involves a unique kind of moral pleasure (as a result of the consciousness of the moral law) and pain (at the prospect of denying/ humiliating the natural inclinations). Kant is even more explicit about the two-sidedness of the felt effect of the moral law later in the same text.

The feeling which arises from the consciousness of this constraint is not pathological, as are those caused by objects of the senses, but practical, i.e., possible through a prior determination of the will and the causality of reason. As submission to a law, i.e., as a command (which constrains the sensuously affected subject), it contains, therefore, no pleasure but rather displeasure proportionate to this constraint. On the other hand, since this constraint is exercised only through the legislation [*Gesetzgebung*] of one's own reason, it also contains something elevating, and the subjective effect on feeling, in so far as pure practical reason is its sole cause, can also be called self-approbation with reference to pure practical reason, for one knows himself to be determined thereto solely by the law and without any interest; he becomes conscious of an altogether different interest which is subjectively produced by the law and which is purely practical and free. (Pr. R 5:81)

Thus, respect is a complex feeling that accompanies the consciousness of the *legislative* (i.e., not executive) constraint of the law.[16] Again, this consciousness of the moral law gives us a combination of feelings of pleasure and pain.

Now, if we take Kant's thinking from the second *Critique* and develop it in terms of his later thinking on pleasure, then we can see that the complex feeling of respect is a part of (i.e., the subjective dimension of) the consciousness of the constraint of the moral law.[17] So, the complex feeling of respect (like all Kantian feelings) has specific cognitive or intentional content. The painful dimension involves a pain *at* the thought of a specific inclination being blocked, and the pleasurable aspect involves a pleasure *at* the thought of acting on the law in a particular kind of way.[18] Notice here, we do not conceive of the moral law in an abstract or general way, but rather represent it embodied in a recommendation for a particular kind of action (e.g., not dishonestly borrowing money). In other words, consciousness of the moral law is consciousness of a specific demand on us as partly rational, partly sensuous beings. The moral law imposes a particular demand on us in any given context by legislating for an action that constrains or challenges the expression of certain inclinations. Kant refers to this as the determination of the will by the moral law—an objective (i.e., legislative) determination that would also be subjective (i.e., executive) were we purely rational creatures.[19] This determination presents us with a proposed action that ought to be done. So, the pleasurable feeling that we experience is experienced at the thought of a particular kind of action, and the painful feeling is experienced at the thought of certain inclinations being denied in the process of so acting. On Kant's mature account of feeling, then, respect is the complex subjective dimension of a representation of a particular kind of action, just as nonmoral pleasures and pains are the subjective dimensions of nonmoral representations.

As I have noted on several occasions above, Kant never directly addresses the question of how respect works to ground moral interest. However, in light of the parallels that exist between moral and nonmoral action, I want to propose that it is the interplay between the pleasurable and painful dimensions of respect that serves to promote moral action. For Kant, acting on the basis of the moral law involves acting in a thoroughly autonomous or self-determined way. It follows that respect is in part an experience of a kind of pleasure at the thought of a self-determined or autonomous (i.e., moral) action. This feeling, since it arises at the prospect (or representation) of a moral action, is essentially an *anticipatory* feeling of pleasure. We saw in the previous chapter that an anticipatory feeling of pleasure is crucial in Kant's understanding of non-moral action. Anticipatory pleasures (i.e., pleasurable representations) influence our choices insofar as they tend to maintain themselves. If the moral and nonmoral cases are parallel, then the feeling of respect affects us insofar as its pleasant dimension tends to maintain itself. Now, moral pleasure at the thought of a self-determined action can best maintain itself if we actually perform a self-determined action.[20] At the same time, the unpleasant feeling that we experience as a result of the prospect of denying inclinations encourages a change of our state of mind. So, the pleasant dimension of the representation encourages us to maintain the associated state of mind by acting on the basis of the moral law, while the painful dimension pushes us away from the state of contemplating the denial of inclinations. The pleasant moral feeling, then, is maintained (and the pain at the representation of a moral act removed) if we act in an autonomous fashion.[21] This feeling at the thought of being autonomous grounds or produces a moral interest insofar as it affects us in the choice of that which gives rise to it. To form a moral interest, then, is to choose self-determination as a basis for action.

It could be objected here that it looks like the complex feeling of respect actually leaves us ambivalent and thus paralyzed: the pleasure at the thought of the moral action encourages us to do the right thing, while the pain at the same thought encourages us to abandon the moral and give in to the inclinations. If this is so, the feeling of respect is not much of an incentive to moral action at all. But it could also be argued (and this must be what Kant has in mind) that the pain at the representation of humiliated inclinations heightens our focus on the pleasure of the moral action. Remember that, for Kant, pain tends to move us away from our current state of mind. Focusing on the positive dimension of the represented action can accomplish this. So, if pain is to affect our moral choices in a positive way, it must be by getting us to focus on the pleasure of moral actions. There is some evidence for this way of interpreting the motivational force of the painful dimension of respect in the fact that Kant never says that the performance of a moral action is followed by pain (i.e., that pain is maintained through the action), but (as we will see immediately below) repeatedly tells us that moral actions are followed by pleasant feelings. This seems to suggest that the moral action itself removes the painful consciousness of the humiliation of the inclinations. My suggestion, again, is that this pain is removed through our focusing on the pleasant dimension of morality.

Now, in order for this interpretation of the way the feeling of respect functions as an incentive to moral action to work, acting for the sake of duty would have to produce (i.e., maintain) a feeling of pleasure. Fortunately, Kant says just this in his (otherwise mysterious) claims to the effect that the performance of a dutiful action is accompanied by a kind of pleasure. For example, in the second *Critique,* Kant says:

> Do we not have a word to denote a satisfaction with existence, an analogue of happiness which necessarily accompanies the consciousness of virtue, and which does not indicate a gratification, as "happiness" does? We do, and this word is "self-contentment" [*Selbstzufriedenheit*], which in its real meaning refers only to negative satisfaction with existence in which one is conscious of needing nothing. Freedom and the consciousness of freedom, as a capacity for following the moral law with an unyielding disposition, is independence from inclinations, at least as motives determining (though not as affecting) our desiring; and so far as I am conscious of freedom in obeying my moral maxims, it is the exclusive source of an unchanging contentment necessarily connected with it and resting on no particular feeling. (Pr. R 5:117–18)

This presence of a kind of pleasure makes sense on Kant's later theory of pleasure: it is the pleasure that is maintained through the moral action. Notice that Kant uses the notion of an "analogue" here again in the second *Critique.* Remember, before the third *Critique,* Kant had not fully worked out how any pleasure associated with morality could differ from nonmoral pleasure/happiness, and so the notion of a feeling that is

analogous to pleasure but somehow unique seems to have suggested itself to him. Self-contentment is Kant's term for the unique kind of feeling that accompanies the performance of a moral action. Respect, on
the other hand, is his term for that complex moral feeling that precedes
this performance.

It must be noted, however, that in the *Groundwork* Kant makes a
slightly different point about a feeling of pleasure that results from
acting morally. In this earlier work, he tells us, "In order to will an action which reason alone prescribes to the sensuously affected rational
being as the action which he ought to will, there is certainly required a
power to instill [*einzuflößen*] a feeling of pleasure or satisfaction [*ein
Gefühl der Lust oder des Wohlgefallens*] in the fulfillment of duty, and
hence here must be a causality of reason to determine sensibility in accordance with its own rational principles" (G 4:460). Notice here that
Kant is noncommittal on the precise nature of the moral feeling; he
says that it is a feeling of pleasure *or* satisfaction. Unfortunately, Kant
does not merely say here that the moral law infuses this feeling of pleasure or satisfaction accompanying, or resulting from, doing one's duty.
He also indicates that there is a *need* for this association of duty and
pleasure in order to ensure that humans, as sensuously affected beings,
pursue this duty. In other words, Kant seems to be saying that moral action requires an *anticipation* of pleasure or satisfaction. His point, then,
appears to be that "there is certainly required a power to instill a feeling of pleasure or satisfaction in the fulfillment of duty" because otherwise we would not anticipate pleasure and would not act morally.
This is a very strange thing for Kant to say, since it clearly heteronomizes
morality.

Now, I argued in previous chapters that an anticipatory pleasure is not
contingent upon the existence of a grounding anticipation of pleasure.
Thus, an anticipatory pleasure can determine choice without any expectation of pleasure in the future. All that is necessary, on the Kantian model,
is that pleasure is somehow associated with the object in question. Along
these lines, we saw (in the posthumous writings example in chapter 2)
that one can be moved to act by a pleasure at the thought of something
in the future that one will not experience, and thus from which one cannot anticipate getting any pleasure. It follows from this that it is at least
conceivable for Kant (on both his earlier and later views on pleasure)

that a moral pleasure moves us without the presence of any anticipation of pleasure. So, Kant does not *need* to say that "there is certainly required a power to instill a feeling of pleasure or satisfaction in the fulfillment of duty." In saying this he mistakenly implies that the fulfillment of duty requires an anticipation of pleasure. Again, all that is required is that there is an *association* of pleasure with one's duty, such that the thought or representation of this duty includes an anticipatory pleasure as a subjective dimension.

Of course, as I also pointed out in previous chapters, Kant overlooks the lack of a need for an anticipation of pleasure in the nonmoral context, and thus it is perhaps no surprise that he does so here again in the moral arena. Having said this, it must also be noted that this is not a mistake that Kant makes again in the moral context. In other words, there is no other place in his mature writings where Kant even implies that there is an anticipation of pleasure at the performance of one's duty. Nevertheless, Kant's misstatement in the *Groundwork* regarding the conditions for the possibility of acting out of duty actually provides further evidence for a parallel between moral and nonmoral action, since the position that he takes in the moral context mirrors the one that he takes in the nonmoral context.

With all of this said, let me return to a passage from the *Metaphysics* already quoted above and see how it is illuminated by the preceding discussion.

> Moral Feeling: This is the susceptibility to feel pleasure or displeasure merely from being aware [*dem Bewußtsein*] that our actions are consistent with or contrary to the law of duty. Every determination of choice proceeds *from* the representation of a possible action *to* the deed through the feeling of pleasure or displeasure, taking an interest in the action or its effect. [*Alle Bestimmung der Willkür aber geht von der Vorstellung der möglichen Handlung durch das Gefühl der Lust oder Unlust, an ihr oder ihrer Wirkung ein Interesse zu nehmen, zur Tat.*] The state of *feeling* here (the way in which inner sense is affected) is either *pathological* or *moral*.—The former is that feeling which precedes the representation of the law; the latter, that which can only follow upon it. (MM 6:399)

In this fully mature passage, Kant speaks of a pleasure—which is made possible by moral feeling—merely "from being aware" that our actions are consistent with the law of duty. Now, Kant clearly means "our *prospective* actions" because he goes on to elaborate on this notion of a moral pleasure in the next sentence, by saying that it *follows* from the *thought* of an action but *precedes* the actual action. The pleasure is a pleasure *at the thought of a prospective action* (i.e., it is the pleasurable dimension of a representation of some future action). It follows, then, that it is an anticipatory pleasure. Moral feeling makes the anticipatory feeling of pleasure possible. Kant goes on to link this anticipatory pleasure with interest. Unfortunately, the precise nature of the link is difficult to grasp from this passage. Indeed, the translation of this passage differs in James Ellington's version, and reads, "through the feeling of pleasure or displeasure *in taking an interest* in the action." This suggests that the experience of pleasure is equivalent to, or even generated by, taking an interest, whereas Mary Gregor's version (correctly, I think) implies a more concrete distinction between the experience of pleasure and the interest. I argued earlier that for Kant this distinction denotes a grounding relation, with the experience of pleasure at the thought of the law providing a basis or foundation for the choice of a moral interest. The account I have just presented provides a reading of this passage by explaining just how this experience of pleasure grounds a moral interest by affecting this choice.

Moral Interests and Maxims

The final step in the production of nonmoral actions—looked at in chapter 4—involves the formation of nonmoral maxims out of interests. With this discussion in mind, let us now turn to Kant's comments on the formation of moral maxims. The act of incorporating an incentive into a rational plan for action is completed by the formation of a maxim around the end with which this incentive is associated and in which we are interested. Now, if the incorporation of incentives were to happen in parallel ways across the moral/nonmoral divide, then this would suggest that the feeling of respect (associated with an action in which we are interested) is incorporated into a maxim. Does Kant indicate at any point that the incorporation of the feeling of respect is the basis for the formation of moral maxims? In fact, Kant says precisely this in the *Religion:*

"This capacity for simple respect for the moral law within us would thus be moral feeling, which in and through itself does not constitute an end of the natural predisposition except so far as it is the motivating force [*Triebfeder*] of the will. Since this is possible only when *the free will incorporates such moral feeling into its maxim,* the property of such a will is good character" (Rel 6:28; emphasis added). A little later Kant repeats this point about respect by referring to the "subjective ground for the adoption into our maxims of this respect as a motivating force [*Triebfeder*]" (Rel 6:28). The complex feeling that is respect gets precisely the same treatment as nonmoral incentives—that is to say, it is incorporated or taken into principled action. These rarely discussed passages raise several difficult questions for those critics who argue that the feeling of respect does not move us to moral choice. If respect were a mere effect of moral choice, as some critics suggest, then why would Kant say that it is an incentive, or motivating force, incorporated into moral maxims? Furthermore, if Kant thinks, as some also maintain, that respect is part of a merely empirical account of action, then why does he say that a *free will* incorporates respect?[22] Finally, if respect motivates as a mere consciousness or recognition of the moral law, then why would Kant say that "the free will incorporates such moral *feeling* into its maxim"? Kant's claims clearly suggest that moral maxims guide and motivate action insofar as they carry a sensible force (i.e., the feeling of respect). The feeling of respect is incorporated into our moral maxims because it is in part a kind of pleasure that tends to maintain itself, and as a result of this incorporation our moral maxims contain a sensible force that makes them viable alternatives to nonmoral maxims.

It should be noted here before we move on that there is a difference between the two passages from the *Religion* just quoted. In one passage, Kant says that respect is incorporated into *a* maxim. In the other, he says that it is incorporated into maxims. This distinction reflects Kant's view (primarily expressed in the *Religion*) that each agent is faced with a fundamental life choice between morality and happiness. Kant understands this fundamental decision as a choice between two maxims. To choose the moral maxim is to make morality a condition for the choice of happiness, and to choose the happiness maxim is to make one's happiness the condition for acting morally. The distinction between incorporating respect into a single maxim and into many maxims can be explained in terms of a hierarchy of moral maxims. Respect is incorporated (through a deep choice) into a fundamental moral maxim which provides a basis for the formation of all subordinate moral maxims. This appears to be Kant's point in the following passage from the *Groundwork* (already partially quoted above): "Now as an act from duty wholly excludes the influence of inclination and therewith every object of the will, nothing remains which can determine the will objectively except law and subjectively except pure respect for this practical law. *This subjective element is the maxim that I should follow such a law even if it thwarts all my inclinations*" (G 4:400–1; emphasis added). Kant says that respect determines the will subjectively, but then he tells us that that which determines subjectively is a maxim. We can conclude from this (in view of the *Religion* passage) that respect is incorporated into the moral maxim that subjectively determines the will to choose subordinate moral maxims. The general moral maxim says, Follow the moral law even if it thwarts your inclinations. This moral maxim carries with it the sensible affect of the feeling of respect and provides a basis for the choice of all other subordinate moral maxims. The ethically committed agent approaches each moral situation equipped with this fundamental maxim, ready to form other dutiful subjective principles on the basis of it.

It seems, then, that all of the main elements present in the production of nonmoral maxims are also present in the production of moral maxims: the capacity for (moral) feeling, concrete and specific feelings of pleasure and pain, interests, and, finally, maxims. Casting Kant's scattered and incomplete comments on respect against the background of his account of nonmoral motivation has helped us to see these comments as part of a systematic understanding of moral motivation. Is there any reason, then, to doubt that Kant saw a fundamental parallel between moral and nonmoral action, such that respect is part of a representation with a pleasurable dimension that maintains itself through the choice of a moral maxim? In concluding, I want to consider and respond to one significant objection to this interpretation.

Acting from Duty

One of the main obstacles to accepting the idea that a kind of pleasure plays a role in causing moral action is Kant's well-known claim that moral actions are performed purely for the sake of duty. This claim seems to imply that moral actions have nothing to do with pleasure at all. So, for Kant, an action is properly moral when we act *from the motive* of duty, and not simply in accordance with duty but *from* some other source, such as pleasure. The important point for Kant is that pleasure does not act as the original motive or cause of moral action. In the *Groundwork,* Kant expresses this point in the following terms: "The first proposition of morality is that to have genuine moral worth, an action must be done from duty. The second proposition is: An action done from duty does not have its moral worth in the purpose which is to be achieved through it but in the maxim whereby it is determined" (G 4:399). If we choose an action because its maxim accords with duty, then our choice has moral worth. Again, the main point is that actions done from duty are actions that are not brought about in view of any anticipated pleasurable effects, but just in view of their status as dutiful actions. Moral interest, then, is an interest in the rightness of certain actions, and an action only has moral worth when it is performed from this interest.[23]

One of the complicating factors here is that, as we saw above, Kant sometimes speaks of a pleasure that is associated with the performance of moral actions—that is, a pleasure that results from acting morally. But even though in a number of places he associates a kind of pleasure with acting morally, he is, at times, very clear about differentiating his position from an eudaimonistic one. In the *Metaphysics,* he attacks the eudaimonists' insistence on connecting morality to happiness.

> When a thoughtful human being has overcome incentives to vice and is aware of having done his often bitter duty, he finds himself in a state that could well be called happiness, a state of contentment and peace of soul in which virtue is its own reward.—Now the *eudaimonist* says: this delight, this happiness is really his motive for acting virtuously. The concept of duty does not determine his will *directly;* he is moved to do his duty only *by means of* the happiness he anticipates.—But since he can expect this reward of virtue only from consciousness of having done his duty, it is clear that the latter must have come first, that is, he must find himself under obligation to do his duty before he thinks that happiness will result from his observance of duty and without thinking of it. A eudaimonist's *etiology* involves

him in a *circle;* that is to say, he can hope to be *happy* (or inwardly blessed) only if he is conscious of having fulfilled his duty, but he can be moved to fulfill his duty only if he foresees that he will be made happy by it.—But there is also a *contradiction* in this subtle reasoning. For on the one hand he ought to fulfill his duty without first asking what effect this will have on his happiness, and so on *moral* grounds; but on the other he can recognize that something is his duty only by whether he can count on gaining happiness by doing it, and so in accordance with a *pathological* principle, which is the direct opposite of the moral principle. (MM 6:377–78)

Kant thinks that the inconsistency or contradiction in the eudaimonist's position is that it seems to call for the agent to act *purely* on the basis of duty in order to be happy. But, since duty is defined in terms of happiness, there is no possibility of acting *purely* from duty. The eudaimonist contradicts himself insofar as his very conception of duty is informed by his notion of happiness. The contradiction arises from (a) implicitly treating duty as though it were separate from happiness, while at the same time (b) grounding duty in happiness. It appears, then, that Kant's criticism of the eudaimonist in this passage really amounts to the familiar one about the grounding of moral *standards* in our pathology. The result of this grounding is that all acts of duty are ultimately about pleasure or happiness.

The key to Kant's position is that pleasure is associated with the fulfillment of duty without being either the basis of moral standards or the point/end of moral actions. Now, the danger in my interpretation is that I have introduced pleasure into the account of how moral actions are motivated and have therefore heteronomized morality (i.e., made it the point of moral actions). How, the critic might ask, can pleasure play a role in motivating us without being aimed at? If one argues that pleasure is associated with acting morally and plays a role in moving us to moral action, then is one not committed to the position that pleasure is being aimed at in moral action? And, of course, if pleasure is aimed at, then the action is not properly moral for Kant.

I have argued on several occasions above that it is conceivable that an anticipatory pleasure moves the agent in the absence of any anticipation of pleasure. Now, in the posthumous writings example presented above, it is clear that pleasure is not anticipated because the agent in question will not be experiencing the relevant end. We do not anticipate any pleasure from admiring our posthumously published works because we will not live to see them. I argued above that such an anticipation of pleasure is not needed in Kant's system, because it is really the pleasure at the thought of an end (i.e., a pleasurable representation of some future object or action) that moves us by causing desires$_1$ that tend to maintain this pleasure. These desires$_1$ can maintain a feeling of pleasure just insofar as it is pleasurable to satisfy a desire$_1$. So, pleasure can move us without any anticipation of pleasure in the future just insofar as it creates a desire$_1$ the satisfaction of which is pleasurable.

However, in the moral context the situation is somewhat different from the writer example, since the agent *will* experience the end in question, and, moreover, the pleasure associated with this end. How, then, can we understand this pleasure as nonmotivational? Well, the pleasure that accompanies the performance of one's duty is nonmotivational if one only achieves this pleasure by actually acting from duty. Kant's position seems to be that unless one actually does something *because* it is one's duty, one will not experience the unique kind of self-contentment that he associates with acting morally. So, if moral pleasure in the performance of one's duty is aimed at, then it will not be felt. We can also think about this point in the following way. The moral feeling of respect includes a kind of pleasure at the thought of a self-determined action. To be self-determined is to be motivated by duty alone (since Kant thinks of inclinations as heteronomous forces). Thus, to act out of the feeling of respect is to act out of duty alone. It follows, then, that the notion of pleasure that is partly constitutive of Kant's concept of respect is a pleasure in acting for a certain reason: duty. In other words, the object of the representation—the subjective dimension of which is the feeling of respect—is a future *action that is done for the sake of duty.* And so, the very concept of respect precludes the possibility of being motivated by an anticipation of pleasure. Kant is explicit about the connection between acting from duty and the feeling of respect in the *Groundwork.* He defines duty there by saying, "Duty is the necessity to do an action from respect for law" (G 4:400). *Kant articulates the very notion of duty in terms of the feeling of respect.* In the second *Critique,* Kant draws the same connection when he distinguishes between acting in accordance with duty and from duty. "And thereon rests the distinction between consciousness of having acted according to duty and from duty, i.e., *from respect for the law*" (Pr. R 5:81; emphasis added). It follows, then, that for Kant acting from duty (or with duty as a reason) is *equivalent* to acting from respect. This can only be because one feels respect as a part of a representation if that representation is of an action done from duty.

So, the anticipatory pleasure that is a part of respect is a pleasure at the thought of acting from duty alone. This feeling maintains itself by determining the higher faculty of desire and causing a moral interest (or intellectual desire$_1$) in acting from duty alone. For Kant, this pleasure is maintained when we act on this interest, since, as we have just seen, acting from duty produces a feeling of self-contentment. This self-contentment is the unique feeling of pleasure that arises from satisfying a moral interest (i.e., desire$_1$). The crucial point here is that there is a difference between the reason we do something and the way in which this reason operates in sensible beings. We choose moral interests and maxims because it is our duty to do so, but the way in which these choices are made involves a feeling of respect. Our choices are made for the sake (or for reasons) of duty, but they are sensibly affected choices, and thus pleasure must be a part of the account of how they happen. When we choose a moral interest from duty we are at the same time acting from the feeling of respect.

The moral law prescribes dutiful actions, and we can either choose a maxim associated with one such action or not. If we choose such a maxim, then we do so either because of the effect of this action, or just because it is our duty. If the latter, then we have chosen to act from duty alone. But we have, at the same time, chosen to act from respect for the law, because this is the subjective dimension of the representation of an action from duty alone. If the representation of the action prescribed by the moral law had also been associated with some nonmoral pleasure and we had chosen a maxim recommending the same action on the basis of this pleasure, then we would have been acting in accordance with duty but not from duty. Notice, in either case—moral or nonmoral—a feeling of pleasure at the thought of an action is incorporated into a maxim. For Kant, there must be some feeling involved here because choosing is incorporating into a maxim and incorporating involves infusing rational principles with feelings. We can see, then, that the account of the feeling of respect as the moral incentive just articulates how the thought of duty actually functions as a motive for limited beings such as humans. When the agent decides upon the moral course of action, she acts from duty if the only feeling that she incorporates is the feeling that is part of the representation of acting on the moral law.

Respect involves a kind of pleasure at the thought of acting from duty alone, and thus the only way that an agent *can maintain this feeling is by actually acting from duty*. It is only if an agent's interest is in the rightness of an action that the feeling of respect can be taken into a maxim. Now, the feeling of respect affects this choice because it is part of a representation that includes pleasure, and thus that tends to maintain itself. So, in a sense, the feeling of respect provides a sensible push to choosing morally. However, we do not act *for the sake of* maintaining this pleasure, because the only way that the pleasure can be maintained is if we act for the sake of duty. So, in acting morally we do not consciously act toward any pleasure. The mechanism by which the thought of a dutiful action is interesting to us does not change the fact that we acted with duty in mind. The feeling of respect just allows the right maxim to be attractive to sensuously affected agents.

• •

REATH AND THE QUESTION OF MOTIVATION

In recent years, the debate about Kant's theory of moral motivation has been dominated by the argument that Kant eventually rejects his initial Humean prejudices about the requirements for the presence of a moral passion or feeling (of some sort) to move the agent. According to this interpretation, Kant champions the idea that our reason can move us without any affective help. This, in short, is how Kant's thesis on the capacity of pure reason to be practical has been read. I have tried to argue that this interpretation is not right. It is certainly true that Kant rejects the doctrine of the primacy of a moral feeling that characterizes the British moral sense theorist position, but it does not follow from this that he renders feeling merely epiphenomenal in the process of moral motivation. Such an interpretation exaggerates the role of reason in Kant's theory of action and does violence to the subtle way in which he attempts to reconcile the rational and the affective. I have tried to reconstruct Kant's thinking on this reconciliation (in both nonmoral and moral spheres) by starting on the affective side of the equation, and showing how Kant's account of rational and free action draws from and builds upon his treatment of desires$_1$ and feelings. In doing so, I developed a full-blown account of what it means to be sensuously affected in acting. This allowed me to throw new light on Kant's theory of moral motivation.

In making my argument, I have avoided focusing in depth on the tensions that exist between the recently dominant interpretation of Kant on moral motivation and my own view. But I will conclude now by taking a representative example of this pervasive position and showing how my treatment provides a corrective to the mistakes that it makes. Perhaps the most important of these mistakes involves driving a wedge between the

rational and the affective dimensions of the Kantian agent. I will argue in
section I that the presence of such a wedge in the interpretation of the
moral incentive of respect does not represent Kant's view.[1] I will go on
to contend in section II that this mistaken interpretation can be traced
to some deep assumptions about the possible theories of action that one
could use to read Kant.

I. REATH ON RESPECT

In his very influential 1989 paper, "Kant's Theory of Moral Sensibility:
Respect for the Moral Law and the Influence of Inclination," Andrews
Reath divides respect into an intellectual aspect and an affective aspect.[2]
He argues that, for Kant, it is the intellectual aspect that moves the agent,
and contends that the affective aspect of respect is the effect of this in-
tellectual aspect's moving the agent.

> The *feeling* of respect is an incentive only in an attenuated sense.
> It is indeed the inner state of a subject who is moved by the
> Moral Law, but the active motivating factor is always the recog-
> nition of the Moral Law. Thus the moral incentive, properly
> speaking, is what was distinguished above as the intellectual
> aspect of respect. The affective aspect is the experience of one's
> natural desires being held in check by the moral conscious-
> ness, and as such, an effect that occurs after, or in conjunction
> with, the determination of the will by the Moral Law. (Reath
> 1989b, 289)

Reath suggests (quite rightly) that the intellectual aspect of respect is the
recognition of the moral law. Kant refers to respect as a kind of consciousness of the moral law in a number of places throughout his works.
For example, in the second *Critique* he says, "The consciousness of a
free submission of the will to the law, combined with an inevitable constraint imposed only by our own reason on all inclinations, is respect for
the law" (Pr. R 5:80). As we saw numerous times in the previous chapter, Reath also has good grounds for saying that respect is, at least in
part, a feeling of some kind. So, even though Kant never says it directly

or explicitly, it is clear that Reath is right in saying that respect has these two sides: cognitive and conative.

More controversially, Reath claims that the mere recognition of the moral law is the "active motivating factor" in moral action. It is this recognition that "determines the will." The feeling aspect of the will is just an effect of this determination. Now, Reath is not altogether explicit on what it means to say that the recognition of the moral law "determines the will." At one point, he writes, "Respect for the Moral Law, in this sense, is the immediate recognition of its authority, or the direct determination of the will by the law. To be moved by, or to act out of, respect is to recognize the Moral Law as a source of value. . . . Respect is the attitude which it is appropriate to have towards a law, in which one acknowledges its authority and is motivated to act accordingly" (Reath 1989b, 287). At first, it appears that Reath is identifying the direct determination of the will by the law with the recognition of the *authority* of the law. It seems, then, that Reath is acknowledging that there is a distinction between the objective (i.e., legislative) and subjective (i.e., executive) determination of the will.[3] But the rest of the passage makes it clear that Reath thinks that determining the will also includes being "moved by" or "act[ing] out of" it. So, for Reath, determining the will includes (presumably as its final stage) choosing a maxim. The implication is that the recognition of the moral law is immediately followed (for the dutiful agent) by the choice to act morally. This means that for the dutiful agent the mere cognitive awareness of the right thing to do leads this agent to choose a moral maxim. Reath confirms the accuracy of this reading later in the article by saying that "in acting from respect, the simple recognition of an obligation determines or guides one's choice" (Reath 1989b, 290). Now, if the feeling of respect is an effect of the determination of the will so understood, it follows that on Reath's account the affective component of respect is the effect of a moral choice. Notice here that there is first the recognition, then the choice, and, finally, the feeling. Although Reath does not divide things in this way explicitly, he must implicitly allow for a distinction between the recognition of the moral law and the choice to act morally, since immoral people often recognize the moral law and yet do not act morally. When Reath says that the affective aspect of respect is "an effect that occurs after, or in conjunction with, the determination of the will by the Moral Law," what he must mean is that this affective aspect occurs after, or in conjunction with, the choice of a moral action.

In dividing the notion of respect in this way, Reath's reading is not faithful to Kant's thinking. For Kant, respect is a single and unified phenomenon. It is difficult to see how it remains single and unified if it is made up of a kind of recognition that *may or may not* lead to a feeling of some sort. Does the agent who recognizes what the moral law demands in a given context (as Kant suggests we always do[4]) and does not act morally only experience *half* of respect? Along the same lines, if the feeling dimension only follows a dutiful choice, then some people might never experience the *feeling* of respect. But everything Kant says on the subject indicates that he thinks that we all experience the *feeling* of respect just insofar as we are conscious of the moral law.

Moreover, Kant's thinking on the relationship between feelings and representations gives us a more plausible account of respect as a unified phenomenon. We first saw in chapter 2 that for Kant all representations have a feeling component or dimension; he calls our sensibility the "subjective aspect of our representations in general" (MM 6:212n). It seems far more likely, in view of this, that the affective dimension of respect is the subjective aspect of our representation of the moral law. So, respect is the consciousness of the power of the moral law, and this consciousness has an affective aspect that is made up of pleasant feelings of awe at our own autonomy, and painful feelings of humiliation at the subjection of our inclinations. There is evidence for this reading of respect as unified in the second *Critique,* when Kant says of respect, "But it is a feeling which is concerned only with the practical, and with the idea of a law simply as to its form and not on account of any object of the law; thus it cannot be reckoned either as enjoyment or pain, yet it produces an interest in obedience to the law" (Pr. R 5:80). Kant draws a direct connection here between a kind of feeling and the cognitive awareness of the law (i.e., "the idea of the law"). Kant also makes it clear that this combination of feeling and awareness produces moral interest, and thus must *precede* moral choice.

The source of the fractured way in which Reath reads respect appears to be his understanding of the notion of determining the will. Reath does not seem to place any great weight on the distinction that Kant draws between the subjective and objective determinations of the will.[5] I looked at this distinction in the introduction, but it is worth reminding the reader again of the role it plays in Kant's thinking. Here is a passage from that part of the second *Critique* upon which Reath otherwise draws heavily: "Thus the moral law, as a formal determining ground of action through practical pure reason, and moreover as a material though purely *objective determining ground of the objects of action (under the name of good and evil)*, is also a *subjective ground of determination*. That is, it is the incentive to this action, since it has an influence on the sensibility of the subject and *effects a feeling which promotes the influence of the law on the will*" (Pr. R 5:75; emphases added). Most of the key elements of my interpretation of respect as the moral incentive are contained in this passage. Kant says that the moral law is both an objective determining ground that tells us what is good and evil, and a subjective determining ground in causing a feeling that promotes our active pursuit of this law. Reath ignores this passage (and similar ones), and the result is that the two dimensions of respect are split asunder as the (intellectual) cause and (affective) effect of the unspecified "determination of the will" to which he refers. On my account, the two aspects of respect remain unified since both are the effects of the legislative (i.e., objective) determination of the will, and both are necessary for the subsequent executive (i.e., subjective) determination.

Reath implicitly acknowledges that his interpretation leaves the two parts of respect more divided than Kant wants them to be when he says, "Though the intellectual and affective aspects of respect at first seem quite different, Kant does not keep them apart" (Reath 1989b, 287). But, having divided the notion of respect as indicated above, Reath attempts to bring the parts back together again in the following passage:

> It turns out that there is a tight connection between these two aspects, due to certain facts about our nature, and this explains why Kant tends to treat them as identical. Our sensible nature is a source of motives that conflict with the moral disposition. . . . Kant thinks that these motives and tendencies are always present to some degree. Thus, whenever the Moral Law is effective, it must overcome contrary motives that originate in sensibility, and will thus produce some feeling. The determination of the will by Moral Law will always be accompanied by an affect.

Moreover, though distinguishable, these aspects of respect need not be phenomenologically distinct, but would be experienced together. (Reath 1989b, 289–90)

There are two distinct claims made here. First, Reath tells us that because we always have to overcome sensible opposition in acting morally, the affective component of respect (i.e., the humiliation of sensible motives) will always be present. Second, he goes on to say that the intellectual and affective aspects, though distinguishable, "would be experienced together." But there does not seem to be any connection between these two points: the argument for the former certainly does not give us any reason to accept the latter. In attempting to explain why Kant treats the two aspects of respect "as identical," Reath just explains why a certain kind of feeling always *follows* the recognition of the moral law (for an agent acting morally). He then simply claims that these two dimensions of respect "would be" experienced together. But, on his own account, there is no reason to think they would necessarily be experienced together at all. The intellectual aspect of respect is a consciousness of the moral law and the affective aspect is the byproduct of the choice to act morally. Thus, the two simply happen to follow one another in the case of a dutiful agent.

II. REATH AND THEORIES OF ACTION IN KANT

Let us now look a little deeper at Reath's argument and try to decipher the fundamental grounds of the difference between his reading of respect and my own. Reath's interpretation of Kant on the two aspects of respect and the notion of determining the will is above all else a product of his commitment to the idea that Kant could not have been suggesting that a moral *feeling* moves the will. This is really the heart of the issue. Reath reads any account that gives feeling a role in moving the agent as a moral sense theory, and he explains that "Kant is careful to make it clear that he is not adopting any sort of moral sense theory" (Reath 1989b, 288). Reath goes so far as to say that when Kant implies or suggests that a feeling moves the agent he is either being careless or inconsistent in his thinking. For example, he writes, "However, Kant's attempt to show how the feeling of respect can be an incentive is somewhat misleading. Strictly speaking, *he should not say* that this feeling is what weakens the influence of inclinations. Since, as we shall see, it is the experience one has when the inclinations are weakened by a superior motive, it presupposes that the inclinations have already been weakened" (Reath 1989b, 288; emphasis added). Reath struggles here to reconcile his interpretation with Kant's words. On my reading, Kant suggests that respect "weakens the influence of inclinations" because he believes that this feeling must play a role in making the decision to choose morally. Even a brief look at the evidence cited in chapter 5 above should convince the reader that relegating this feeling to something that happens *after* a choice has already been made renders an awful lot of what Kant says "somewhat misleading."

But why is Reath—to the point of arguing that Kant sometimes slips up—so opposed to the view that feeling plays a role in moving the agent? Given that he acknowledges that Kant sometimes suggests things to this effect, why does he not even consider the possibility that this suggestion accurately reflects Kant's position? The reason for this is implicit in the way Reath characterizes the view according to which feeling is effective. Referring to this view, he tells us, "Kant does not think the Moral Law determines the will through a quasi-mechanical or affective force" (Reath 1989b, 290). So, Reath equates being moved by an affective force with being moved quasi-mechanically. This interpretation makes up one of only two models of action that Reath entertains by way of reading Kant. On the one hand, incentives directly determine choice, and thus we are "mechanically" impelled to act on the basis of the strongest incentive (i.e., force). On the other hand, action is governed by a "principle of election" whereby we elect any incentive that is going to move us (i.e., Reath's version of the Incorporation Thesis). Reath puts this distinction in the following way:

> Moral motivation does not require, or occur through any feeling that exists independently of the moral consciousness. In addition, we saw that, while an affect is produced when the Moral Law determines the will, it is not this affect that motivates. The picture underlying these ideas is that, in acting from respect, the simple recognition of an obligation determines or guides one's choice. This is to be opposed to a model which would understand the

moral motive to operate by exerting a force on the will. More general grounds for this interpretation are supplied by Kant's conception of the freedom of the will. According to his "principle of election," an incentive never determines the will directly, but only through a choice made by the individual which can be expressed as the adoption of a maxim. This would seem to rule out the idea that the will is determined solely by the force that an incentive might have, or that actions should be understood as resulting from the balance of forces acting on the will. (Reath 1989b, 290)

So, respect cannot motivate as a feeling, because if it does, then an incentive is directly determining the will, and Kant argues that incentives only determine the will when they are elected or chosen.

But Reath's account begs the question as to why these are the only two possibilities for understanding action in Kant. Why is it not possible to propose that the feeling of respect motivates moral choice without appealing to a "balance of forces" model of agency? I have shown how both moral and nonmoral incentives *influence* choice through the exercise of an affective force. On my account, nonmoral actions are chosen because they promise more pleasure than their competitors, though the agent can always do otherwise than choose them on this basis. Moral actions are chosen because the thought of these actions is also connected with pleasure—though not in view of any expected pleasure. Instead, moral ends are associated with pleasure in virtue of our respect for the law. The association of pleasure with any end (moral or nonmoral) means that the thought of this end is a pleasurable representation (i.e., it has a pleasurable subjective dimension). Since, as per Kant's definition of pleasure, all pleasures tend to maintain themselves, it follows that the thought of such an end has motivational power. Now, even in the context of nonmoral actions this theory of motivation involves a rich conjunction of the rational and the affective, since the amount of pleasure that we experience upon thinking of an end depends to some extent on our conception of happiness and our understanding of the place of this end in this conception. Thus, the motivational power of any given representation is a function of both our sensibility and our understanding of happiness (and, indeed, means-ends relations). The choice of a moral or nonmoral end can, on this model, be a question of the most forceful or strongest feeling experienced—but it does not always have to be, because as we saw in chapter 3, the agent can always do otherwise than choose according to this strongest feeling.

In a sense, my account of moral motivation is an articulation of precisely what Kant means when he says that choices are *sensuously affected*. On the other hand, Reath's failure to consider this third possibility for understanding the role of feeling in action makes it difficult for him to deal with this notion of being sensuously affected. It is hard to see what place there is in Reath's account for the pathological weight of inclinations as they strike the individual.[6] At times, Reath does seem to suggest that there is some kind of role for feelings in motivation, but he does not go on to explore any specifics. At one point, he writes, "Kant can allow an incentive to have an affective force of some sort, but the role assigned to such force in motivation and the explanation of action must be limited so as to leave room for the notion of choice. Thus, we may think of respect for the law as one incentive in competition with others, against which it sometimes wins out. But rather than prevailing against its competitors by exerting the greater force on the will, its influence comes from providing a certain kind of reason for choice" (Reath 1989b, 290). Reath is right to say that Kant allows incentives some affective force and that the role of feeling must leave some room for choice. Unfortunately, he never elaborates on the nature of the affective force that incentives have. Moreover, it is not at all clear how his claims in the second part of this passage allow feeling any role in choosing actions at all.

One of the tough questions that Reath must face in light of this account is why any one particular action is chosen over another. What determines choice on Reath's account? Reath asks himself the same question and develops a surprising answer.

> How then do inclinations influence choice? Kant's view, I want to argue, is that one chooses to act on an incentive of any kind by regarding it as providing a sufficient reason for action, where that is a reason acceptable from the standpoint of others, not just that of the agent. Simply stated, inclinations influence choices by being regarded as sources of reasons which can be cited in some form to make your actions acceptable to others. . . . They must be viewed as reasons which would justify or explain the

action from a point of view which individuals other than the
agent can take up (e.g., the members of some community). Thus,
the interpretation proposed is that all choice occurs on quasi-
moral grounds, or proceeds from reasons that resemble moral
reasons in form. . . . Here the role of the maxim is to express
the reason for action in a form which can be assessed and cited
to others. (Reath 1989b, 296)

The key point here is that inclinations do not influence choice in view
of their pathological makeup. Instead, Reath argues that inclinations
influence choice when they are converted into reasons for action that
are acceptable to the "members of some community." Leaving aside
the problematic connection that Reath draws between this kind of test
for acceptability and Kant's moral test, this interpretation is difficult to
accept mainly because it does not get much in the way of support from
Kant's works. Perhaps more importantly, it leaves so much of what Kant
does say unexplained. For example, it does not address the issue of what
Kant means when he says that our choices are sensuously affected.[7] This
is not to say that on Kant's model (as I read it) the community is irrelevant when it comes to the influence our inclinations have on us. A case
could easily be made that the community influences our choices from inclinations by entering into the formation of our conception of happiness.
Kant would probably agree that we typically do not stray from social
norms in forming our conceptions of happiness—and thus in deciding
which inclinations are important and which are less so, or not at all. And,
as we saw in chapter 4, our conception of happiness affects our choices
by affecting the issue of whether or not we feel pleasure at the thought
of the object of any given inclination. Those ends that are seen as a
means to happiness are thereby associated with pleasure, while those that
are not seen as a means to happiness are not associated with pleasure.

Reath appears, then, to be importing a foreign understanding of how
actions are justified/motivated into his reading of Kant. Now, it might be
argued that Reath's account provides us with a more *plausible* understanding of how rational actions (moral and nonmoral) are justified and
motivated; this is an issue for a different debate. But I think that I have
shown in this study that Reath, and those scholars who follow him, have
not provided us with an authentically Kantian account of action.

NOTES

························

INTRODUCTION

1. Though I will not present a detailed survey of these varying interpretations, I will engage directly with some of them at various points in my study. In particular, I will focus in my conclusion on Andrews Reath's interpretation and supplement the argument of this book with a critique of his position. Other significant recent contributors to the ongoing controversy include Henry Allison, Lewis White Beck, Daniel Guevara, Paul Guyer, Larry Herrera, A. Murray MacBeath, Richard McCarty, Josefine Nauckhoff, A. T. Nuyen, Onora O'Neill, H. J. Paton, Nancy Sherman, Robert Wolff, and Allen Wood. Part of the reason for the volume and diversity of interpretations of Kant's theory of moral motivation is that this theory actually gives rise to a cluster of closely related but distinct issues, not all of which are discussed here. For example, I will not take up the question of Kant's overdetermination of the moral motive. Does Kant, by positing a moral motive that is wholly distinct from any inclination to moral action, overdetermine and therefore problematize moral motivation? Can an act that is accompanied by an inclination or desire that is sufficient to cause this act also be done from the motive of duty? For excellent discussions of these issues, see Herman 1993, 1–22, and Guevara 2000, 9–48.

2. As many have noted, Kant does not use the term "pathological" to denote something diseased. "Pathological" comes from the Greek *pathos,* and refers neutrally to the feeling dimension of the human psyche.

3. For two succinct but quite comprehensive surveys of this debate, see Herrera 2000 and Nauckhoff 2003.

4. The main proponents of this view and the variations thereof include Henry Allison, Paul Guyer, Christine Korsgaard, A. Murray MacBeath, Onora O'Neill, and Andrews Reath.

5. The primary defenders of this position are Larry Herrera, Richard McCarty, Josefine Nauckhoff, and A. T. Nuyen.

6. Lewis White Beck first makes this argument. See Beck 1960, 221–22.

7. See *Lectures on Metaphysics* 28:228.

8. See, for example, Herrera 2000; Nauckhoff 2003; McCarty 1993; Nuyen 1991.

9. Of course, this applies to the alternative interpretation as well. Neither side has adequately reconstructed Kant's theory of moral action.

10. To my knowledge, there is no fully worked out account of respect along these lines. Daniel Guevara, however, has suggested this as a possibility in correspondence with the author.

11. It is in part for this reason that I postpone looking closely at any of the current interpretations of Kant on moral motivation until the conclusion. Most of these readings take a direct approach but present only part of the evidence and ignore, or explain away, the rest.

12. Guevara (2000) develops this reading.

13. It is "*somehow*" caused because the moral law is nonsensible (noumenal) and the feeling of respect is sensible, and thus applying the concept of causality to this connection is problematic. The question of how, or whether, there is a causal relation between noumena and phenomena has been a source of disagreement among Kant scholars. For an interesting discussion of this issue, see Westphal 1997.

14. Herrera (2000) discusses this position and Reath's objections to it.

15. It is a "purported" hedonism because some scholars—such as Reath, Allison, and Korsgaard—contend that Kant is not a hedonist at all.

16. This is a division that Kant inherited both from the ethical thinking of his time and from the curricular division of philosophy within German universities. There is some debate about Kant's shifting understanding of this division from the mid-1780s to the 1790s, particularly concerning the nature of the division between a "metaphysics of morals" and "practical anthropology." In the *Groundwork* (1785), Kant indicates that the former has no empirical dimension, but simply involves the a priori deduction of duties (after the groundwork for this deduction is laid through the positing of the first principle of morality). But in the *Metaphysics* (1797), Kant seems to introduce empirical considerations into the deduction of duties. For a discussion of this issue, see Wood 1999, 193–96.

17. For a useful account of Kant's distinctions among anthropology, moral anthropology, and pragmatic anthropology, see Frierson 2003, 48–51. Roughly speaking, Frierson tells us that anthropology is the study of human beings as empirical beings, moral anthropology studies the empirical conditions that aid in promoting morality, and pragmatic anthropology includes moral anthropology and is simply the study of human beings with some practical purpose or application in mind. I think that this way of thinking about the divisions is correct, though I do not think that Kant is either consistent in applying these distinctions or clear about how the various parts of anthropology relate. I will return to this issue.

18. See *Critique of Practical Reason* 5:39.

19. I am thinking, in particular, of Frierson 2003, Grenberg 2001, Louden 2000, Munzel 1999, Sullivan 1995, Sussman 2001, Wilson 1997, and Wood 1991.

20. See Stark 1997, 15–37. According to Stark, Kant lectured twenty-four times on anthropology between 1772 and 1796. He published his

manual for this course in 1798 as *Anthropology from a Pragmatic Point of View.*

21. For a more thorough discussion of this question and some slightly different explanations, see Louden 2000, 6–7. Louden suggests, for example, that lack of interest in Kant's empirical ethics can be traced to the fact that he never finished a systematic treatment of this subject.

22. See, for example, Solomon and Higgins 1991.

23. See *Critique of Pure Reason* A 533/B 561.

24. Frierson distinguishes between two manifestations of this question. First, there is the general question of how the world of causally determined events can have anything to do with Kant's transcendentally free agent. Frierson focuses on the second, more specific question of how empirical lessons might be relevant to moral improvement without the will being causally influenced by these lessons. See Frierson 2003, 1–6.

25. In general, I will use the notes taken on Kant's lectures (*Lectures on Ethics, Lectures on Metaphysics,* and *Lectures on Anthropology*) to either support or elaborate on ideas found in the published texts. I *start* my account here with a passage from Kant's *Lectures on Ethics* because (as I will argue) this passage provides a useful key to understanding (and elaborating on) Kant's somewhat vague published references to anthropology as the study of the "helping and hindering" effects of human psychology on morality.

26. I should note, however, that I share Louden's concern that in his actual anthropological writings Kant never discusses explicitly and directly "what in [his] practical philosophy texts [he calls] 'moral anthropology' . . . showing how this . . . empirical part of ethics relates . . . to the non-empirical" (Louden 2003, 62). Thus, I am not making the claim that Kant's anthropology systematically pursues the task that he set out for it. I will argue, however, that we can take Kant's central anthropological discussions and apply them to the question of how the moral law functions. (I also return to the various classifications of anthropology below.)

27. See *Metaphysics* 6:408. Or, to take another example, Kant discusses "egoism" as a hindrance to morality in both the *Anthropology* 7:128–31, and the *Lectures on Anthropology* 25:735, 859–61, 1215–20.

28. Moral anthropology is part of practical education. As Kant writes in the *Education,* "Practical or moral training is that which teaches a man how to live as a free being. (We call anything 'practical' which has reference to freedom)" (E 9:455).

29. It should be noted at this point that in his *Logic* Kant presents a distinct method of classifying knowledge, which he refers to as the "world concept [*Weltbegriff*]" (L 9:24). According to this concept of the sciences, philosophy is not classified in terms of its source or the objects it studies but in terms of its purpose: it is the science that aims at the "ultimate ends of human reason" (L 9:24). He explains that philosophy is the science that

relates "all cognition and every use of reason to the ultimate end of human reason" (L 9:24). In other words, philosophy is that discipline the practical goal of which is the institutionalization of the ends of reason in life. With this in mind, Kant writes:

> The field of philosophy in this cosmopolitan meaning may be summed up in the following questions:
>
> 1. What can I know?
> 2. What ought I to do?
> 3. What may I hope?
> 4. What is man?
>
> The first question is answered by metaphysics, the second by morality, the third by religion, and the fourth by anthropology. At bottom all this could be reckoned to be anthropology, because the first three questions are related to the last. (L 9:25)

On this understanding, anthropology addresses the question of what man is and thus subsumes the other disciplines insofar as our knowledge, morals, and hopes are all expressions of the kind of creatures that we are. Thus, anthropology includes within itself the study of all that man knows, is, ought to be, and hopes to be. Surely such a study conceives of man as a free being.

30. Louden agrees, contending that Kant does not stick to this distinction in a systematic way. See Louden 2000, 72.

31. Wood makes much of this role of freedom in Kant's anthropology. He tells us here that Kant's philosophy in general might lead one to anticipate that his empirical study of humans would exclude "freedom altogether and [treat] human behavior as merely a part of the mechanism of nature" (Wood 1999, 180). But, as the passage just quoted above shows, Wood does not think that Kant's anthropology satisfies this expectation. Wood elaborates in a later work, writing, "Although Kant never pretends to seek or find empirical proofs of human freedom, his empirical anthropology always proceeds on the fundamental presupposition that human beings are free, and throughout it interprets the empirical observations it makes on the basis of this presupposition" (Wood 2003, 44). My position is very much in line with Wood's. For a reading of Kant's critique of determinism in empirical psychology, see Westphal 1995. On the other hand, in his unpublished manuscript "Kant's Empirical Account of Human Action," Patrick Frierson argues that Kant's empirical psychology is thoroughly deterministic.

32. See also *Lectures on Metaphysics* 28:269 where Kant repeats the very same idea. For Kant, practical freedom is distinct from transcendental freedom. I will return to this distinction in greater detail in chapter 3.

33. Of course, it is not my intention to suggest that Kant's anthropological studies are restricted *solely* to the investigation of human psychology and

the problems that this psychology creates for the promotion of morality. Wood (1999) argues that Kant's conception of anthropology is initially identical to empirical psychology but expands in the 1770s to include all of the various issues discussed in the *Anthropology*. Clearly, Kant's moral anthropology also includes the study of the social, racial, and educational factors relevant to morality. One of Kant's favorite examples of such a social factor is "polite society." (See the *Anthropology* 7:151–53, and *Lectures on Anthropology* 25:930–31. See also Frierson 2003, 57–58.) He argues that polite society is an important social tool in the development of a moral will. His argument seems to be that politeness, insofar as it often requires us to deny inappropriate urges or impulses, allows us to identify and even cultivate our capacity for self-mastery. Notice here, however, that politeness only has an effect on morality through the psychological effect of enhancing self-mastery. In order to grasp the effects of politeness, then, we must understand the psychology of self-mastery and how this psychology relates to moral actions. Furthermore, even a brief analysis of Kant's discussions of education indicates that they, too, hinge upon an understanding of the psychology of children and the need to mold this psychology in a certain way. These examples suggest that what is perhaps *most essential* in moral anthropology is the psychology of the agent and the bearing of this psychology on the agent's morality.

34. *Lectures on Anthropology*, 25:1211 (translation from Louden 2000, 73).

35. Louden presents a fourfold breakdown of the "bridging effort" that empirical ethics makes between nature and freedom. These are all ways in which the study of anthropology is relevant for Kant's ethics. Thus, empirical ethics (a) provides psychological knowledge of human nature that is important for understanding how the moral law can be applied, (b) helps "to prepare human beings for a sovereignty in which reason alone shall have authority" (CJ 5:433), (c) provides the knowledge necessary to develop a successful approach to ethical education, and (d) provides a long-term orientation for action by highlighting the path of moral progress. See Louden 2003, 25–26.

36. See also the second *Critique* 5:72.

37. Jacobs (2003) presents the intriguing view that Kant's concept of character provides us with a conjunction of the empirical and the intelligible. "If pragmatic anthropology oscillates between physiological and practical perspectives, and between a doctrine of prudence and applied morals, then it is in the concept of character that Kant will eventually attempt to find unity and locate, in an 'absolute' form, the meeting place of the empirical and intelligible characters" (119). Character reveals "both the basic psychological constitution of a person and the unmistakable traces of an intelligibly autonomous self" (120). Jacobs charts the development of this notion of character through Kant's lectures on anthropology. I will not explore this concept further here,

but I think that it may provide an interesting way of developing some of the thoughts that are laid out in what follows.

38. This is where my account differs most obviously from those such as Korsgaard's. An unfortunate consequence of her position is that, qua noumenal, the practical standpoint de-prioritizes knowledge to such an extent that free action is virtually unknowable. But Kant does not seem to treat practically free action in this way. The phenomenal/noumenal distinction, then, differs from the practical/theoretical distinction (as I understand it) insofar as we cannot say anything about Kant's noumenal realm, but we can (and Kant does) say many things about the practical.

39. "Given Kant's argument in the analogies, this means that we could not speak meaningfully of something happening in or to this agent or of its being determined by antecedent conditions" (Allison 1990, 30).

40. Kant draws close links between the practical use of reason and the intelligible world throughout his ethical writings because the former grounds our cognition of, and commitment to, the latter. In these discussions, Kant always links the practical with the intelligible and the theoretical with the sensible. But the intelligible, according to this division, is associated with the moral law, or the capacity to be absolutely self-determining. In other words, the intelligible is linked to the rationality of a purely rational being. But insofar as the practical standpoint applies to us as imperfectly rational, it includes both the intelligible and sensible. See, for example, the second *Critique* 5:105. For a contrary reading, see Allison 1990, 36–41.

41. It is here that my account differs most noticeably from Frierson's. Earlier I noted that Frierson—along with some early critics—is concerned with how anthropology can be relevant to morality in view of transcendental freedom. My response, upon which I will elaborate in chapter 3, is that anthropology is relevant to moral actions understood as an expression of practical, and not transcendental, freedom.

42. This notion is picked up on and developed in Kant's famous account of autonomy as that "property of [the will] by which it is a law to itself independent of every property of the objects of its volition" (G 4:440). This notion of autonomy is not undermined by anything that I say concerning practical freedom.

43. See, for example, *Religion within the Limits of Reason Alone* 6:21, where Kant discusses the inscrutability of our deepest choices of maxims. This is essentially the inscrutability of human agency as spontaneous first cause. There is obviously much more to be said here and I will return to this issue in chapter 3.

44. Ultimately, Kant also talks about our reason as a faculty of desire, and thus he distinguishes between a higher and lower faculty of desire. I will return to these issues in chapters 1 and 4. For now, I am talking about the faculty of desire insofar as it is independent of our rationality (i.e., the lower faculty of desire).

45. Jeanine Grenberg (2001) and George Schrader (1976) provide two noteworthy contributions in this area.

46. Kant comes closest to such an identification when he refers to a feeling (such as the feeling of love) as an inclination. I will return to this conflation in a note in the next chapter.

47. See Allison 1990, 5.

48. Gerold Prauss (1983) argues that Kant's practical philosophy fails because he does not have a sufficiently worked out theory of action upon which to ground his ethical thinking. In this study, I am attempting to reconstruct some of the essential elements of just such a theory.

CHAPTER I

1. See Grenberg 2001. The increased interest to which Grenberg refers includes both attempts to clarify Allison's interpretation and what follows from it, and negative reactions against certain dimensions of his view. Grenberg's account is very much in the first vein, while McCarty (1994) and Herrera (2000) react critically to a number of Allison's arguments.

2. In Allison 1990, for example, there is no sustained analysis of inclinations, passions, affects, or instincts, even though Part II of this book is called "Moral Agency and Moral Psychology." Moreover, even though the Incorporation Thesis is the centerpiece of his argument, and this thesis is essentially a claim about the incorporation of *incentives,* the notion of an incentive itself is only briefly addressed about halfway through the text (see 121). The Incorporation Thesis facilitates this lack of focus on the agent's psychology just insofar as maxims are treated as rational *translations* of the various forces that go to make up this psychology—and Allison is, so to speak, more interested in the translation than in the original. The distinction that Allison draws between the end or object of an action and the ground or reason for adopting that end is telling in this context. He says about this distinction:

> The same distinction, which is rooted in the Incorporation Thesis, also enables us to understand Kant's connection of heteronomy with the principle of happiness or self-love. As Reath has likewise noted, what is crucial here is that this is the principle on which heteronomous agents act and . . . not the end or object of their action. To say that it is the principle on which heteronomous agents act, or in Kant's terms, the "determining ground of the will," is to say that it provides the ultimate norm or criterion governing choice. In other words, Kant's central claim . . . is that all heteronomous theories are committed to a model of choice or deliberation in which the maximization of satisfaction (however that be construed) is the standard in terms of which specific maxims or courses of action are to be judged. (103)

Allison never returns to the question of how the maximization of satisfaction *should* be construed. It appears, then, that the analysis of heteronomy in terms of principles and not ends allows him to ignore the details of desiring and feeling. Allison does not make any argument to this effect, but this seems to account in part for his failure to pay attention to what Kant calls our pathology.

3. The division that I am drawing here between pathology and reason is not quite the same as the distinction drawn in the Introduction between empirical and a priori ethics. The main reason for this is that the latter is a division within *ethics*, while in this chapter I am using the former distinction in a discussion that is restricted to the nonmoral realm.

4. Similarly, in the second *Critique*, Kant writes, "The faculty of desire is the faculty such a being has of causing, through its ideas, the reality of the objects of these ideas" (Pr. R 5:9n).

5. Presumably, an agent can bring things into existence in a variety of ways—through constructing, moving, grasping, pouring, studying, writing, etc.

6. For a discussion of the merits of phenomenological—as opposed to nonphenomenological—accounts of desire, see Smith 1994, 105.

7. Although I do not have the space to address this issue here, I do acknowledge that in the contemporary literature even this much is controversial as an analysis of our reasons for acting. See, for example, Bittner 2001 for an attack on the desire/belief account of reasons for acting.

8. The power to bring something about does not mean that we will always be successful in bringing this thing about. In other words, we do not always get what we have the power to get (i.e., what we desire). But we would not even conceive of trying to get something unless we possessed the deep assumption that we can produce things.

9. Kant uses the Latin term *nisus* here and thereby points to the influence of the Stoics on this part of his thinking. For more on Kant and the Stoics, see Seidler 1981.

10. Kant also makes it clear in the *Metaphysics* that a wish is a determination of the faculty of desire and thus a desire$_1$. He tells us that if the faculty of desire "is not joined with this consciousness [of the ability to bring about its object] its act is called a wish" (MM 6:213).

11. For some of the best discussions of the distinction between *Wille* and *Willkür*, see Allison 1990, 129–36; Beck 1960, 177–81; and Meerbote 1984, 69–89.

12. So, for example, even in the First Book of the *Religion*—where Kant does draw some distinctions between inclinations, instincts, emotions, and passions—he continues to refer to inclinations in the most general sense. See the *Religion* 6:27, and 35.

13. This kind of classification of inclination can be better understood if we consider that Kant's point in this passage is to distinguish inclination from

interest (a distinction to which I will return). Interest is the dependence of the will on reason. I will return to the issue of the determination of the faculty of desire by sensation in the next chapter.

14. Allison does acknowledge the presence of this more narrow conception of inclination, but he tends to emphasize the broader notion.

15. I will translate "*Affekt*" as "affect," rather than as "emotion," throughout this work. In the third *Critique* 5:272–73, Kant distinguishes between emotions generally (*Rührungen*) and affects (*Affekten*), with the latter being more violent.

16. Kant also distinguishes between inclination and fear in the *Groundwork* 4:401n. This distinction seems to chart a basic division between being attracted to, and repulsed by, various things.

17. In writing of instincts, Kant has the impulses toward food, shelter, and procreation in mind. Interestingly, though, Kant regards the impulse to self-preservation as an inclination and not as an instinct. In the *Groundwork* 4:397, he tells us that "everyone has a direct inclination" to self-preservation. But is our urge to survive not on the same level as our instincts for food, shelter, and procreation? After all, it could easily be argued that one does not need to experience any pleasure in life in order to want to maintain one's existence, just as one does not need to experience the pleasure of food in order to want it. Of course, Kant could be using "inclination" in the broad sense. In this case, instincts are inclinations that do not require an experience of pleasure in order to come into existence. On the other hand, the use of "inclination" in the narrow sense is actually defensible in this context. Kant could argue that it is impossible to feel no pleasure in life. Alternatively, he could respond that a being that has experienced a life of uninterrupted pain will not have an urge to self-preservation. Either way, Kant's classification of self-preservation as an inclination is at least defensible.

18. Kant's description of inclinations as insistent (*beharrlichen*)—and earlier in the *Metaphysics* (6:408) as lasting (*bleibenden*)—should not be taken to denote that there are short-term, or nonlasting, inclinations. Instead, and this is especially clear from the context in the *Metaphysics* 6:408, Kant is just emphasizing a feature of inclinations—namely, that they are long-lasting.

19. Another possibility is that the *Religion* passage refers to inclinations in the broader sense. This may not work, though, because if the broader sense includes the narrow sense (which it must), then the theory of inclination formation in the *Religion* passage should include the one expressed in the *Metaphysics* passage.

20. Kant is influenced here by the Stoics, who believe that responsibility for allowing passions to take over lies with the agent.

21. For now, let us understand Kant's principle of happiness to be the satisfaction of a coherent system of our inclinations. I will return to this notion at some length in chapter 4.

22. This passage raises a question about Kant's consistency in employing his psychological distinctions. Kant tells us here that the sexual impulse is a passion, while in the *Religion* passage that we looked at earlier in this section it is referred to as an instinct. It may be possible to resolve this difficulty by considering the following passage from the *Metaphysics:* "Sexual inclination is also called 'love' (in the narrowest sense of the word) and is, in fact, the strongest possible sensible pleasure [*Sinnenlust*] in an object. It is not merely sensitive pleasure, as in objects that are pleasing in mere reflection on them (receptivity to which is called taste). It is rather pleasure from the enjoyment of another person, which therefore belongs to the *faculty of desire* and indeed, to its highest stage, passion" (MM 6:426). The explicit connection between this passage and the one from the *Anthropology* shows that Kant does have some consistent conception of sexual love in mind. When Kant talks of the sexual impulse as an *instinct* in the *Religion* he is referring to the basic reproductive urge, as opposed to the desire to use another person's body for one's sexual pleasure. It is to this latter tendency that he is referring in both the *Anthropology* and the *Metaphysics*. This interpretation is supported if one considers that in the same section of the *Religion* Kant directly associates the sexual impulse with reproduction when he writes that mankind has a predisposition toward "the propagation of the species, through the sexual impulse, and for the care of the offspring so begotten" (Rel 6:27). So, Kant thinks that the sexual urge to reproduce is an instinct, while the urge to take pleasure from sex with another person is a passion (and thus an inclination).

But, we might ask, to what does a distinction such as this really amount? In other words, what psychological basis, if any, does Kant have for drawing this distinction? His point cannot be that we are not born seeking to use another's body for pleasure, since we are not born wanting to reproduce either. The crux of the distinction is that without an initial experience of pleasure with another, the sexual passion would not be formed. Kant does not think that this is true of the urge to reproduce. In actual fact, Kant's classification makes a lot of sense if one considers cases in which an initial experience of sex is not pleasurable. Consider the victim of a sexual assault. Studies have shown that individuals whose first sexual experiences are negative in this way can have difficulty in forming (what are considered) normal sexual desires (see Lisak 1994). But these same individuals' desire to reproduce is, typically, not affected by this experience. Kant's insight is, perhaps, further supported by the plausibility of the idea that people often do not initially have sex for pleasure out of a passion for this sex, but rather out of social pressure or curiosity or any number of social influences. The passion is properly generated only when the experience is found to be pleasant.

23. For a more comprehensive account of the passions, see Wood 1999, 250–82.

24. See Wood 1991, 328–35, for an excellent discussion of the connection between Kant's anthropology and his theory of history.

25. See Wood 1991 for more on Kant's notion of "unsociable sociability."

26. The social passion of ambition connects with Kant's notion of self-conceit (*Eigendünkel*). Self-conceit is essentially a desire for esteem in the eyes of others; it is ordinary self-love and egoism gone awry. In order to get this esteem from others, we have to be better than these others or, when this fails, to manipulate them into believing that we are superior to them. For more on Kant's notion of self-conceit see the second *Critique* 5:74.

27. See Beck 1960, 93.

28. See *Lectures on Metaphysics* 28:245.

29. See also *Metaphysics* 6:449–52.

30. I will address this development in more detail in the next chapter. See Zuckert 2002.

31. Although I will argue in the next chapter that for Kant all desires$_1$ are aimed at pleasure, it should be noted that the fact that feelings of pleasure or pain play a role in the origins of inclinations tells us nothing about whether these feelings are also the object of inclinations. See Reath 1989a, 47–48, for some examples of how pleasure might function as the origin but not object of an inclination.

32. I will return to this in chapters 2 and 4. Even though Kant distinguishes between feeling and desire/inclination, he is not rigid about drawing this distinction at all times. Kant defines love as a feeling, saying that it is a "pleasure joined immediately to the representation of an object's existence" (MM 6:402). After drawing the distinction between feeling love and acting in a loving way, Kant goes on to say, "To do good to other human beings insofar as we can is a duty, whether one loves them or not" (MM 6:402). The implication here is that feelings of love can lead us to perform benevolent actions, but that even if this feeling is not present we still have a duty to act benevolently. Kant says, "Love is a matter of feeling, not of *willing*, and I cannot love because I *will* to, still less because I *ought* to (I cannot be constrained to love); so a duty to love is an absurdity. But benevolence, as conduct, can be subject to a law of duty" (MM 6:401–2). Now, in the second *Critique*, Kant makes the same point, except that he tells us that love qua *inclination* cannot be a duty. He writes, "The possibility of such a command as, 'Love God above all and thy neighbor as thyself,' agrees very well with this. For as a command, it requires respect for a law which orders love and does not leave it to arbitrary choice to make love the principle. But love to God as inclination (pathological love) is impossible, for He is not an object of the senses. The latter is indeed possible toward men, but it cannot be commanded, for it is not possible for man to love someone merely on command" (Pr. R 5:83). Similarly, in the *Groundwork*, Kant draws a distinction between practical love (i.e., performing

love-related acts out of duty) and pathological love, and says of the latter that "love as an inclination cannot be commanded" (G 4:399). The *relevant* contrast in these passages is between acting in a loving way, and the feeling of or inclination to love. Kant is clearly making the same point in all three texts, *but classifying love differently.* I think that this classificatory looseness is a product of the closeness of the relation that Kant sees between feeling and inclination.

33. Kant also distinguishes the two on the basis of their phenomenology: "Emotion is like an intoxicant which can be slept off; passion is to be regarded as an insanity which broods over an idea that is imbedding itself deeper and deeper" (A 7:253). Thus, emotions are more fleeting than passions, which tend (as inclinations) to be drawn out and obsessive.

34. This fits quite well with Kant's Rousseauian account of the origins of social passions. See Wood 1991.

CHAPTER 2

1. I will return to this "misconception" of nonmoral freedom in Kant in the next chapter.

2. The relationship between the Incorporation Thesis and the objection to a hedonistic reading of Kant is a complex one. I will return to this question in chapter 4.

3. See Beck 1984, Irwin 1984, and Wood 1984. For another treatment of psychological hedonism in Kant, see Phillips Griffiths 1991.

4. According to Reath (1989a), Kant thinks that pleasure is either the cause of desire or the principle governing our choice of actions—it is never the object of desire. I am focusing on the first of these claims. According to the second claim, pleasure is the result of the satisfaction of desires, and thus to say that pleasure provides a principle or criterion governing choice is really just to say that the *satisfaction of desires* provides a principle or criterion governing choice. I will return to this understanding of pleasure in a different context below, but for now it is sufficient to point out that Reath's analysis simply ignores all of those cases in which Kant refers to pleasure as an object aimed at or desired. Christine Korsgaard holds a position similar to Allison's and Reath's in "Kant's Analysis of Obligation: The Argument of *Groundwork* I" and "Kant's Formula of Humanity" (both in Korsgaard 1996). She also argues that pleasure is not an object of action but a principle governing choice. However, she does acknowledge in "Kant's Formula of Humanity" that, in places in the second *Critique,* Kant seems committed to "a more conventional sort of hedonism" (131n2).

5. Again, I will postpone discussing the question of the rationality of agency until chapters 3 and 4. Notice here, I am not arguing that hedonism is the *right* theory of motivation, but just that it is Kant's theory.

6. There is more to be said on the relationship between interests and desires, but because I am just focusing on desire formation I will not explore this issue further here. I will turn to this relationship in chapter 4.

7. This is evidence that Reath does not address in his paper.

8. In the case of moral actions, the practical law (i.e., the categorical imperative) determines the agent's conception of the good.

9. I am, of course, excluding critics such as Reath, Korsgaard, and Allison from this characterization.

10. See Beck 1960, Irwin 1984, Meerbote 1984, and Wood 1984.

11. Other commentators seem to be aware of the distinction between the various roles that Kant assigns to pleasure in the formation of desires, but do not pause to give this distinction any consideration. For example, Wood (1984) argues that for Kant all desires aim at pleasure. However, in Wood 1999, he focuses more on the role of the experience of pleasure in the formation of desires. He never discusses the relationship between these two roles. To take another case, Paul Guyer in trying to clarify the distinction between pleasure and interest writes, "This suggests that even if an interest is founded on *pleasure or the expectation of pleasure,* it cannot be equated with such a feeling of delight" (Guyer 1993, 163; emphasis added). Guyer does not appear to see any point of contention here, such that it almost seems as though he *identifies* the experience of pleasure with the expectation of pleasure. Similarly, in his essay "Kant on Desire and Moral Pleasure," Mark Packer slides between two uses of pleasure without explicitly noting any distinction. Notice, for example, the ambiguity in the following passage:

> What is morally significant about Kant's understanding of inclination is not merely its origin in the natural and causal (instead of the purely rational) domain of human existence; rather, when inclination is the motive to action, *the thought of the pleasurable object or experience* precedes and conditions the relevant desire and the ensuing conduct. But this order obtains only when it is inclination that is the sole motive to action. There are other cases where the order of this relation will be reversed, so that a *pleasurable experience follows from, rather than precedes* desire's engagement with an object or event. This will occur when an agent intends to perform a task successfully, for example, solving a problem in mathematics, and only after the achievement of the goal feels contentment with a job well done. (Packer 1989, 434; emphases added)

In the middle of making this useful distinction between an anticipation of pleasure as a motive force and pleasure as a consequence, Packer makes a subtle and, ultimately, unexplained move. The implication of the last sentence quoted is that in the case of inclination a pleasurable *experience* precedes desire. But this is not what Packer had said earlier when he referred to the "*thought of* the pleasurable object or experience" preceding desire. He never explains the mysterious move to the second formulation.

12. See my discussion of the faculty of desire in chapter 1.

13. These considerations arise in large part out of a response to an earlier version of this chapter by Patrick Frierson at the APA Central Division meeting in Chicago, 2004.

14. See, for example, the *Lectures on Metaphysics* 29:880.

15. In chapter 1 we saw that maxims play a role in the formation of passions. On this account, then, it is not just an idea but rather a full-fledged principle that is involved in the formation of a desire$_1$.

16. It is possible to have an anticipation of pleasure based on someone else's recommendation. For example, a friend might tell you that a film is good. If you trust her opinion, you might have an anticipation of pleasure at the thought of watching it, and consequently form a desire to see it.

17. In a lecture from 1784–85, Kant speaks of "satisfying your inclinations and taste for pleasure" (LE 27:276). I think that the fact that there is a distinction drawn between the satisfaction of inclinations and the taste for pleasure provides further evidence for my hedonistic interpretation. See note 4 above.

18. Far from it being a superfluous pleasure, Kant actually thinks that anticipatory pleasure is the strongest and most effective pleasure that we feel. See Meld Shell 2003, esp. 218.

19. This is how Kant treats them in the second *Critique* 5:9n, when he defines the two notions together.

20. Kant first introduces the notion of a pleasure at the thought of an object in the second *Critique*. It is in this work that he is beginning to shift toward his mature understanding of pleasure.

21. This, incidentally, seems to be the emerging conceptual background that informs Kant when he tells us in the second *Critique* 5:22 that happiness is a life of *uninterrupted (ununterbrochen)* pleasure.

22. See the second *Critique* 5:72, 5:74, and 5:75, as well as the *Metaphysics* 6:211.

23. For more on the relationship between pleasure and pain in Kant, see Meld Shell 2003.

CHAPTER 3

1. The following well-known commentators suggest this interpretation in (at least) these works: Potter 1974, Wood 1984, Korsgaard 1996, Ginsborg 1998, Engstrom 2002. (However, Korsgaard takes back any such suggestion in Korsgaard 1998.)

2. Nelson Potter argues for this most clearly in Potter 1974. His argument (strongly echoed in Wood 1984) is a response to the classic criticism

of Kant's theory of freedom, first leveled by Carl Reinhold and later associated with Henry Sidgwick. Reinhold and Sidgwick argue that Kant requires two concepts of freedom: a "good" freedom (i.e., the freedom to act morally) and a "neutral" freedom (i.e., the freedom that allows us to choose between morality and immorality). They maintain that Kant *unwittingly* uses freedom in these two senses, and thus that he maintains that an immoral action is both free and not free at the same time. More recently, Lewis White Beck and John Silber independently revive the positions of Reinhold and Sidgwick, but argue that Kant avoids the inconsistency charge since he associates "good" freedom with *Wille* and "neutral" freedom with *Willkür* (*Wille* and *Willkür* being two dimensions of the one will). See Beck 1960 and Silber 1960.

3. These two dimensions of a free choice are linked to Kant's concepts of *Wille* and *Willkür*, respectively. In this chapter, I am going to avoid using this distinction as much as possible, in order to avoid the suggestion that I am simply employing this division to resolve the problem of two freedoms in Kant in the same way that Beck and Silber do (see note 2 above).

4. I will return to Kant's concept of happiness at greater length in the next chapter.

5. See note 11 below.

6. It should be noted here that this account seems to contradict Kant's view that all humans, by necessity, seek happiness as an end. For example, Kant writes in the *Metaphysics*, "It is unavoidable for human nature to wish for and seek happiness" (MM 6:388). This suggests that there is at least one end that is not freely chosen. There is no easy solution to this problem, as Robert N. Johnson's insightful article, "Happiness as a Natural End" (2002), makes clear. My position in this chapter is that Kant does *not* mean that we cannot but choose objects that we think are good for our happiness. I will return to this issue in the next chapter.

7. Some critics argue that for Kant practical freedom is the freedom of the turnspit. That is to say, practical freedom is a compatibilist notion of freedom. The central piece of evidence for this is in Kant's *Lectures on Metaphysics*, where he first contrasts practical freedom and transcendental freedom (LM 28:257), and then, a little later on, contrasts a merely relative or conditioned spontaneity (i.e., the spontaneity of a turnspit) with transcendental freedom (LM 28:267). The argument is that these contrasts are one and the same, and hence that practical freedom is a conditioned spontaneity. I will not explore this issue any further since I think that Allison's criticism of this argument is correct (Allison 1990, 54–66). It seems quite clear from Allison's textual evidence that Kant's notion of practical freedom is an incompatibilist notion.

8. Allison's view is shared, in the main, by Andrews Reath and by the later views of Christine Korsgaard. The main similarity between these thinkers is

that they focus on the role of the Incorporation Thesis in grounding Kant's notion of nonmoral freedom. Allison and Reath are the most outspoken critics of the long-held view that Kant's theory of nonmoral motivation is deterministic.

9. I will return to this passage and, in particular, to the notion of incentives in the next chapter.

10. See *Metaphysics* 6:211.

11. The fact that we do not always *know* the best means to our maximal pleasure does not create room for the kind of freedom in which Kant is interested. Our susceptibility to pleasure means that whatever *seems* most pleasurable to us (even if we are not sure) will determine action. And what it is that seems most pleasurable to us will be determined by our susceptibility to pleasure and the limits of our knowledge. The person who smokes thirty cigars a day does so because of the pleasure that he associates with smoking relative to the pleasure that he associates with his health. That his knowledge of the health effects of smoking this many cigars is very limited does nothing (on its own) to introduce a notion of freedom here. His decision to continue smoking will be determined by his susceptibility to different kinds of pleasure and the limits of his knowledge. Even if he knows all that he could know about the health effects of smoking cigars, it might still be the case that he gets more pleasure from smoking than from protecting his health. In this case, he will continue to smoke.

12. See Engstrom 1993.

13. This is not to say that Allison does not present textual evidence to show that Kant thinks that practical freedom is a spontaneous kind of freedom. In fact, as I mentioned in note 7 above, Allison presents a good case for just this interpretation in Allison 1990, 54–66. The disagreement that I have with Allison is over (a) the kind of spontaneity that Kant thinks is entailed in the concept of practical freedom, and (b) the basis upon which this spontaneity is posited. Allison argues for a distinct nonmoral kind of spontaneity. I do not think that the Incorporation Thesis alone justifies this position.

14. See note 6 above.

15. It is with this in mind that Kant writes in the third *Critique* that passions "belong to the faculty of desire, and are inclinations that make all determinability of the faculty of desire by means of principles difficult or impossible" (CJ 5:272n). One of the principles to which Kant refers here is the principle of happiness. So, passions make it "difficult or impossible" to choose nonmoral maxims in light of one's concept of happiness.

16. For a good introduction to the central issues concerning this argument, see Allison 1990, 240–48.

17. These two dimensions of the concept of moral freedom should not be confused with the two dimensions of moral choice noted above: the governing principle and the actual choice.

18. This reading helps to make sense of Kant's references to grades or degrees of freedom. So, for example, in the *Metaphysics,* Kant writes, "The less a human being can be constrained by natural means and the more he can be constrained morally . . . *so much the more free he is*" (MM 6:382n; emphasis added). Kant's point here seems to be that the agent who cannot resist natural temptation is *less* free than the agent who can to some extent. This talk of degrees of freedom only makes sense if we think of nonmoral freedom as a limited or lesser form of moral freedom; as we will see below, this is precisely my point.

19. In making this claim, I am in agreement with Allison's interpretation of these passages in Allison 1983, 315–19, and Allison 1990, 57–58. Allison's central point is that the connection that Kant makes between transcendental freedom and practical freedom in the first *Critique* is a conceptual and not an ontological one. Transcendental freedom provides the conceptual (not ontological) ground for practical freedom.

20. We will see in chapter 5 that there are two distinct senses in which we can be sensuously affected.

21. This does not introduce a second incompatible notion of freedom, as Reinhold and Sidgwick argue (see note 2 above). Rather, it calls upon a deeper analysis of the original and overarching moral concept of freedom.

22. It should be noted here that moral choices involve nonmoral dimensions. For example, in choosing to give money to charity we must decide when we will give it, where we will give it, how we will give it, and a host of other nonmoral details. Thus, moral choices, insofar as they involve some nonmoral choices, also involve the exercise of the capacity to do otherwise.

CHAPTER 4

1. It should be noted that these maxims are not (necessarily) consciously chosen, but insofar as one could decide to abandon any of them, they are, in principle, objects of choice. I will return to this issue at greater length in a note below.

2. See, for example, Baron 1993.

3. This point is worthy of note since Kant discusses the incorporation of incentives into maxims and the existence of weakness of the will in the same part of the *Religion* (6:24 and 6:29).

4. In chapter 3, we saw Kant tell us that *all* ends are freely chosen.

5. I say "relatively uncontroversial" because scholars disagree over the scope and longevity of maxims. For example, Rüdiger Bittner (1974) argues that maxims refer to the most general life-rules, while others argue that maxims can refer to single actions. On the longevity issue, Manfred Kuehn presents the most radical reading when he says that something is only a

maxim "if the person who formulated it is willing to live by it for the rest of his life. Constancy and firmness are required characteristics of maxims. Once accepted, they must not be revoked—ever" (Kuehn 2001, 146). My account goes against the basic thrust of these interpretations, and in this sense it might be seen as controversial. For recent noteworthy treatments of Kant on maxims, see Bubner 2001, Kitcher 2003, and McCarty 2002.

6. I am going to leave Kant's rules or imperatives of skill out of my account here since they do not really impact the question of weakness of the will. Kant gives the following examples of such rules: "The precepts to be followed by a physician in order to cure his patient and by a poisoner to bring about certain death" (G 4:415).

7. Robert Johnson (1998) argues that Kant professes two distinct kinds of maxims: justifying maxims and nonjustifying maxims. This distinction is not the same as the one that I lay out. Leaving aside questions regarding evidence for Johnson's account, this paper will show that, in fact, there is no need for such a distinction between maxims. Instead, we can account for the possibility of nonmoral weakness of the will in Kant in light of the fact that there are distinct senses in which nonmoral maxims *prudentially* justify action for the agent. It is in view of these distinct senses that the possibility of acting in a way that is not good (in some sense) arises.

8. As we saw in the Introduction, Kant thinks of objective principles as standards of action, and subjective principles (or maxims) as motives to action. The objective principle tells us what we ought to do (morally or prudentially), resulting in the objective determination of the will, while the subjective principle carries motivational force, resulting in the subjective determination of the will.

9. See Beck 1960, 84–85, for a discussion of the sense in which the hypothetical imperative is an objective principle of practical reason.

10. In speaking of "subjectively justifying" an action, I am shifting the sense of "subjective" slightly from the sense used earlier (see note 8 above). In this case, the term "subjective" refers to the limited applicability of the principle (i.e., that it only holds for the particular agent in question). Objective principles, on the other hand, are standards of action that Kant thinks are "valid for every rational being" (G 4:420n). Hence, the subjective/objective distinction has a couple of uses in Kant's thinking. It can refer to the *motivation/standard* distinction, or it can refer to the *valid for me/valid for all rational beings* distinction.

11. As noted above, I will focus in more depth on the issue of maxim formation in section II of this chapter.

12. This account is indebted to Richard McCarty's analysis of incentives in McCarty 2006.

13. We will see in chapter 5 that moral interests are produced when the categorical imperative determines the will.

14. See chapter 3, note 6. For interesting discussions of some of the complexities that surround Kant's concept of happiness, see O'Connor 1982, Paton 1945, Wike 1994, and Wood 2001.

15. So, in total there are three notions of happiness: (1) uninterrupted agreeableness; (2) satisfaction of all inclinations; (3) satisfaction of a subset of inclinations. Paton (1945) divides these notions by contrasting the first with the second and the third (which he pairs). Wike (1994), however, focuses on the contrast between the second and the third. My reading attempts to reconcile all three notions.

16. In places, Kant indicates that happiness plays a very active role in our lives as a kind of quasi-regulative Ideal. He expresses this understanding most clearly in a fragment: "Happiness is something thought, not something felt. Moreover, it is not a thought which can be taken from experience; rather, it is this thought which makes the experience possible" (LM 29:278).

17. In the same passage from the third *Critique,* Kant uses health as his example of an end that just pleases as a means to some other end. In his lectures, Kant illustrates this point using the example of money. "Our satisfaction or dissatisfaction is either mediate or immediate; the former is intellectual, the latter sensible. Something pleases me mediately when it pleases not in itself, but rather only as a means to an immediate satisfaction. It is no special object of pleasure but rather an object of reason, which recognizes that I will partake in a pleasure through this, e.g., I have a mediate satisfaction in money" (LM 29:891).

18. As I argued in chapter 1, the gulf between Kant's psychology and his theory of rationality is not as great as some commentators would have us believe. We saw there that Kant's views regarding the role of maxims in the development of passions undermines the notion that there is a radical divide between these two realms.

19. Of course, it does not follow from the fact that there are two such dimensions to the formation of maxims that both of these stages must be actively or explicitly present in the case of every particular action. Thus, every time we desire to wash our hands, we do not first take an interest in doing so, then posit a maxim, etc. Nor do we explicitly call a maxim to mind whenever we act. But, for Kant, it is nevertheless true that we always act on the basis of a maxim, even in the case of weak actions, or of apparently unreflective actions like washing our hands. Washing hands can only be considered a practically free action if it is governed by a maxim. It is only in virtue of the (perhaps unconscious) presence of a maxim governing hand washing that the desire to wash our hands does not *necessitate* hand washing, but merely *affects* us in the decision to do so. So, insofar as the first two dimensions of rational action (taking an interest and forming a maxim) are packed into the very notion of acting on a maxim, they are presupposed by actions like washing hands.

20. It must, however, be noted that in the Vigilantius lectures from the mid-1790s, Kant says things to indicate that an interest is not really distinct from the pleasure experienced at the thought of something. In spite of the distinction that Kant draws between the faculty of pleasure and the faculty of desire, he often comes close to identifying pleasure and desire$_1$ in his lectures. In the *Lectures on Metaphysics* (29:1009), this seems to translate into a closeness between pleasure and interest. Ultimately, an interest certainly involves pleasure at the thought of something, but as we have seen, it also includes more.

21. These kinds of interests raise interesting questions. How can an end be pleasant in itself and as a *means* to happiness if happiness is a composite of pleasures? Does the fact that the end is pleasant in itself not automatically mean that it is a *part* of happiness (since happiness is a composite of pleasures)? How can we also speak of it as a *means* to happiness? The answer to these questions hinges upon whether or not we use Kant's more rational formulation of happiness. On this formulation, happiness is not simply the satisfaction of all of the pleasures that we have, but of some ordered set of these pleasures. For example, happiness might be the maximal pleasure that we get from a life of education and study, or from a life of adventure and travel. An end can contribute to happiness (and thus be a means to it) insofar as it contributes to our maximal pleasure when we reach it. By the same token, an end can take away from our maximal pleasure if reaching it somehow reduces the possibility of reaching other ends that make up the totality of our happiness. For example, if one's notion of happiness is associated with the maximal pleasure derived from a life of stability and family, but one also desires to explore outer space, then achieving the latter end will not be good as a means to one's happiness. Achieving the end in question might increase one's immediate quotient of pleasure but ultimately reduce one's happiness.

22. Kant's account does not seem to leave room for interests in ends that are neither good nor bad for happiness. His doctrinal division of the fundamental principles of action between morality and happiness seems to rule out the possibility of a nonmoral interest that is unrelated to happiness. So, all of our nonmoral actions impact happiness negatively or positively; they all take happiness into consideration in some way.

23. Jeanine Grenberg (2001) seems to suggest that this is not a possibility when she argues that taking an interest is equivalent to either morally or prudentially deciding that some end is good.

24. Though in the case of the formation of desires$_1$ there is no choice—pleasure simply causes desire$_1$.

25. Indeed, the view that the presence of a pleasant feeling determines choice can be found in Kant's earliest writings. In "A New Elucidation of the First Principles of Metaphysical Cognition," Kant endorses the commonly

held view that "the power to perform an action is suspended in a state of indifference relative to each of the two directions in which it could realize itself, and that it is determined exclusively by a pleasurable inclination towards the blandishments which arise from our representations" (1:401). Kant goes on to discuss and endorse the claim that "it is the being pleased which . . . determines the action" (1:401).

26. The other determination of the higher faculty of desire—that is to say, the other kind of intellectual desire$_1$—is a moral desire$_1$. See note that follows; we will also return to this in the next chapter.

27. It must be noted here that the rational purity of these nonmoral intellectual desires$_1$ (and, hence, their classification under the higher faculty of desire) appears to be compromised by Kant's notion of happiness. Kant's concept of happiness is a sort of hybrid of sensibility and rationality. Earlier, I defined this concept as the maximal (sensible) pleasure that we can get from the satisfaction of an organized system of our inclinations. This is a composite conception with two distinct poles that are almost always represented separately in Kant's actual comments. On the one hand, Kant refers to happiness as the greatest amount of uninterrupted pleasure possible. The account of happiness as the satisfaction of the sum of all of our inclinations can be grouped with this characterization. These formulations present us with a *sensible* understanding of happiness as the maximal (or continual) pleasure that we can get by satisfying every inclination that we have whenever we have it. On the other hand, according to Kant's more *rational* formulation, happiness involves the satisfaction of a subset of our inclinations—a subset that we rationally organize into a whole. This is Kant's rational articulation of happiness (or, if you accept my attempt to reconcile Kant's accounts, the rational pole of his account) in the sense that reason must play a role in actually determining what happiness is for each individual by comparing and reconciling the various pleasures that make up the systematic whole. Now, depending on which account of happiness (or dimension of the single notion) Kant focuses on, intellectual desires$_1$ for nonmoral ends are more or less rational. Of course, this amounts to saying that these desires$_1$ belong *more or less* to the higher faculty of desire. Consider the following passage from the second *Critique*, in which Kant seems to rule out any classification of our nonmoral reason as a higher faculty of desire:

> The principle of one's happiness, however much reason and understanding may be used in it, contains no other determinants for the will than those which belong to the lower faculty of desire. Either, then, no higher faculty of desire exists, or else pure reason alone must of itself be practical, i.e. it must be able to determine the will by the mere form of the practical rule without presupposing any feeling or consequently any idea of the pleasant or the unpleasant

> as the matter of the faculty of desire and as the empirical condition
> of its principles. Then only is reason a truly higher faculty of desire,
> but still only in so far as it determines the will by itself and not in
> the service of the inclinations. (Pr. R 5:24–25)

Kant's argument here suggests that only reason in its moral capacity (i.e.,
only reason as it is expressed in the categorical imperative) can be a "truly
higher faculty of desire." The implication is that the production of intellectual desires$_1$ through the hypothetical imperative is *not* the work of a higher
faculty of desire, because our conception of happiness is fundamentally made
up of immediate, or sensible, pleasures. So, it seems that the ambiguity in
Kant's texts regarding the classification of nonmoral reason (i.e., whether or
not it is a higher faculty of desire) goes back to the ambiguity at the heart
of his conception of happiness (i.e., the extent to which it is sensible or rational). Although this does not bear directly on the question of the moral
law as a higher faculty of desire, it does undermine the rigidity of Kant's distinction between the higher and lower faculties of desire. Again, this distinction is mainly about the basic origin of the desire$_1$ produced, and we will see
in the next chapter that in spite of this distinction both faculties share much
in common.

28. I do not mean to suggest here that this process is self-consciously deliberative. This is just a theoretical elaboration of a model case of maxim
formation. In reality, some maxims may be simply assumed or adopted from
one's parents or environment. We might imagine that in such cases there is
a certain pleasure associated with simply mimicking maxims held by authority figures. An agent might not be aware of the moment at which she assumed the maxim, or even that she has the maxim, but since she is capable
of choosing to reject it at any given moment, then it is, in theory, chosen.

29. Though our accounts are not identical, I must acknowledge a debt on
this issue to Jeanine Grenberg's (2001) impressive analysis of Kant's theory
of action.

30. In chapter 1, we saw Kant discuss the role of maxims and reason in
the formation of passions. We are in a better position now to understand
how this might happen. Kant writes, "A passion is a sensible desire that has
become a lasting [*bleibenden*] inclination (e.g., hatred as opposed to anger).
The calm with which one gives oneself up to it permits reflection and allows
the mind to form principles upon it and so, if inclination lights upon something contrary to the law, to brood upon it, to get it rooted deeply, and so
to take up what is evil (as something premeditated) into its maxim" (MM
6:408). Passions are formed when we reflect upon certain inclinations and
choose maxims based on this reflection. Kant tells us in the *Anthropology*,
"Passion always presupposes a maxim of the subject, namely, to act according to a purpose prescribed for him by his inclination. Passion, therefore, is

always associated with the purposes of reason" (A 7:266). All of this is possible because the formation of maxims is about taking an interest in ends and actions associated with our desires$_1$. These interests can then go on to play a role in the formation of other desires$_1$ (i.e., passions) because there is a pleasure associated with the thought of the end of our interests, and this pleasure can determine the faculty of desire and lead to further desires$_1$.

CHAPTER 5

1. See the second *Critique* 5:23–24, 75, and 117.

2. See Introduction and chapter 4 for earlier arguments justifying this approach. In the Introduction, I argued not only that an account of nonmoral action was *useful* in helping us to understand Kant's treatment of respect, but, more strongly, that it was only against the background of an account of sensible action that respect could be understood. See "Empirical Ethics and A Priori Ethics" in the Introduction.

3. This brief catalogue is not intended to be a comprehensive survey of the various positions that have been taken on Kant's notion of respect. For a slightly different approach to classifying these positions, see Nauckhoff 2003, 57–58nn3, 4, 5, and 6.

4. See Guyer 1993 (esp. 362–63) and Ameriks 1987.

5. See Reath 1989b, 289–90, and Sherman 1990, 176. Allison (1990, 127) and O'Neill (1975, 111) present variations on this view, according to which it is some kind of intellectual recognition of the moral law that functions as a motive to moral action.

6. See Walker 1989, 98.

7. See Herrera 2000, McCarty 1993, Nauckhoff 2003, and Nuyen 1991.

8. I mentioned in the previous chapter that there is some ambiguity in Kant's account of the higher faculty of desire, insofar as he sometimes classifies the desires$_1$ that are produced by the hypothetical imperative as belonging to the higher faculty of desire.

9. Gregor's translation.

10. I will return to this issue of the cognitive content of respect below and in my conclusion.

11. A. T. Nuyen presents a different interpretation of the role of respect when he refers to Kant's discussion of respect in the second *Critique* and says, "At the very least then, we can interpret Kant as saying that the moral feeling of respect for the moral law is an additional incentive to act morally" (Nuyen 1991, 39). He then quotes Kant: "Thus the moral law, as a formal determining ground of action through practical pure reason, and moreover as a material though purely objective determining ground of the objects of action, is also a subjective ground of determination. That is, it is the incentive to this action, since it has an influence on the sensibility of the subject

and effects a feeling which promotes the influence of the law on the will" (Pr. R 5:78). Nuyen concludes from this passage that "Kant's moral motivation does include a non-cognitive element after all. It is Kant's view that the law motivates through practical reason *as well as* through a feeling that it effects" (Nuyen 1991, 39). But the "non-cognitive element" is not an "additional incentive" that exists "*as well as*" the objective determination of practical reason. It is true that Kant believes that we have both an objective and subjective ground determining action, but it is not the case that they so determine by somehow coming together and combining to produce enough motivational power to determine an action. Nuyen makes it seem that both reason and feeling together are needed to motivate the human agent. Instead, I contend, Kant's view is that the objective ground is somehow converted into a subjective ground, into something that interests us as human agents. In the *Metaphysics,* Kant writes that in a moral person "feelings arising from sensible impressions lose their influence on moral feeling only because respect for the law is more powerful than all such feelings together" (MM 6:408). He does not say that moral feeling *and* reason together combat sensible feelings, just that moral feeling does. It should be pointed out here that the face-off between moral and nonmoral feelings is not simply determined by the balance of forces. As I argued in chapter 3, there is room in Kant's view for the idea that we can choose (morally and nonmorally) against those feelings that carry the greatest weight: we can always do otherwise.

12. At the same time, of course, Kant thinks that our practically free choices can also express transcendental or autonomous (i.e., moral) freedom. That is to say, sensibly affected actions can also display the power of pure reason to cause moral actions.

13. See also the second *Critique* 5:74, 78, 117. Kant claims in these passages that the moral law "causes" us to have moral feelings. Of course, the very concept of the moral law "causing" anything is inherently problematic given the link between the moral realm and the noumenal (i.e., the realm in which notions like causality are, by definition, not applicable). For a helpful discussion of this topic, see Westphal 1997.

14. Even though respect involves feelings of pleasure and Kant changes his views on pleasure around 1790, it does not follow that he changes his thinking on respect as a moral incentive. We will see that Kant's pre-1790 treatment allows us an understanding *that* a moral feeling must precede moral action, while his post-1790 thinking affords us a richer understanding of just *how* this feeling leads to moral action.

15. Note also that Kant says that no feeling is "prior to the moral law," acting "as its basis." This is further evidence for the claim that when Kant denies feeling, he is denying it as a *legislative* factor.

16. In the Introduction, we saw Kant say that "The direct determination of the will by law and the consciousness of this determination is respect"

(G 4:401n). It is clear from Kant's account in the second *Critique* that what he should have said is that the consciousness of the determination by the law is the consciousness of respect.

17. See note 15 above on this. There is no evidence to suggest that Kant's later thinking on pleasure leads him to change his mind on respect. In fact, as I argued above, the only major difference it makes is that it allows Kant to differentiate the moral feeling from nonmoral feelings without appeal to the language of "analogues." Otherwise, it just provides us with a more robust sense of just *how* respect actually moves the agent without "aiming" at pleasure.

18. We will see that the pleasure is a pleasure at the thought of *acting from duty.*

19. See the section on objective/subjective determination in the Introduction.

20. Kant does not consider the possibility of maintaining pleasure through sustained contemplation. He seems to assume that as practical, engaged agents we are moved by pleasure to take action in the world.

21. Notice here, Kant thinks that a self-determined (or autonomous) action is an action performed *for the sake of* the moral law. So, the pleasant experience at the thought of the moral law moves us to act for the sake of this law. This point will be very relevant in the final section of this chapter.

22. See McCarty 1993, 430.

23. For a discussion of moral *worth* and its relation to acting from duty, see Herman 1993, 1–22.

CONCLUSION

1. We will see that as a result of this wedge the commentator upon whom I focus must gloss over interpretive infelicities in order to force his account into line with Kant's own words.

2. Henry Allison draws on this article several times in Allison 1990.

3. I will return to this issue below. See also the introduction, "Subjective and Objective Determinations of the Will."

4. See *Religion* 6:36.

5. At the start of his article, Reath explains that an incentive is "a subjective determining ground" of the will "in the sense that it is that in the subject which determines the will." But then he goes on to say that, "though incentives are 'subjective' in the above sense, they can include reasons that are objectively valid" (Reath 1989b, 285). Presumably, then, a subjective determining ground that is objectively valid can also be considered an objective determining ground. In this case, there is no real distinction between subjective and objective determining grounds of the will. Now, though this is certainly one way in which Kant uses the distinction between subjective and objective determinations of the will, it is clearly not the only one, and Reath is remiss is not taking note of this.

6. Kant typically introduces the notion of being sensuously (or pathologically) affected by contrasting it with being determined by our sensibility (or pathology). For example, in the second *Critique*, he refers to our will as "pathologically affected (though not pathologically determined—and thus still free)" (Pr. R 5:32). Reath is, of course, right to deny that Kant believes that we are pathologically determined, and if this is what the "balance of forces" model of action suggests, then this model is not a good reading of Kant either. But in denying that feeling as such plays any role in moving us, Reath is surely going too far; he provides no explanation for what Kant might mean by saying that our actions are pathologically *affected*.

7. Reath appeals to the following passage for evidence. Kant says that "we find our pathologically determined self, although by its maxims it is wholly incapable of giving universal laws, striving to give its pretensions priority and to make them acceptable as first and original claims, just as if it were our entire self. This propensity to make oneself, according to subjective determining grounds of one's choice, into an objective determining ground of the will in general can be called self-love" (Pr. R 5:77). Reath glosses this passage by saying, "Here self-love is described as the tendency to treat subjective grounds of choice as objective reasons. That is, one's inclinations, which may provide valid reasons to the subject, are treated as reasons that can be valid for anyone, and could thus lead others to accept the action" (Reath 1989b, 298). But does the passage quoted really provide evidence for Reath's account? The important point Kant is trying to make is that self-love involves treating ends that are good for me as good as such. The question of whether or not other people approve of these ends is not really relevant to the psychology of the agent engaged in self-love. Such an agent does not factor others' perceptions into her thinking so much as she ignores others' perceptions, and thus elevates the status of her own ends by default. There is nothing here to indicate that inclinations must somehow be seen as approved of by a community before they can be acted upon.

REFERENCES

....

KANT SOURCES

Apart from the *Critique of Pure Reason,* all references to Kant are to the volume and page number of *Kants gesammelte Schriften,* edited by Deutschen Akademie der Wissenschaften zu Berlin (formerly the Königlichen Preussischen Akademie der Wissenschaften), 29 vols. (Berlin: Walter de Gruyter, 1902–), referred to below as "KGS" and known generally as the *Akademie-Ausgabe.* References to the *Critique of Pure Reason* are to the standard A and B pagination of the first and second editions. Specific translations, editions, and abbreviations used are as follows:

Anthropology from a Pragmatic Point of View (A). Translated by Victor L. Dowdell. Carbondale: Southern Illinois Press, 1978 (KGS 7).
Critique of the Power of Judgment (CJ). Translated by Paul Guyer and Eric Matthews. Cambridge: Cambridge University Press, 2000 (KGS 5).
Critique of Practical Reason (Pr. R). Translated by Lewis White Beck. Chicago: Chicago University Press, 1949 (KGS 5).
Critique of Pure Reason (Pu. R). Translated by Norman Kemp Smith. London: Macmillan, 1956 (KGS 4 and 3, A and B).
Education (E). Translated by Annette Churton. Ann Arbor: University of Michigan Press, 1960 (KGS 9).
Foundations of the Metaphysics of Morals (G). Translated by Lewis White Beck. Englewood Cliffs, N.J.: Prentice Hall, 1997 (KGS 4). (This will be referred to as the *Groundwork* throughout.)
Lectures on Ethics (LE). Translated by Peter Heath. Edited by Peter Heath and J. B. Schneewind. New York: Cambridge University Press, 1997 (KGS 27 and 29).
Lectures on Metaphysics (LM). Translated and edited by Karl Ameriks and Steve Naragon. New York: Cambridge University Press, 1997 (KGS 28–29).
Logic (L). Translated by Robert S. Hartman and Wolfgang Schwarz. Indianapolis: Bobbs-Merrill, 1974 (KGS 9).
Metaphysics of Morals (MM). Translated by Mary Gregor. New York: Cambridge University Press, 1996 (KGS 6).
Prolegomena to Any Future Metaphysics (Prol). Translated by Lewis White Beck. Indianapolis: Bobbs-Merrill, 1950 (KGS 4).

Reflexionen (R) (KGS 17–19).

Religion within the Limits of Reason Alone (Rel). Translated by Theodore M. Greene and Hoyt H. Hudson. New York: Harper Torchbooks, 1960 (KGS 6).

Theoretical Philosophy 1755–1770. Translated and edited by David Walford in collaboration with Ralf Meerbote. New York: Cambridge University Press, 1992 (KGS 1).

SECONDARY SOURCES

Allison, Henry. 1983. *Kant's Transcendental Idealism*. New Haven, Conn.: Yale University Press.

———. 1990. *Kant's Theory of Freedom*. New York: Cambridge University Press.

———. 1996. *Idealism and Freedom*. New York: Cambridge University Press.

Ameriks, Karl. 1987. "The Hegelian Critique of Kantian Morality." In *Essays on Kant*, ed. Bernard den Ouden and Marcia Moen, 179–212. New York: Peter Lang.

Audi, Robert, ed. 1999. *The Cambridge Dictionary of Philosophy*. 2nd ed. New York: Cambridge University Press.

Baron, Marcia. 1993. "Freedom, Frailty, and Impurity." *Inquiry* 36 (4): 431–41.

Beck, Lewis White. 1960. *A Commentary on Kant's "Critique of Practical Reason."* Chicago: University of Chicago Press.

———. 1984. "What Have We Learned from Kant?" In Wood 1984, 17–30.

Bittner, Rüdiger. 1974. "Maximen." In Funke and Kopper 1974, 485–98.

———. 2001. *Doing Things for Reasons*. New York: Oxford University Press.

Bubner, Rüdiger. 2001. "Another Look at Maxims." In Cicovacki 2001, 245–60.

Carnois, Bernard. 1987. *The Coherence of Kant's Doctrine of Freedom*. Trans. David Booth. Chicago: University of Chicago Press.

Cicovacki, Predrag, ed. 2001. *Kant's Legacy: Essays in Honor of Lewis White Beck*. Rochester, N.Y.: University of Rochester Press.

Engstrom, Stephen. 1993. "Allison on Rational Agency." *Inquiry* 36 (4): 405–18.

———. 2002. "The Inner Freedom of Virtue." In Timmons 2002, 289–316.

Frierson, Patrick. 2003. *Freedom and Anthropology in Kant's Moral Philosophy*. New York: Cambridge University Press.

———. n.d. "Kant's Empirical Account of Human Action." Unpublished manuscript.

Funke, Gerhard, and Joachim Kopper, eds. 1974. *Akten des 4. Internationalen Kant-Kongresses*. Berlin: de Gruyter.

Ginsborg, Hannah. 1998. "Korsgaard on Choosing Non-moral Ends." *Ethics* 109 (1): 5–21.

Green, Theodore H. 1888. *Collected Works*. Vol. 2. Ed. R. L. Nettleship. London: Longmans, Green.

Grenberg, Jeanine. 2001. "Feeling, Desire and Interest in Kant's Theory of Action." *Kant-Studien* 92 (2): 153–79.

Guevara, Daniel. 2000. *Kant's Theory of Moral Motivation*. Boulder, Colo.: Westview.

Guyer, Paul. 1993. *Kant and the Experience of Freedom: Essays on Aesthetics and Morality*. New York: Cambridge University Press.

Herman, Barbara. 1993. *The Practice of Moral Judgment*. Cambridge, Mass.: Harvard University Press.

Herrera, Larry. 2000. "Kant on the Moral *Triebfeder*." *Kant-Studien* 91 (4): 395–410.

Hinman, Lawrence. 1983. "On the Purity of Our Moral Motives: A Critique of Kant's Account of the Emotions and Acting for the Sake of Duty." *The Monist: An International Quarterly Journal of General Philosophical Inquiry* 66 (2): 251–67.

Irwin, Terence. 1984. "Morality and Personality: Kant and Green." In Wood 1984, 31–56.

Jacobs, Brian. 2003. "Kantian Character and the Science of Humanity." In Jacobs and Kain 2003, 105–35.

Jacobs, Brian, and Patrick Kain, eds. 2003. *Essays on Kant's Anthropology*. New York: Cambridge University Press.

Johnson, Robert N. 1998. "Weakness Incorporated." *History of Philosophy Quarterly* 15 (3): 349–67.

———. 2002. "Happiness as a Natural End." In Timmons 2002, 317–30.

Kitcher, Patricia. 2003. "What Is a Maxim?" *Philosophical Topics* 31 (1–2): 215–43.

Korsgaard, Christine. 1996. *Creating the Kingdom of Ends*. New York: Cambridge University Press.

———. 1998. "Motivation, Metaphysics, and the Value of the Self: A Reply to Ginsborg, Guyer, and Schneewind." *Ethics* 109 (1): 49–66.

Kuehn, Manfred. 2001. *Kant: A Biography*. Cambridge: Cambridge University Press.

Lisak, David. 1994. "The Psychological Impact of Sexual Abuse: Content Analysis of Interviews with Male Survivors." *Journal of Traumatic Stress* 7:525–48.

Louden, Robert B. 2000. *Kant's Impure Ethics: From Rational Beings to Human Beings*. New York: Oxford University Press.

———. 2003. "The Second Part of Morals." In Jacobs and Kain 2003, 60–84.

MacBeath, A. Murray. 1973. "Kant and Moral Feeling." *Kant-Studien* 64 (3): 283–314.

McCarty, Richard. 1993. "Kantian Moral Motivation and the Feeling of Respect." *Journal of the History of Philosophy* 31 (3): 421–35.

———. 1994. "Motivation and Moral Choice in Kant's Theory of Rational Agency." *Kant-Studien* 85 (1): 15–31.

———. 2002. "The Maxims Problem." *Journal of Philosophy* 99 (1): 29–44.

———. 2006. "Maxims in Kant's Practical Philosophy." *Journal of the History of Philosophy* 44 (1): 65–83.

Meerbote, Ralf. 1984. "Commentary: Kant on Freedom and the Rational and Morally Good Will." In Wood 1984, 57–72.

Meld Shell, Susan. 2003. "Kant's 'True Economy of Human Nature.'" In Jacobs and Kain 2003, 194–229.

Mellin, Georg Samuel. 1970. *Encyclopädisches Wörterbuch der kritischen Philosophie*. Vol. 1. Repr. ed., 6 vols. Aalen: Scientia Verlag. (Orig. pub. 1797.)

Munzel, G. Felicitas. 1999. *Kant's Conception of Moral Character: The "Critical" Link of Morality, Anthropology, and Reflective Judgment*. Chicago: University of Chicago Press.

Nauckhoff, Josefine. 2003. "Incentives and Interests in Kant's Moral Psychology." *History of Philosophy Quarterly* 20 (1): 41–60.

Nuyen, A. T. 1991. "Sense, Passions and Morals in Hume and Kant." *Kant-Studien* 82 (1):29–41.

O'Connor, Daniel. 1982. "Kant's Conception of Happiness." *Journal of Value Inquiry* 16 (3): 189–205.

O'Neill, Onora. 1975. *Acting on Principle*. New York: Columbia University Press.

Packer, Mark. 1989. "Kant on Desire and Moral Pleasure." *Journal of the History of Ideas* 50 (3): 429–42.

Paton, H. J. 1945. "Kant's Idea of the Good." In *Proceedings of the Aristotelian Society*, n.s., 45:1–25.

Phillips Griffiths, A. 1991. "Kant's Psychological Hedonism." *Philosophy* 66 (256): 207–16.

Potter, Nelson. 1974. "Does Kant Have Two Concepts of Freedom?" In Funke and Kopper 1974, 590–96.

Prauss, Gerold. 1983. *Kant über Freiheit als Autonomie*. Frankfurt am Main: Vittorio Klostermann.

Reath, Andrews. 1989a. "Hedonism, Heteronomy and Kant's Principle of Happiness." *Pacific Philosophical Quarterly* 70 (1): 42–72.

———. 1989b. "Kant's Theory of Moral Sensibility: Respect for the Moral Law and the Influence of Inclination." *Kant-Studien* 80 (3): 284–302.

Schrader, George. 1976. "The Status of Feeling in Kant's Philosophy." *Proceedings of the Ottawa Congress on Kant in the Anglo-American and Continental Traditions*, 143–64. Ottawa: University of Ottawa Press.

Seidler, Michael. 1981. "Kant and the Stoics on the Emotional Life." *Philosophy Research Archives* 7:1–56.

Sherman, Nancy. 1990. "The Place of Emotions in Kantian Morality." In *Identity, Character, and Morality: Essays in Moral Psychology*, ed. Owen Flanagan and Amélie Oksenberg Rorty, 149–72. Cambridge, Mass.: MIT Press.

Silber, John. 1960. "The Ethical Significance of Kant's *Religion*." Introduction to Immanuel Kant, *Religion within the Limits of Reason Alone*. New York: Harper Torchbooks.

Smith, Michael. 1994. *The Moral Problem*. Oxford: Blackwell.

Solomon, Robert C., and Kathleen M. Higgins. 1991. "The Virtue of (Erotic) Love." In *The Philosophy of (Erotic) Love*, ed. Robert C. Solomon and Kathleen M. Higgins, 1–12. Lawrence: University Press of Kansas.

Stark, Werner. 1997. "Kant's Lectures on Anthropology." Paper presented at the Central Division Meeting, American Philosophical Association, Pittsburgh.

Sullivan, Roger. 1995. "The Influence of Kant's Anthropology on His Moral Theory." *Review of Metaphysics* 49 (September): 77–94.

Sussman, David. 2001. *The Idea of Humanity: Anthropology and Anthroponomy in Kant's Ethics*. New York: Routledge.

Timmons, Mark, ed. 2002. *Kant's Metaphysics of Morals: Interpretative Essays*. New York: Oxford University Press.

Walker, Ralph. 1989. "*Achtung* in the *Grundlegung*." In *Grundlegung zur Metaphysik der Sitten*, ed. Otfried Höffe, 97–116. Frankfurt am Main: Vittorio Klostermann.

Westphal, Kenneth. 1995. "Kant's Critique of Determinism in Empirical Psychology." In *Proceedings of the Eighth International Kant Congress*, vol. 2, part 1, ed. Hoke Robinson, 357–70. Milwaukee, Wis.: Marquette University Press.

———. 1997. "Noumenal Causality Reconsidered: Affection, Agency, and Meaning in Kant." *Canadian Journal of Philosophy* 27 (2): 209–45.

Wike, Victoria S. 1994. *Kant on Happiness in Ethics*. New York: State University of New York Press.

Wilson, Holly. 1997. "Kant's Integration of Morality and Anthropology." *Kant-Studien* 88 (1): 87–104.

Wood, Allen, ed. 1984. *Self and Nature in Kant's Philosophy*. Ithaca, NY: Cornell University Press.

———. 1984. "Kant's Compatibilism." In Wood 1984, 73–101.

———. 1991. "Unsociable Sociability: The Anthropological Basis of Kantian Ethics." *Philosophical Topics* 19 (1): 325–51.

———. 1999. *Kant's Ethical Thought*. New York: Cambridge University Press.

———. 2001. "Kant versus Eudaimonism." In Cicovacki 2001, 261–82.

———. 2003. "Kant and the Problem of Human Nature." In Jacobs and Kain 2003, 38–60.

Zuckert, Rachel. 2002. "A New Look at Kant's Theory of Pleasure." *Journal of Aesthetics and Art Criticism* 60 (3): 239–52.

INDEX